HIGH STAKES & DANGEROUS MEN
THE UFO STORY

Neil Daniels

HIGH STAKES & DANGEROUS MEN

THE UFO STORY

AN UNAUTHORISED BIOGRAPHY

Neil Daniels

soundcheck books

the stories behind the sounds

First published in Great Britain in 2013
by Soundcheck Books LLP, 88 Northchurch Road, London, N1 3NY.

Copyright © Neil Daniels 2013

ISBN: 978-0-9571442-6-2
All rights reserved. No part of this book may be reproduced or
transmitted in any form or by any means, electronic or mechanical,
including photocopying, recording, or any information storage and
retrieval system without permission in writing from the publisher.

This book is sold subject to the condition that it shall not, by way of
trade or otherwise, be lent, resold, hired out or otherwise circulated
without the publisher's prior consent in any form of binding or
cover other than that in which it is published and without a similar
condition being imposed on the subsequent purchaser.

Every effort has been made to contact copyright holders of
photographic and other resource material used in this book. Some
were unreachable. If they contact the publishers we will endeavour
to credit them in reprints and future editions.

A CIP record for this book is available from the British Library

Book design: Benn Linfield (www.bennlinfield.co.uk)

Printed by Bell & Bain Ltd, Glasgow

CONTENTS

FOREWORD

BY EDDIE TRUNK

Many have asked me about my fascination and rabid support of UFO. Especially here in the USA, where the band never really broke through at the level they did in Europe and other parts of the world. The answer is really quite simple: of all the bands I grew up loving, no other band's music still holds up and moves me as much today as when I first heard UFO. It frustrates me that so few really know the band's catalogue, or, in some cases, are even aware of whom the band is, so, to that end, I have done my best to help spread the word. Simply a fan trying to help the band gain more fans, more than forty years later. Better late than never! And it is clearly working.

Ever since talking so much about UFO on my two radio shows and TV show *That Metal Show* on VH-1, I average at least an email, tweet, or fan exchange a day that thanks me for turning them on to the group's music. Now don't get me wrong, I'm aware that UFO certainly has their fans. But too often they are way off the radar for most when it comes to discussing great hard rock. Many fans ask me where to start when it comes to the band's music since the catalogue is so expansive. My answer is always the same: *Strangers In The Night*. Not only do I feel it's the greatest live album ever, but my favourite album ever made.

For me there are three definitive eras of UFO. Of course the Schenker era from *Phenomenon* is usually the most celebrated. However, I equally love the Paul Chapman era. Paul "Tonka" Chapman was highly underrated, filling Michael's shoes and playing with great melody and a looser style that I really love. That material was a bit more commercial leaning at times, but no less brilliant in my view. The final great era is the band's current line-up with Vinnie Moore handling guitar. Vinnie does an amazing job playing the band's early catalogue, and with him UFO has made four solid studio albums that sees them leaning in a more bluesy direction. Even though Pete Way is greatly missed, the UFO line-up of Mogg/Parker/ Raymond/Moore has created some great music in the band's twilight years.

Phil Mogg remains the one member to be a part of every era of UFO and is one of rock's greatest voices and writers. I still get the same thrill going to see UFO now as I did when I was in high school seeing them for the first time.

UFO's music is simply timeless, and, for me, they have created the greatest melodic hard rock ever.

Eddie Trunk
www.eddietrunk.com

INTRODUCTION

BY THE AUTHOR

"It is so important however as a band to keep moving forward so we take our influences and the things that give the UFO sound and try to keep progressing as a band."

Paul Raymond[1]

Formed in 1969, UFO has existed for over 40 years and yet, despite the reverence they have earned, the influential albums they have released and the scandalous tales that have followed them around the world for over five decades, UFO are sadly not as well-known or as popular as they should be. Many rock fans would argue that UFO should be a much bigger band, especially in the States where they could, at one point in the late 1970s, fill those enormous 15,000 seater venues.

In many respects, they are underdogs and they're all the better for it. There's no question that UFO are one of the most influential rock bands of all time. Like Uriah Heep and Nazareth, UFO are rock stalwarts.

UFO have earned the respect and adulation of some of the world's most popular and best-selling rock bands, from Slash of Guns N' Roses to Metallica and Iron Maiden to Pearl Jam. There are a number of UFO's songs such as "Lights Out", "Only You Can Rock Me", "Doctor Doctor" and "Love To Love" that are hailed as some of the most influential rock songs of all time. A fair few of their albums – *Lights Out*, *Obsession* and *Strangers In The Night*, in particular – are often touted as some of the greatest rock albums ever.

So, why don't UFO receive the sort of mass mainstream attention that is frequently given to, say, Led Zeppelin, The Who, Queen or AC/DC? Even Status Quo – a band with a similarly turbulent career to that of UFO – are far better known worldwide. Perhaps UFO are better off this way? Why is it that UFO and Quo are attacked by snooty critics for supposedly repeating the same musical formula, while AC/DC are hailed as rock icons? Perhaps flying under the mainstream radar is the best place for bands such as UFO? After all, the fans probably would not want it any other way.

Akin to most long-standing rock bands, UFO's career has gone through a number of different eras. Firstly, there is what could be termed the space rock era; the band's first two studio albums and their first live album were essentially space rock, psychedelic albums. Secondly, there is the most important and influential era of the band when Michael Schenker joined in 1973 and departed in 1978. It is the era of the band's career which most fans hold in the highest regard. It was an incredibly creative, consistent and thrilling time when the band were at the top of their game and seemingly unstoppable both in the studio and onstage.

However, it ended with a bump, much to the dismay of fans the world over. This was succeeded by the Paul Chapman era, which lasted until 1983 when that particular line-up folded. The band subsequently went on a hiatus. The following period was undoubtedly the least consistent with a number of line-up changes, although 1991's *High Stakes & Dangerous Men* incarnation deserves far more attention than it was originally given. However, it wasn't meant to be and the band reformed with Michael Schenker in 1993. The second and final Schenker era ended in 2002.

After some downtime, the band re-united with new guitarist Vinnie Moore and a highly creative and successful period of the band commenced, which continues to this day (although this particular period did see the departure of original bassist and all-round rock legend, Mr Pete Way). The band currently consists of Phil Mogg, Andy Parker, Paul Raymond and Vinnie Moore, but with a succession of bassists completing the rhythm section in the studio and onstage. It is without question the strongest, not to say most consistent, line-up the band has had since the late 1970s Schenker era. Vinnie Moore has certainly proven himself to be a vital addition to the band and their recent 'resurrection'.

Stories of substance abuse, wild antics, violence and nasty arguments have dogged the band throughout much of their career, but it is difficult to distinguish fact from fiction in the UFO story and, until Mogg or Way decide to write their own book, those tales will remain unsubstantiated, though part of rock folklore. Many of the stories will be true and they'll probably be more shocking than the contents of Stephen Davis' gossipy Led Zeppelin biography *Hammer Of The Gods* or Mötley Crüe's scandalous rock 'n' roll band memoir, *The Dirt*. If anything, such stories add to the aura, mystique, success, failure and charm of a rock band, particularly with UFO, whose exploits have been documented for years in various publications. A roguish band through and through that has always lived on the edge, UFO have created their own set of rules and lived life on their terms.

However, with the exception of Martin Popoff's *Shoot Out The Lights*, book shelves are bereft of UFO material. This biography chronicles the story of the band from the beginning to the present day, with an emphasis on dissecting the studio material, detailing the band's influences, as well as the numerous subsequent bands they have themselves influenced. The book may have been written independently and some may scorn the term "unauthorised biography", but *High Stakes & Dangerous Men* was written in tribute to one of the greatest British rock bands of all time and is by no means meant to tarnish the band's reputation in any way. Quite the opposite, in fact. It is a celebration of their music. Would an authorised biography tell the true story? Some would argue that it would, yet others, including me, would refute such claims, but that is a lengthy debate best left for another time.

My hope for *High Stakes & Dangerous Men* is that it will cause older readers to revisit the band's albums, whilst younger readers will perhaps discover periods of the band's career with which they were, perhaps, not overly familiar.

I've used a vast array of research, spanning the full length of their career, including firsthand interviews with former members, personnel, associates and fans. Details of these can be located on the acknowledgements page.

The story of UFO begins in 1969 and, while this book closes in the present day, UFO will no doubt continue to exist for many years to come. *High Stakes & Dangerous Men* charts the highs and lows of this great bunch of misfits, but ultimately it is a book which honours their music. Let it roll!

Neil Daniels
neildanielsbooks.tumblr.com
neildanielsbooks.wordpress.com

CHAPTER
ONE

Unidentified Flying Object –
The Early Space Rock Years
(1969–1972)

"We try to do more than just play music –
we entertain."

Phil Mogg[2]

On 16 October 2009, UFO set foot onstage at Chicago's famed music venue House Of Blues, a chain of legendary rock venues which exist in various American cities. Singer Phil Mogg was in great shape, both physically and vocally. It was if he had hardly aged despite his indulgent lifestyle, but Mogg is a rock 'n' roll trooper. He was joined by his cohorts, drummer Andy Parker, guitarist/keyboardist Paul Raymond, guitarist Vinnie Moore and bassist Rob de Luca.

Chicago was once a pivotal market for UFO: in the 1970s they played to 15,000 people each night at the city's largest venues. The band has gone through many eras in their often tumultuous 40 plus year career, which now spans six decades. UFO's history dates back to their origins in London, back in 1969; the year when Led Zeppelin released their debut album.

Many bands go through name changes and line-up amendments before they settle on their permanent moniker and UFO were no exception.

A band called the Boyfriends was formed at the tail-end of the 1960s by guitarist Mick Bolton, bassist Pete Way and drummer Tic Torrazo, which went through various name changes itself from Hocus Pocus to The Good, The Bad, The Ugly and the more succinct Acid. Torrazo was soon replaced by Colin Turner, who himself was replaced by drummer Andy Parker after they met at a college gig in Cheshunt, when singer Phil Mogg joined the fold.

1

Specifically, it was in August 1969 when aspiring singer Mogg was introduced to musicians Way and Parker by Bolton. The trio had mostly been jamming in Bolton's parents' home in Enfield, North London when they met Mogg. Still in their teens, it was when Mogg moved into a house with the trio that he started singing professionally and thus fronted the band which soon became known as UFO. They began rehearsing at places such as the Fishmonger's Arms in Wood Green, North London before they performed in front of an audience. An important encounter with Noel Moore of Beacon Records, at the UFO club in London in October 1969, caused the band to rename their outfit UFO. It was a name that fitted the post-hippie *zeitgeist*.

The newly christened UFO made their first live appearance at Fagin's Blues Workshop in late 1969; a legendary British rock band was born that day. They soon began playing on the pub and club circuit in the London area, playing sets of around 45 minutes. Beggars can't be choosers and so they supported any band that would give them the time of day; one of those bands was Caravan, a progressive rock outfit from the Canterbury area.

Mick Bolton remains the least well-known member of the first sighting of UFO. Ultimately the core of the band was Mogg, Way and Parker, while the chemistry between Mogg and Way would emphatically be the driving force behind their future success.

Phil Mogg was born Phillip John Mogg on 15 April 1948 in Wood Green, North London. The British blues boom of the 1960s had an enormous influence on the young Mogg. Guitar players such as Eric Clapton, John Mayall, Jimmy Page and Jeff Beck had mixed American black blues with other influences such as rock 'n' roll and made their own electrifying brand of blues-based rock. "I discovered the blues from the English blues and then I wondered where all this stuff was coming from," Mogg told Todd K. Smith of *Cutting Edge Rocks* many years later. "I started to investigate and discovered Howlin' Wolf, Muddy Waters, Big Bill Broonzy, Big Mama Thornton – that whole lot. Hearing voices as big as those singers was amazing to me."[3]

Ironically, it was not only British music fans and budding musicians that discovered the American black blues musicians through the British bands, but their American peers also discovered their musical heritage, which had been, thus far, neglected. In short, the Brits had taught the Americans about their musical roots.

2

The 1960s provided a cultural and social revolution and Britain, it seemed, had finally begun to recover from the devastating effects of World War II. The 1960s was an age of mass consumerism, fashion, music and drugs. Words like "counterculture", "bohemian" and "beatnik" were being thrown around by a new liberalised youth much to the horror of the elder conservative generation. There had also been a major musical movement in Liverpool in the North West of England spearheaded by The Beatles. The British Blues Boom and the Liverpool Merseybeat bands were an inspiration to youngsters like Mogg but his primary influences – surrogate singing teachers if you like – were the likes of Sonny Boy Williamson, Muddy Waters and Howlin' Wolf and more contemporary singers such as Joe Cocker, Steve Marriott, Arthur Brown and Terry Reid. Mogg would watch the likes of Muddy Waters and John Mayall's Bluesbreakers at The Marquee Club on London's Wardour Street.

Mogg actually started out as a drummer before switching to bass, attempting to copy his idol Jack Bruce of Cream. Mogg wasn't especially talented at either instrument so he started singing which, again, was an attempt at sounding like his blues bassist/singer hero Bruce. Mogg's parents didn't think he would be successful as a musician but in time the cocky young London lad would prove his worth.

Meeting Way and Parker that day, via Mick Bolton, was essentially a life-changing encounter. In terms of enduring popularity and significance, the encounter is not as frequently written about as, say, the day Paul McCartney met John Lennon at a church fete in Woolton Village, Merseyside on 6 July 1957, or when Mick Jagger met Keith Richards at Dartford train station on 17 October 1961. Nonetheless, for enthusiasts of hard rock and fans of UFO it was certainly a red letter day.

Pete Way was born Peter Frederick Way on 7 August 1951 in Enfield, Middlesex. He was a keen hand on the bass guitar before UFO formed, having played in several high school bands with some local kids, but nothing professional. Way's defining moment came on 18 October 1968 when, aged 18, he saw Led Zeppelin (then known as the New Yardbirds) at London's Marquee Club. He'd also offered his services as a session player to other artists, which proved to be a great training ground for UFO. "My mum always warned me about loud music," Pete Way would later tell the *NME*'s Bob Edmands. "Always told me to turn down my record player. She would have told me to turn my amp down as well."[4]

Way was in awe of Led Zeppelin's self-titled debut, which was released in the UK through Atlantic Records in March 1969 (two months later than in the States). Led Zeppelin would not only influence UFO and their peers but future generations of rock bands to come, of course, and to have seen them at the Marquee rather than a stadium is claim to fame in itself.

Way's school friend, Andy Parker, was born Andrew Maynard Parker on 21 March 1952 in Cheshunt, Hertfordshire. Parker first began playing drums at aged 7 and got his first drum kit at 17, the same age at which he signed on with Mogg and Way in UFO. As a child, before the early days of UFO, Parker would pound and bang on anything from buckets to pots and pans just to get a sound. He was from a musical family, so it was likely that he would end up in the music industry in some capacity. "My mother always had to sing," he later explained. "She was a church goer. Coming out of the post-war-babies kind of thing, my parents struggled for a while but, when they had the money, they gave my sister and I piano lessons. My sister's extremely gifted as a pianist."[5]

However, it was because of his sister that he never took drum lessons. As is often the case with the infants of a family, he could never live up to the standards of an elder sibling. Parker did not want to take piano lessons knowing full well that he would never be as skilled as his sister. However, his mother refused to pay for drum lessons, so he did it all by himself.

Joining UFO was a Godsend. One of his idols was the Led Zeppelin drummer John Bonham. Similarly to The Who, whose drummer Keith Moon was as equally manic as Bonzo, Led Zeppelin was powered by drums just as much as guitars. Parker looked up to Bonham as a hero as soon as he heard "Good Times, Bad Times". Bonham's style and approach was exactly what Parker was looking for, whilst he also admired Mitch Mitchell from the Jimi Hendrix Experience and Ginger Baker from Cream.

Parker's father, on the other hand, wanted him to pursue a career in the electronics industry believing, correctly, that computers would play a vital role in the world's future. However, they weren't to play much of a role in his son's future direction.

Speaking in 2012, Parker recalled his youth and early influences: "It's just my style that I developed over the years. I like that big drum sound, not loads of intricate fills, not loads of odd time signatures, just basically I like it that Bonham leaves space for everybody else, and he doesn't overplay, leaves space for everybody and it's [*sic*] makes it more exciting and create[s] a good framework for the guys to show off."[6]

With the first line-up of UFO now established, they were gratified to learn that Equals' guitarist Eddy Grant was something of a fan of the band and it was he who arranged to get them signed to Beacon Records, as he was branching out into management and production work. Beacon Records, run by the Antiguan born American businessman Milton Samuel, was behind the band from the word go. Samuel also signed a band called the Show Stoppers who were best known for the 1967 song, "Ain't Nothin' But A Houseparty".

UFO's debut album, *UFO 1,* was the band's first stepping stone. Produced by Doug Flett and Guy Fletcher for Beacon Records, *UFO 1* features, naturally, Phil Mogg, bassist Pete Way, guitarist Mick Bolton and drummer Andy Parker. How did Flett and Fletcher come into the picture? Paul Rich, a music publisher whose clients included the songwriter-producer Flett, had arranged a meeting for him in June 1970 with Samuel, chairman of Beacon Records, a small EMI distributed label. Eddy Grant had produced a few tracks for the band, but they were not quite suitable for what they had in mind. Flett met with the band and liked their raw, edgy rock sound. Flett and Samuel subsequently arranged the contracts resulting in Flett getting the producer's chair for UFO's debut offering.

As is often the case with traditional producers, Flett routined the band with several of their own original compositions and three cover versions that Flett handpicked. A cover of Eddie Cochran's "C'mon Everybody" was chosen for the final selection knowing that Cochran's other classic "Summertime Blues" had been covered many times, most famously by The Who. One of the first songs Pete Way ever wrote was "Follow You Home" which would also make it to the final cut.

Flett's budget was £500. Even by 1970s standards it was a tiny amount of cash to make a commercial sounding release. Flett and the band recorded *UFO 1* at Jackson Studios and received significant support from Malcolm Jackson. It took them just two days to record the album; all tracks were recorded live with just a minor amount of overdubbing before they mixed the tracks on the third day. Flett and the band received some positive feedback from Milton Samuel, who even got some foreign distribution deals including Motown's rock imprint Rare Earth in the USA for a reported $20,000 advance.

I contacted Doug Flett to be interviewed for this book but he directed me towards his website *dougflett.com* and said in an email: "At this distance from events I don't have anything to add to my comments on my website. I can say that Guy had nothing what so ever to do with the band or the production. In those days we shared credits on whatever came up."[7]

After the release of the album, Milton Samuel moved to Jamaica to run a club over there before dying a few years later of cancer. According to Flett's website, neither he nor the band "received a cent in royalties."

UFO 1 opens with the eerie instrumental "Unidentified Flying Object" which is very reminiscent of Hawkwind. "Boogie" (originally named "Boogie For George" on the 1970 LP) is a 1950s style rocker with some guitars that were undoubtedly inspired by The Shadows. "C'mon Everybody" is a raucous romp with some excellent drums and guitars, whereas "Shake It About" is a bluesy and curiously groovy little number. "(Come Away) Melinda", which was popularised by the late gruff voiced American singer Tim Rose, in 1967, is a dreamy five minute number with some oddly laidback vocals from Mogg.

"Timothy" is a much needed rocker and possibly the album's standout track; the band are on fire especially during the middle section, which is undoubtedly influenced by the blues-rock trio Cream. "Follow You Home" isn't sure if it's a rocker or a psychedelic song but Parker's drums are excellent. "Treacle People" is another spacey effort; it's a little too laidback and dreamy. "Who Do You Love?", originally a Bo Diddley song, shows that UFO were very much a drums led band during this era. They may have been influenced in choosing this by the Quicksilver Messenger Service, who covered it a year previously on their wonderful live jam *Happy Trails*. The closing track, "Evil", is mid-paced blues similar to Black Sabbath's "Evil Woman", which itself is a cover of the 1969 Crow song "Evil Woman (Don't Play Your Games With Me)".

UFO's debut album is an interesting release from an historical perspective but, while the musicianship has held up, it ultimately lacks focus and thrills. The production does not exactly sparkle, either. The band fused their varied influences together for their debut *opus* from Bo Diddley to Eddie Cochran by way of Quicksilver. UFO were essentially divided between R&B, rock 'n' roll and blues, and it shows in the slightly muddled sound of their first full-length release.

Although the band delves into arty space rock and 1960s psychedelia, they also take stabs at blues rock with influences that predictably include Led Zeppelin, The Who and the great American blues rock outfit, Blue Cheer.

The band's energy and rawness was undeniable on the debut album. What they perhaps lacked in creativity they more than made up for with enthusiasm and energy. However, this incarnation of UFO evidently leaned more towards the psychedelic than the blues. They were a confused band, unsure of which style of music to create. "We were torn between doing something that was bluesy or acid," Mogg later admitted, "Drugs were starting to come out, dope and all that stuff and the Roundhouse [in London] was all psychedelic."[8]

Psychedelia, indeed, was alive and tripping, but Free had released the classic hard blues rock album *Fire And Water* in mid-1970, and slowly but surely UFO would edge towards such a harder bluesier sound. To be fair to them, UFO had only been playing together for a short time and hadn't had much opportunity to hone their own style. *UFO 1* was released in October 1970. It did not chart in the UK or USA.

In terms of singles in various territories, "Shake It About" was released with the B-side "Evil" in 1970, as was "(Come Away) Melinda" with "Unidentified Flying Object"; "Boogie For George" with "Treacle People" and "C'mon Everybody" with "Timothy". "Boogie For George" was re-released in 1971 with "Follow You Home".

UFO 1 was put out there with little fanfare, which goes some way to explaining the poor sales of the album which, in the UK, were around 3,700. It would linger in relative obscurity for years to come; only talked about by the most ardent UFO fan. Writing on the popular music reference website, *All Music*, Jason Anderson states: "The uneven mixes and amateur performances that some listeners might find quaint or innocent could be distracting to others. In their pre-Michael Schenker days, the British band made a much more experimental noise that reflected psychedelic as well as R&B influences pitched with a dark resonance."

The album was later reissued as *Unidentified Flying Object* with four of the five tracks from the band's second album and also features a cover image of the band's 1980s line-up much to the annoyance of fans. The album was also reissued as *Flying – The Early Years* in 2004 and *All The Hits & More – The Early Days*.

In hindsight, *UFO I* was merely a stepping stone to bigger, better and bolder rock based albums. Debut releases by the likes of Black Sabbath and Blue Cheer may have gone down in the history books for all the right reasons, but some fans would argue it took Deep Purple three albums before their made their first hard rock masterpiece with *In Rock* in 1970. *UFO 1* is not the UFO that we now know and love, and it's just as well they developed a new sound later in the decade, because it's arguable that they would have otherwise faded into obscurity.

Following the release of their debut album, UFO went back into the studio to work on what became *UFO 2: Flying*, although the initial title was actually *Star Storm*. It was another rushed job for the band as time was of the essence. However, they had progressed as musicians in a relatively short space of time, so they could cope with such haste. For the second release, they already knew that they wanted to create longer songs rather than the relatively short three or four minute tracks that comprised the first album. Essentially the band had evolved quickly under the guidance of Beacon boss, Milton Samuel. After all, their debut *opus* had only been released in October 1970 while its follow-up was arranged for a late 1971 arrival.

UFO 2: Flying, which is also known as *UFO 2* or *Flying*, was recorded at London's Nova Studios with producers Doug Flett and Guy Fletcher, or rather Doug Flett flying solo as producer according to his website, as previously mentioned. Flett used a sixteen-track mixing desk. *UFO 2: Flying* consists of the 26:30 long title track as well as the 18:54 long 'Star Storm', and such was the aura of the songs that the album was sub-titled *Space Rock*. "We want to develop melody, lyric, beat and rhythm to a state of equal importance," Mogg said to *Beat Instrumental Magazine* at the time.[9]

UFO 2: Flying opens with "Silver Bird", an almost seven minute long epic with notable shifts in pace; there are no vocals and the guitars are excellent. It's just about bearable. 'Star Storm' is something of an endurance test for the listener although it does show how underrated Mick Bolton (still) is as a guitarist. Mogg's vocals come in towards the end of the track. "Prince Kajuku" is a frantic three and a half minute number that is a slight nod towards the rock band UFO would subsequently become. "The Coming Of

Prince Kajuku" is something of a come down after the raucousness of the previous song, but it's almost tranquil ambient opening shows another side to the band. "Flying" is a lengthy 26 minutes and 30 second long song which has some interesting chord sequences, but it's not the type of song which UFO excels at.

Ultimately, UFO's second album is a flawed piece of work. It is obvious in hindsight that they were trying to find their footing. *UFO 2: Flying* was released in October 1971, exactly a year after the band's debut album. "Prince Kajuku" was issued as a single with the B-side "The Coming Of Prince Kajuku". As with the band's first release, *UFO 2* did not trouble the charts either in the UK or USA.

As with the band's debut, *UFO 2: Flying* hardly set the critics' pulses racing either. The album gained little prominence in the UK and is all but forgotten about except by the more enthusiastic fans (and many of those prefer to forget this era of the band's history in favour of latter day glories).

UFO 1 and its subsequent release are both space rock themed albums, albeit with a hard rock edge that would become the band's trademark sound. However, these two releases are light years away from what the band would produce later in the decade. It was later reissued with the first album as *Flying – The Early Years.*

Historically, the album has little significance except within the realms of serious followers of the band, and perhaps Hawkwind fans and enthusiasts of space rock. Critic Richard Foss makes an interesting point on the *All Music* website when he says: "It's fairly obvious that if Bolton had stayed at the helm then UFO would have never had the pop fame that they later achieved, but it can be interesting to try to imagine what kind of music they might have made as they grew even more accomplished."

Preceding the album's release, the band headed to Japan in September for a promotional road jaunt. They arrived at Sapporo Airport on 18 September followed by a press conference and gig in Mugen on 21 September, and from there gigs were arranged at the Osaka Prefectural Gymnasium and Hibiya Outdoor Music Hall on 23 and 25 September. They performed "Prince Kajuku", "Silver Bird", "C'mon Everybody", "'Boogie

For George", "Follow You Home" and "Who Do You Love". The three dates cost Japan's Toshiba Records almost £10,000 but the fee proved to be worthwhile as a shade shy of 10,000 people turned up for the Osaka gig and 23,000 fans turned up to see the band perform in Hibiya. "Japanese audiences are great. They will accept anything that's done well. They haven't been told what's trendy to like and dislike," Mick Bolton told the *NME*'s Roger St Pierre at the time.[10]

The first album which, as we've seen, didn't exactly fly off the shelves in the UK, shifted a massive 135,000 copies in Japan. Unsurprisingly, the band flew back to East Asia in October 1971 for a two week jaunt with Three Dog Night. The tour was reported to be worth £15,000. UFO were already making a name for themselves as a feisty live act. "We have noticed that people seem more into the music if you move about," Way told the *Melody Maker*'s Mike Guy at the time. "When they go out to see a group, they expect more than what they hear on a record."[11]

Although both albums were shunned in the UK and USA, UFO went down a storm in Germany where "Boogie For George" from *UFO 1* peaked at Number 30 in the official German singles chart and "Prince Kajuku" from *UFO 2: Flying* hit Number 26. Germany wasn't the only country to latch onto UFO before the UK: in Japan they scored a hit with "C'mon Everybody" and consequently they released their first live album, simply called *Live*, in Japan in 1971. They were still teenagers when they toured Japan, which in their eyes felt like Beatlemania. In Germany alone, they had a couple of million album sales of the first two studio releases and *Live,* but success did not come globally. Despite the lack of interest in UFO in the UK, the band did get a minor endorsement by renowned DJ John Peel.

Live, which was later reissued as *UFO Lands In Tokyo* and *UFO Live In Japan*, was recorded in Japan in 1971 and produced by the band with Milton Samuel. The original Japanese release was titled *U.F.O Landed Japan*. Mostly consisting of covers and songs from the band's first two blues space rock textured albums, *Live* is an interesting release.

Live opens with an awesome version of "C'mon Everybody" that Cochran himself would have been proud of; it's fast and furious and the audience are very much in the groove. "Who Do You Love" is a frantic blues rocker with a taut rhythm section which proved that the first line-up of the band had chemistry onstage. "Loving Cup" has more than a passing nod to Mogg's hero, Jack Bruce. The duo of "Prince Kajuku"/"The Coming

Of Prince Kajuku" are far bluesier onstage than they are on the recorded versions. Bolton is on fire and Parker has always deserved more praise as a drummer. "Boogie For George" is a chaotic onstage riff-fest while the closing track, "Follow You Home", is preceded briefly by a version of The Kinks' "You Really Got Me" (which also ripples through the song) to get the audience pumped up before the end of the gig. It's a sweat-inducing climax to a tantalising glimpse of what UFO were like back in the early 1970s.

It's a suitably energetic and, at times, fiery live album. Some would argue, justifiably, that UFO were much better onstage than in the studio. Later releases of the album include a bonus track: the single edit of "Loving Cup".

With not a great deal of original material at that point in their history, the band did extended versions of five of the six songs on the record, while "Loving Cup" is a cover of a song by American blues guitarist Paul Butterfield. It's interesting to listen to this period of the band's history in a pre-punk context and at a time when progressive rock was still in its youth. Certainly, this period of the band's career is rarely touched upon by prog rock enthusiasts and critics of the genre.

The band's live approach would change considerably in the coming years, shifting away from jam style blues to a guitar led hard rock sound. Speaking a year later, Phil Mogg spoke to *Melody Maker*'s Chris Welch about his perception of the band then: "Oh ... I suppose you could say we were sexual and possibly slightly bizarre. There aren't many bands around like us. We are quite theatrical in our presentation."[12]

The recording features the original line-up of UFO (Mogg, Way, Bolton and Parker) and was the last album to feature Mick Bolton.

Live was released in 1971, originally by Toshiba Musical Industries/ Stateside Records. It eventually went Gold in both the USA and UK due to subsequent reissues as well as the band's growing fanbase and reputation later. *Live* was released outside of Japan in 1972 under various titles and on different labels, such as Nova Records in Germany. Some contemporary reports suggest that the band were unaware of its release at the time.

Regardless of its history, it remains an important piece of the band's career as it is the only officially released live document featuring Mick Bolton. Those first three albums netted the band sales of three million in Japan, Germany and France yet they remained relatively unknown in the UK. As the Bible tells us, a prophet is without honour in his own country; this was true for UFO.

Live gained little notice in the domestic music press either. Historically, the recording brought an end to this particular era of the band's sound. Their albums may not have given them a great deal of coverage in the UK, but they had begun to make some splashes in the press with their energetic live performances. Not everyone was convinced though. Chris Welch writing for *Melody Maker* in 1972 was scathing: "They are unmusical, blatantly sexual, and cheerful copyists of the Funk-Cooper school (although they reject most of this assessment as 'unfair'). I thought they were one of the worse bands seen in several weeks." Ouch!

The band figured that they had to change a few things if they were to ever compete with the likes of Deep Purple, Black Sabbath and Led Zeppelin. The space rock sound had to be ditched. Speaking about their lack of chart success in the UK, Phil Mogg spoke to the *NME*'s Roger St Pierre in January 1972: "I don't know. Perhaps it's because the public has become a little tired of progressive rock groups and we're a progressive rock group. But we do avoid the usual clichés and try to give the public something more than just freaky sounds."[13]

In January 1972, after arguments with Mogg and Parker, Mick Bolton left UFO and the band began their quest for a new lead guitarist. They needed somebody to give them a much needed edge; some grit and verve. Ex-Blodwyn Pig and future Motörhead guitarist Larry Wallis was perceived to tick all the boxes and joined UFO in February 1972.

Wallis was hired after answering an ad in *Melody Maker*, a rather vague one, which read "Gigantic Rock Band. No Names. Needs A Guitarist. You've Got To Look Great." Wallis went to the audition, which was held by Pete Way and Andy Parker, but Phil Mogg was not present for some reason. He'd never heard of UFO (although he did not let on to the band). However, he looked trendy for the time, even getting a compliment from Way on account of his long hair and cool hippy-like attire. At the audition, Wallis played a version of "Driving South" from *The Jimi Hendrix Experience Album*, which he'd heard the night before on John Peel's radio show.

At this time the band was managed by Mark Hannau who, for one reason or another, had stopped managing Curved Air. UFO felt he couldn't take them to the heights they yearned for so they started making contacts, one of whom was Wilf Wright at Chrysalis Records. Wright, who also managed ex-Procol Harum axe maestro Robin Trower, got the band some gigs in Italy. They simply had to aim their music at other markets besides those in Japan and Germany, where they already had a large following.

Larry Wallis: "He [Wright] signed us a publishing deal for £8,000, which was a respectable amount in those days. We were about to go off on a tour of Germany, so naturally we spent the money on a sound system bigger than anyone else's and a second hand Bentley." The tour ended when the German gangsters running one of the shows nicked the Bentley. Apparently Mark Hannau made them believe they were going to stay in Germany and tour for them.[14]

It has been said that Wallis' abrupt departure from UFO came about after he got drunk one night and told Mogg what he really thought of him. Of course, Mogg was not going to take any bullshit and Wallis got his marching orders in October 1972. Way and Parker were disappointed about Mogg's decision as they rather liked Wallis. The roadies were disappointed too and even dropped off Wallis' amp at his parent's house.

However, this created an argument between Wallis and Wright. Wright said the amp belonged to the band and was not his to keep. Wallis refused to give it back, but Wright reportedly asked him what would happen if the police were given an anonymous tip-off about where Wallis' dope was stashed at his parents' house. Wallis was furious about this threat and called Wright every name under the sun.

Although Way and Parker liked Wallis, the original Holy Trinity of Mogg, Way and Parker was not going to be broken. Wallis remains best known as a member of the Pink Fairies despite his tenure in UFO and his contribution to Motörhead's debut album *On Parole* (which was recorded in 1975 but not actually released until 1979). He was also a house producer for Stiff Records in the mid-1970s, releasing his own single "Police Car" on the label.

The band set about replacing Wallis. Next up was ex-Skinny Cat and future Whitesnake guitarist Bernie Marsden, who was just 21 years old at the time of his initiation into UFO in November 1972. A gig review written by Barbara Drillsma (the publication is unknown) from the band's first visit to Liverpool, where they played at the legendary Cavern Club in December, said: "Bernie Marsden and bass guitarist Pete Way got some fine interplay going, particularly in numbers like 'Galactic Love' and 'Rock 'n' Roll Car' and were strong in 'Do It.'"

Beginning with Wallis and continuing with Marsden, UFO had begun to move towards the blues and away from the psychedelic, acid space rock sound. However, the band would soon join forces with a guitarist who would ultimately change the sound of the band forever and become one of the most iconic guitarists in hard rock history.

CHAPTER
TWO

UFO's Rise To Prominence –
The Michael Schenker Years Part 1
(1973–1976)

*"This is a rock band. The thing is that you are what you do.
When you become great [it's] because you are great.
You are not great if you play once every tenth year or so."*

Pete Way[15]

Sometime in 1973, UFO hooked up with producer Dave Edmunds to record a batch of demos, including the Bernie Marsden co-written track "Oh My", at Rockfield Studios in Monmouthshire. Edmunds told the band to think about hiring his guitarist cousin Paul Chapman, which they did later. Such was the strength of the demos that they secured a new record deal. Rockfield was not yet the legendary recording studio it would become (thanks to bands such as Queen who would later record there) and was at the time very basic.

The band were housed in a local cottage on a secluded farm with minimal heating, which suffice to say was very different from life in the Big Smoke. As well as "Oh My", the demos captured the bare bones of what would become "Doctor Doctor", "Sixteen" and "Rock 'n' Roll" and also a cover of "Move Over", originally a Janis Joplin song. The band were not overly enthusiastic about the demos and went back on the road playing clubs around Britain as well as residencies at The Marquee Club in London. They also ventured over to Europe and it was in Germany when UFO met the Scorpions for the first time.

In June 1973, UFO lured the 18-year-old German guitarist Michael Schenker from Scorpions, Germany's greatest hard rock export. Fate seemed to play a part in this.

Opening for Scorpions that summer (some reports have suggested July 13 as the first date of the tour), UFO were a man down as Marsden was held up back in England due to reported passport problems. Schenker stepped into the breach for two nights. "So there we were, no guitarist and no gear," Mogg told the American magazine *Scene*. "But the show had to go on. We'd sold a lot of advance tickets, and if we hadn't gone on, they quite likely would have smashed the place up."[16]

Marsden – who later admitted he refused to go because he could no longer stand being in the band – arrived in Germany as quickly as he could to continue with the rest of the tour, only for him to be permanently replaced by Schenker once the tour ended.

UFO's set list was "Move Over", "C'mon Everybody", "Looking For An Easy Life", "Sixteen (Crystal Light)" and "Boogie For George". They knew how to handle the crowds, as Mogg told *Melody Maker*'s Chris Welch back in 1972 when referring to their success in Japan where they once played to 20,000 fans: "We've already been through the superstar treatment, so we're not unready. Our main aim is not so much 'success' as to communicate with our audiences."[17]

Leaving UFO for good in June, Marsden went on to join ex-Jethro Tull bassist Glenn Cornick in Wild Turkey, but it is his time in Whitesnake that Marsden remains best known for. Marsden recorded a demo with UFO called "Give Her The Gun" and also appears on the 1993 UFO compilation, *The Decca Years*. Marsden's experience in UFO, although brief, turned him into a professional player, for which he remains thankful. "Oh, Bernie's just an easy going, nice guy to get on with. I think we were a little too wild for Bernie," Pete Way said. "Bernie's like 'Hello?' and we're like 'Where's the drugs? Give us a drink!' David Coverdale once said to Bernie 'What are they like then, those guys?' and Bernie said 'Oh, you wouldn't believe!'"[18]

UFO were a very bluesy band at that point, a sort of British Allman Brothers Band, but Marsden knew his days were numbered. Phil Mogg would later recall an anecdote from the Marsden era: "... Bernie was great, Bernie was very funny ... except when he took his shoes off and put them under the [heater] in [winter]. He used to make the car really smelly. Once he took off his shoes and fell asleep, and Pete Way tied them up with plastic bags and threw them out of the window, so we didn't have to suffer. Bernie was good, we really had fun touring. It was that kind of tour when there's six of you in a car and you're not earning any money, so it's more fun."[19]

Michael Schenker was born on 10 January 1955 in Sarstedt, Lower Saxony in Germany. The general story goes that the future of Schenker's life was forever changed when, one day, his older brother Rudolf brought home a Gibson Flying V. Schenker was captivated by the instrument and in time perfected the electrifying Flying V sound. However, it has been said that Schenker initially played a Les Paul.

Schenker spoke about his early influences to the *Chicago Daily Herald's* Joel Reese many years later: "I would call it original – as original as it gets. I copied other people – Jeff Beck, Eric Clapton, Jimmy Page, Leslie West, Johnny Winter – when I started, but I also knew early I wanted to take it my own way, which I did. It involves a lot of melody."[20]

Michael had Aryan good looks and blond hair, and a mastery of the fretboard which surpassed even that of Rudolf, 16 years his senior.

While Rudolf craved to be in one of the greatest bands in the world, his younger brother yearned to be one of the world's best guitarists. "We could not have fulfilled our visions as accurately as we did if we had not done it that way," Michael explained to Jeb Wright of *Classic Rock Revisited* 40 years later. "It was important for both of us to go our different ways. His vision is very strong but my vision requires different surroundings and a different type of momentum; it is a different journey."[21]

Michael played in the amateur bands The Enervates, Cry and Copernicus before joining Scorpions. He made his live debut with Rudolf and Scorpions in a local club in Germany on New Year's Eve, 1969. Scorpions became a fully fledged professional band in 1971. As a full-time member of the rock outfit, Michael contributed to Scorpions' debut album *Lonesome Crow*, released in 1972. With Rudolf's blessing, Michael joined UFO despite not being able to speak English; his guitar did the talking for him. Schenker's replacement in Scorpions was no slouch either – Uli Jon Roth.

1974's *Fly To The Rainbow* also features songs written by Michael Schenker but *Lonesome Crow* is the only Scorpions album to feature Schenker as a full-time member. Mogg and Way must have thought all their Christmas' had come at once getting Schenker in the band. They knew that with him onboard they would be able to craft an entirely new sound for the band; a sound that was driven almost entirely by the guitar. Goodbye space rock, hello hard rock.

It was during his initial tenure in Scorpions when Schenker developed a musical identity of his own that was both visual and musical. Schenker spoke to *Hard Roxx*'s Matthew Honey in 1997: "... I was on stage with the Scorpions and about to play a lead break. I broke a string so I ripped my brother's Flying V guitar off him and carried on with my solo and I realised that that combination was what I wanted: the Marshal 50W and the Flying V. I developed this tone that I really liked listening to and I just stuck with it."[22]

When Schenker first came over to England, he shared a flat with Phil Mogg in Palmers Green, North London. Mogg has retold one story about Schenker stealing a rabbit from someone's back garden a few doors down the road. Its owners were fattening the bunny up for Christmas but Schenker wanted to prevent its grisly fate. He took the rabbit back to the flat, but it shat all over the place which infuriated the pair.

"He will bring us luck. We will make it work with him at last," Mogg said of Schenker to German magazine *Bravo* at the time.[23]

In November 1973 the band headed back to Germany for another round of dates with Scorpions as support, which made for an interesting story considering the recent line-up amendments between both bands.

This version of UFO set to work on some demos for their upcoming studio album and, in 1974, the band officially signed to Chrysalis Records, which, with the addition of Schenker, would change the band's fortunes on a global level. Indeed, UFO would record their best work for Chrysalis and, under the guidance of new manager Wilf Wright, UFO would get their first big break. Similarly to UFO, Chrysalis had formed in 1969 and had some of the country's best rock acts on their books including, Jethro Tull, Ten Years After, Rory Gallagher and Procol Harum. With a new label backing them and a new producer in the shape of Ten Years After's bassist Leo Lyons, UFO's future was suddenly looking bright.

With Schenker as the guitarist, UFO set to work on their third studio album, the record which most fans consider to be the true beginning of the band.

Phenomenon was recorded at Morgan Studios in London with Lyons as producer. Lyons was a seasoned musician and producer having spent the best part of eleven years touring and recording. He had also co-produced a total of six Ten Years After albums, and had been working at his home recording studio with Frankie Miller before hooking up with UFO. The bassist had also performed at Woodstock in 1969 and featured on the Isle Of Wight Festival bill the following year. Lyons was joined by engineer Mike Bobak who had previously worked with Rod Stewart and The Faces.

Lyons explains: "... basically, they'd sold a few records in Germany and with Ten Years After I was signed to Chrysalis Records, I'd been doing some production work for them. They asked me if I would go in the studio for a day with UFO and work on a couple of songs with them, which I did. I had a farm in Chipping Norton and so I booked Chipping Norton Studios for a day, but it turned out to be half a day because they'd turned up late. We got two tracks and Chrysalis wanted to see how they were. I guess they wanted to see how I was with them and what they thought about me. They liked it and so I got the record. The brief was, well, you know, they sell a few records in Germany, here's the project and £1500 and go in a make a record. I didn't get the impression that any of them were expecting anything."[24]

Based in Willesden, North-West London, Morgan Studios had hosted recording sessions for luminaries such as Thin Lizzy, Yes, Mott The Hoople and Jethro Tull. Also, Morgan Studios had a bar which helped! Ozzy Osbourne and John Bonham would sometimes drop by and make everyone laugh out loud with some hilarious stories, and entertain everyone with their generally mischievous rock 'n' roll personalities.

This forthcoming release would mark the beginning of what was, for many fans, the definitive line-up of UFO: singer Phil Mogg, bassist Pete Way, drummer Andy Parker and guitarist Michael Schenker.

It was a thrill to work with Lyons, because he gave the band free rein to play whatever they liked. However, the band only had ten days to complete the album. Luckily, they were tight, having played so many club dates in the past and, given that Schenker was also a wizard on the guitar, things moved rather quickly. With Lyons' background in guitar-based rock, he knew the importance of a memorable guitar solo which is why he was on the band's side when they did not chop the solo in half during "Rock Bottom" (though this made it less radio friendly).

Still only 18 years old, Schenker was an obsessive when it came to working on the second album of his career. He would build up countless takes before he settled on a riff or guitar part that he felt was suitable enough for the tracks. The band didn't mind the fact that Schenker's English was almost non-existent at this point, because his playing was so bloody good. Lyons spoke German so he would act as a translator and got along fine with the guitarist.

Lyons: "I don't think there was too much translating. It was just trying to understand what he wanted, what the problem was. Basically, he played a bit of music and he'd say, 'What do you think?' I'd say, 'That was great' and he'd say, 'Yeah, maybe.' Schenker's one of those guys that is a perfectionist. He'd work at solos which you can probably figure [out] from listening. They're all very melodic. He'd work on his solos. He'd come in and play them to me and make a few suggestions. We'd put it together and do 20 or 30 takes and put together all the bits he liked. Usually the second or third take I would have accepted."[25]

Schenker always came up with truly stunning melodic solos in the studio, which compare favourably to the fretboard masturbation that so many of his contemporaries delighted in. He was a strict guitarist that knew which part of a song should contain the right guitar hook. He thought about every riff, mulling over it until he was truly happy with it. Unlike Bernie Marsden, Schenker is not a blues player but he has a sense of melody and an innovative style of playing which is what interested Mogg and Way in the first place, and it was those skills that Schenker brought to the party.

While Schenker brought a German rock sound to the band, Mogg and Way threw in their British-American influences by the way of The Who and the Small Faces. Marsden was certainly far more blues orientated than Schenker and for the time even too bluesy for UFO. Schenker offered a new beginning for the band with his sophisticated sense of melody and timing.

"Pete was always the guy that had a million excuses as to why he turned up late," recalls Lyons. "Andy was a very underrated player. Nobody talks about him. When you're talking about a rock band, the basis of a rock band stands or falls on its drummer. Andy was a damned good drummer. Phil, I still think he's a great singer, and I liked a lot of the songs we did."[26]

"Rock Bottom", the album's standout song and a track that would become a firm fan favourite, was written in a rehearsal studio. Schenker was working on some riffs while Mogg was reading a newspaper. The story goes that Mogg said he'd stop Schenker playing when he heard a nifty riff. Schenker launched into the riff that would form the basis for 'Rock Bottom' and Mogg jumped up shouting, "That's it!"

Although the bulk of the album was recorded at Morgan Studios, Lyons chose to record "Let It Roll" and "High Flyer" at Wessex Studios in Highbury, North London, which he managed at the time. The band were more comfortable at Morgan, but Lyons would occasionally get criticised for not using Wessex enough.

Phenomenon opens with the hard rock stomp of "Oh My" before the dulcet guitar chords of "Crystal Light" come into play. "Doctor Doctor" is now a classic and needs no analysis. "Space Child" is a catchy mid-paced affair with some wonderful guitar passages. "Rock Bottom" – as with "Doctor Doctor" – is one of the most recognised songs in rock music. "Too Young To Know" shows off Mogg's vocal prowess and Parker's restrained drums. "Time On My Hands" has Schenker's melodic touch on the guitars stamped all over it. "Built For Comfort" is a bluesy number with an almost funky groove while Mogg's vocals resemble Paul Rodgers of Free. "Lipstick Traces" is a slower affair with no vocals. Finally, "Queen Of The Deep" closes the album in style with some excellent interplay between guitars, bass and drums.

Phenomenon has its faults but it undoubtedly set the benchmark for the future sound of the band, and it was obvious that certain traits were now coming together to create UFO's now iconic hard rock sound.

In terms of the songwriting credits, six of the ten songs are credited as Schenker/Mogg with "Too Young To Know" billed as Mogg/Way and "Oh My" as Schenker/Mogg/Way/Parker. "Built For Comfort" is a cover of the Willie Dixon blues number. It was fairly obvious that despite being the newbie in the band Schenker was not going to sit back and let the rest of the group take control.

The album cover was designed by the famed Hipgnosis team spearheaded by Storm Thorgerson who sadly passed away in 2013. *Phenomenon* was released in May 1974. It didn't chart in the UK but stuck at 202 in the US album charts, thus missing out by a whisker on the all-important *Billboard* 200.

Various songs were released as singles in different territories: "Give Her The Gun" with "Sweet Little Thing" was released in Germany in 1974;

"Doctor Doctor" with "Lipstick Traces" came out in March preceding the album's May release and "Rock Bottom" followed suit in 1974. "Rock Bottom" with "Doctor Doctor" and "High Flyer" (from the forthcoming album, *Force It*) gained a release in 1975.

The album was later reissued in 2007 with a selection of bonus tracks, including the demos "Sixteen" and "Oh My", the single A-side "Give Her The Gun", the B-side "Sweet Little Thing", the previously unreleased "Sixteen" and a live recording of "Doctor Doctor" from 1974. "Give Her The Gun" and "Sweet Little Thing" feature the talents of guitarist Bernie Marsden prior to the presence of Michael Schenker.

Phenomenon was released to mostly positive reviews, although there were some complaints from critics about the album's production. Nevertheless, *Phenomenon* started it all for the band and many fans prefer to think of this album as the band's true debut.

Pete Makowski was critical of the album's first two songs, calling them "awful" in *Sounds* though he continued to praise most of the songs: "But if you do hear them, don't let it put you off the album cause it's quite good and shows promising flickers of what the band could develop into." Over in the USA, *Billboard* was enthusiastic about the release: "The first English band to appear in some time that seems to be able to handle rock without succumbing to the most outrageous commercialism."

An important recording for the band in so many ways, *Phenomenon* contains some of the band's most enduring songs with fan favourites such as "Doctor Doctor" and "Rock Bottom". The guitar attack of Michael Schenker was truly unmistakable and the key ingredient which the first two UFO albums blatantly lacked.

What did Chrysalis make of the album?

Lyons: "They liked it. They put it out in America and Jerry Moss from A&M called up and said: 'I think you've got a really big record here.' It started to get airplay and it started to get into the shops. Chris Wright [Chrysalis] called me up and said: 'Congratulations, you've got a hit record. It's great.' I said: 'I'm on tour in America right now. Can I help with it?' I called up their Sales Rep in the States and I said: 'I'm in the States. The band aren't here but I can do some interviews or whatever you want.' I said 'It's great. It's happening. It's at the bottom of the charts.' He [Wright] said 'It won't go any further, we haven't shipped enough.' That's when I realised they didn't expect it to do what it did."[27]

The album's legacy is assured as it has gone down as a classic hard rock album and it remains steady back catalogue after all these years. *Phenomenon* has since become a cherished album amongst rock fans, notably with the heavy metal band Iron Maiden. When Blaze Bayley joined the band in the mid 1990s replacing Bruce Dickinson, they covered "Doctor Doctor" live. With Dickinson back in the fold, during the *Dance Of Death* world tour of 2003 to 2004 they'd play the original version as an intro to tell fans that Maiden were about to begin their show. Maiden's version of "Doctor Doctor" can be found in the *Eddie's Archive* box-set in the *Best Of The B-sides* collection. It was originally included as a B-side to the Blaze Bayley fronted "Lord Of The Flies" single in 1996.

"We were a team of people that were going to show the record company that there was something to offer," says Lyons summarising his thoughts on the album. "To do a record that stood up and that I thought was good. I still do think it's a good record."[28]

The band hit the road to promote *Phenomenon* in 1974. During the band's performances, Mogg introduced material from the new album as "from our first album" letting everyone know that *Phenomenon* saw their reinvention. They were a hard rock band and emphatically not a space rock orientated outfit.

The band had played their first live show of 1974 in January at the Linkebeek Festival in Belgium, before they embarked on an extensive series of dates in Britain and mainland Europe. They opened with "Oh My" before working their way through "Doctor Doctor", "Built For Comfort", "Give Her The Gun", "Space Child", a cover of the John Lennon song "Cold Turkey", and "Rock Bottom". They recruited Welsh born guitarist Paul Chapman in April.

Nicknamed "Tonka" after the company which made indestructible toys, Chapman was born Paul William Chapman in Cardiff, Wales on 9 June, 1954. Aged just 16, Chapman joined the Irish blues rock band Skid Row in December 1971, replacing Gary Moore. His first real band was the Welsh rock outfit Universe, but Skid Row was in a different league all together. Chapman's stint in Skid Row was short-lived, lasting until July of the following year. He moved on to a band called Kimla Taz from December

1972 to mid 1974. Having seen an advertisement in *Melody Maker* by UFO, who wanted a second guitarist to strengthen their live sound, Chapman auditioned at the Unity Theatre in London. Chapman helped strengthen the band's guitar sound during their many club dates throughout the year.

Cliques had developed in the band, which happens with every outfit. On the road, Schenker and Chapman would share a room, while Mogg kipped in the same room as Way thus leaving Parker on his own. Chapman got on well with Schenker, while Way or Parker used to bitch to him in private about how bored they were of the band. Nevertheless, there was also camaraderie and a sense of fun in the band and Way, especially, acquired a reputation for some rock 'n' roll antics and *Spinal Tap*-like moments. Mogg and Way dubbed Parker "No Neck" on account of his physical appearance.

Phil Mogg: "That's why we're a looser organisation than many. We go through a series of sagas every day. You know, half out of it, missing planes, checking into wrong hotels."[29]

They also made several important appearances at the BBC, before touring the USA in October for the first time, supporting Steppenwolf amongst other artists. UFO played their first show at the famed LA hotspot, the Whiskey A-Go-Go during the tour and also performed on Don Kirshner's TV music show. Going from The Marquee Club in London to the Whisky A-Go-Go was a big change for the band and they got a kick out of staying at the Sunset Marquis Hotel. The USA and the sense of euphoria the band felt whilst touring on the other side of the Atlantic would impact on the band's upcoming material.

Phenomenon was the first of a series of classic 1970s hard rock albums delivered by UFO. Still continuing a seemingly never ending series of small live dates around the UK, they set to work on their next album. However, the band printed a public apology in the 10 December, 1974 issue of *Melody Maker* which read: "UFO would like to apologise to fans and promoters for the cancellation of their dates at short notice due to their American tour. See Y'all soon." 1974 did, however, end with a gig at Nottingham Boat Club. They were still a world away from headlining such venues as Hammersmith Odeon.

Chapman did not record an album with UFO although he did tour and, as such, helped the band promote *Phenomenon*. He can be heard on several tracks on the *BBC – In Session And Live* collection that was released many years later. Due to difficulties with the band and the fact that Chapman failed to turn up for a gig, Chapman's tenure would only last until January 1975 when he went on to found IONA, which would evolve into Lone Star where he stayed until mid-1978. Chapman was young and arrogant and enjoyed getting pissed. Even by his own admission he wasn't too professional back then, but he wasn't even 20 years old, so who can blame him?

The solitary Schenker guitar sound would be an iconic part of UFO's musical identity throughout the rest of the decade. The twin guitar attack worked well for UFO although it wasn't in the Judas Priest or Wishbone Ash duelling guitarists mould, where both axemen would take turns on the lead breaks. Schenker was far too protective of his riffs to allow that to happen! Instead, Chapman added some background strength. It was a great gig for the young Welsh player, but perhaps the timing just wasn't right given his youthfulness and attitude. However, this won't be the last we hear about Chapman.

1975's *Force It* was recorded at Morgan Studios in London with producer Leo Lyons in just two weeks. The band were familiar with working to a tight schedule having recorded *Phenomenon* in just ten days. They also roped in the talents of Lyons' Ten Years After colleague Chick Churchill on keyboards, thus making first use of the instrument on a UFO album. It was the band's idea, as they felt that a selection of songs would benefit from some keyboards. The band even considered asking Churchill to join them as a fully-fledged member, but Churchill enjoyed the finer things in life which put him out of UFO's price range! A chain smoker, he would always have a ciggie in his mouth whilst playing the Hammond organ. Churchill was a keen golfer too, which wasn't high on the list of UFO's hobbies and interests. When they rehearsed together at the Twickenham Rugby Club the band knew the relationship would not last.

Chrysalis left the band and producer alone while they worked on the new album, which was just as well because they had a lot to deal with in the studio. "Working in a studio is very stressful," says Lyons on the growing tension within the camp. "It brings out the worst in people. There were moments on the UFO records where everything was going great and it's a tremendous buzz. Everybody's stressed. If you go and get a take and the take doesn't sound right, the guitar doesn't sound right, there's an insecurity. You get a guy that can't quite play the part right and keeps going wrong in the same place."[30]

It was the first UFO album where Parker used the double bass drum kit, which gave an extra kick to "Shoot Shoot" and "Let It Roll". James Dewar from Robin Trower's band added vocal harmonies to a couple of the tracks. Such was the tight-knit rapport between Lyons and the band, that they asked him if he wanted to manage them. Lyons assumed the role of UFO's manager, but only for about ten days.

Lyons: "Sometime during that period the band came to me without Phil Mogg and asked me to manage them. That's when I realised that there was a little bit of tension. I was gonna manage them but we resolved that problem. The guy [Gary Holton] that was gonna join them was in [the TV show] *Auf Wiedersehen Pet* [Holton's role as Wayne in the popular TV show was post the Heavy Metal Kids and just before his untimely death from drink and drugs in 1985]. I knew that there were weird things going on. They weren't in control of their own money; they'd ended up in debt. You can't not work and then have three drivers and three BMWs to drive around on tour. You've gotta drive around in the van.

'This is the problem that Michael had. He said: 'They're using my publishing money and just spending it.' I knew Pete well. He stayed at an apartment I had in London for a while. I think Pete's idea was, well, the record company will never pay us so let's just roll up a debt. That's really what the grief was between Michael and Phil. I told them all this. I said: 'You're gonna end up in debt; you haven't got any money. Put your feet on the ground and kick up from there.' They called me up a week later and said: 'Actually, we don't want you to manage us.' That was fair enough. We still remained friends. I went in the studio and did the *Waysted* record with them. At that point in time Andy said: 'Fucking hell, I wished we had've listened to you.' There were obviously things going on."[31]

The band were focused on continuing the hard rock sound which *Phenomenon* had been the blueprint for. Such was Schenker's dedication to UFO that he turned down an opportunity to audition for the Rolling Stones (presumably to replace Mick Taylor). There were some inevitable tensions in the band. Mogg and Way had been together since the late 1960s so they would obviously side with each other, which left Schenker out on a limb. Parker was, wisely, quite happy to let them get on with it!

Given the language barrier it must have been difficult for Schenker to express himself articulately. Schenker and Mogg – both of whom shared a famously fiery temperament – were often at war with each other.

Schenker/Mogg dominated the songwriting credits, although Way penned "Too Much Of Nothing" when they needed another song for *Force It* and Mogg didn't have any lyrics left. Lyons and the rest of the band liked the backing track for "Too Much Of Nothing" so Way penned some lyrics. "Shoot Shoot" and "Mother Mary" are credited as Schenker/Mogg/Way/Parker compositions proving that every member of the band had something to say.

Lyons: "One of the guys would come up with a riff and I'd really produce an instrumental and not know what the song is about until Phil came in with the lyrics, which I don't like to do. Phil would come in with the lyrics at the last minute. That's always stuck out in my mind. Even today when I'm working in the studio I always make people put the vocal down so that we know what we're going to do, so that was always weird. I enjoyed it. I look back on it; very fond, great times."[32]

However, the band was hit by some bad luck as they wrapped up recording in February. Schenker collapsed in the studio and was hospitalised with a serious liver condition. He was told to spend six weeks in hospital followed by a couple of months rest at his London flat. He could not stand being in hospital. "The other three UFOs, Phil, Andy and Pete have proved genuine friends these days. They have come to see me almost every day and not for a second considered to abandon me to pursue their own career," Schenker told Germany's *Pop* magazine.[33]

Obviously the band had to alter their plans and touring commitments, but by June Schenker was fit and ready to rock.

As with the band's other albums of the 1970s, the artwork for *Force It* was designed by Hipgnosis. The cover for *Force It* depicts a couple making out in a bath tub. There is a surrealist element to the artwork with several bath tubs scattered about the bathroom. There is a play on words here, of course, as faucet is the American word for a tap. The artwork was risky for the time and because of the amount of flesh on display was almost banned – well, it was the 1970s, a non-PC age, but also surprisingly prudish too. It was toned down for the USA release, where they were even more prudish. One point of interest, is that the gender of the couple remained a cause of debate amongst UFO fans, but the couple turned out to be Genesis P.

Orridge and his then girlfriend Cosey Fanni Tutti; both were later in the avant-garde band Throbbing Gristle.

Force It opens with the truly awesome "Let It Roll" before "Shoot Shoot", an even better song, kicks in. This is a great way to open the band's second Schenker album. "High Flyer" has one of those unmistakably dulcet guitar intros that Schenker excelled at during this era, while Mogg's voice is simply intoxicating. "Love Lost Love" is a toe-tapping, sing-along number with some staggered guitars. "Out In The Street" opens with some piano keys and a fine vocal performance from Mogg before the band come into play. It's a wonderful, almost understated number. "Mother Mary" has become a staple of the band's live set and a classic song in UFO's impressive catalogue. The aforementioned "Too Much Of Nothing" is a pounding rocker while "Dance Your Life Away" is a groovy little number. The closing track, "This Kid's" (Including "Between The Walls"), is a hard rocking stomper and an excellent choice to end the album.

Force It is a step up from *Phenomenon* with some classic rock songs and virtuoso musicianship. It was released in July 1975 and was the band's first album to chart in the USA making it to Number 76 (some reports suggest Number 71) in the *Billboard* 200. Strangely it didn't trouble the UK chart, thus proving the old dictum that prophets are without honour in their own country. The album gave birth to two singles: "Shoot Shoot" with "Love Lost Love" and "High Flyer" with "Let It Roll".

The album was reissued in 2007 with various bonus tracks, including the previously unreleased "A Million Miles" and live versions of "Mother Mary", "Out In The Street", "Shoot Shoot", "Let It Roll" and "This Kid's".

Force It was received with open arms by most critics, many of whom rated it higher than *Phenomenon*. Schenker had handed the band a new sound on a plate and it had worked a treat.

Melody Maker stated: "UFO sound a cut above most of the bands currently doing the rounds with a brash style. Much of this is because of guitarist Michael Schenker, who manages to avoid the usual heavy rock clichés and shows refreshing creativity at times." *Record Mirror* said: "*Phenomenon* has something of a Wishbone Ash feel, but this album has more bite, more raunch." While *Sounds'* Geoff Barton enthused: "*Force It* is a raucous, pounding album, the sort that will shake those delicate china ornaments on your mantelpiece apart and then progressively reduce them to fine dust."

Over in the States, Robert Christgau, the self-appointed "Dean Of American Rock Critics", said of the album in his famed *Consumer Guides*: "Heavy metal that's not hard to take? What? Well, the whole first side moves so smartly you could almost mistake it for rock and roll."

Historically, *Force It* belongs up there with UFO's strongest releases and, while it is not perfect, it is an album that fans continue to adore to this day.

>———

When they weren't in the studio working on *Force It*, most of 1975 was spent on the road. With Schenker back to match fitness, the band resumed touring to promote *Force It* with a series of gigs around mainland Europe. However, after a successful opening slot at a high-profile festival in Dusseldorf in front of 8,000 fans, the band were plagued by a series of mishaps. In France, they could not perform at the Mullhouse because the voltage of the venue was too low and, due to the gig's cancellation, disgruntled fans threw stones and bottles at the tour bus. The band escaped unscathed, fortunately. In Nuremberg, Bavaria, the band's crate of cables and wires was stolen, and in Ludwigshafen the band's car caught fire. While in Baden-Baden, UFO's gig was so wild that Mogg was hit by Way's bass and had to go to hospital where his reported five centimetre head wound was sewn. Despite the problems, the band's shows were well-received with at least 1,000 fans in attendance at every gig.

"Perhaps all this bad luck is a sign of something good coming soon," Schenker told Germany's *Pop* magazine at the time. "We have reached the bad luck summit – from now on it can only get better."[34]

With seemingly no time to waste, UFO followed the well-received *Force It* opus with album number five, *No Heavy Petting*. After using keyboards on *Force It*, UFO decided to repeat the exercise. It would be the first album to feature a full-time keyboard playing band member in the shape of Danny Peyronel (as well as harnessing his talents as a harmony vocalist and co-songwriter).

The story behind Peyronel's introduction to UFO is certainly a fortuitous one. Peyronel was friends with the late Paul Varley, drummer with The Rats and Streak. Varley also happened to be good mates with UFO, especially Pete Way. Born in Buenos Aires in 1953, Daniel Augusto Peyronel joined the Heavy Metal Kids in 1973 and made his live debut at

London's Marquee Club. It was Peyronel's second professional outfit after The Rats. On tour in the US, Peyronel first saw UFO on TV on a show called *Don Kirshner's In Concert*. Peyronel pointed out to his roommate that his friend Paul Varley was mates with UFO.

Peyronel explained to me: "Bizarrely, coincidentally almost, as soon as I got back to London, Paul popped round the flat I shared in Chelsea with my girl, Alexandra (still my girl!), with Pete in tow. They came up and Pete and I just hit it off instantly. I invited him to a gig we were doing at The Roundhouse in Chalk Farm, London, and we had drinks in the dressing room. He asked me if I might put down some keys on the next album, etc."[35]

Peyronel was ready to join UFO due to tensions that had mounted in the Kids. Peyronel even recommended a new replacement: Jackie Clinton's keyboardist, John Sinclair.

Peyronel: "I telephoned Alexandra when I reached my decision, having told the lads I would of course fulfil my commitments for the rest of the tour, which would end in Glasgow a week later. I asked her to phone the lovely Laura at Chrysalis and find out if the UFO boys might be in Europe. She did. They were. And they asked if I might be dropped off in Cologne and hook up with them? They had a Wurlitzer in the truck, and a song from *Force It* that they could not do live without keys, so would I help them out? Of course I was thrilled to do so. They dropped me off in front of the hotel ... I remember Michael sitting on the steps welcoming me.

'That night was a free night so we just partied and had a great time. Next day we ran through 'Out In The Street' in the soundcheck and I joined them onstage for the song, and for the encore, 'C'mon Everybody'. It was just total magic."[36]

He rehearsed all their songs by ordering UFO's back catalogue from the Chrysalis office. The band headed to Germany for a tour and by the time the gigs were completed Peyronel had mastered every chord.

Peyronel: "UFO were really big in Germany at the time, and it was a packed house of some 3,000 plus [people], something I wasn't used to! The after show festivities were really brilliant and Pete told me right there and then that as soon as we were back in the UK, if I wanted the job it was mine. So if there is such a thing as Karma, I must have done something right. My move to UFO was the first step in a career that took me to wonderful places. "[37]

Peyronel made his debut as an official member of UFO at Reading Festival in August, playing on the Friday (August 22) which was headlined by Hawkwind and also featured Dr Feelgood.

The slightly tweaked version of UFO turned their attentions to the USA, specifically focussing on the second half of the year with a series of gigs in October and November supporting Edgar Winter Group. During this time, the band recorded some live broadcasts at the famed New York City Record Plant Studios on September 1 which, as with the *BBC In Session And Live*, would become heavily bootlegged over the coming years. The live session saw the band perform a cover of the Small Faces' "All Or Nothing" and Willie Dixon's "Built For Comfort" while the rest of the material was made up of tracks from *Phenomenon* and *Force It*.

On the road, the band's set list was a solid collection of hard rock heavyweights and usually looked like this: "Let It Roll", "Doctor Doctor", "Oh My", "Built For Comfort", "Give Her The Gun", "Space Child", "This Kid's", "Shoot Shoot", "Rock Bottom", "Prince Kajuku", "Boogie For George", "C'mon Everybody" and "Back To The USA".

The band's live performances for 1975 climaxed with a gig at The Roundhouse. The evening was dubbed "The Heaviest Night Of The Year" by promoter John Curd of Straight Music and, with performances from Stray, UFO, Judas Priest and Strife, the claim was no exaggeration.

UFO, if anything, had a cult following in Britain. Much of their time was spent touring Europe and Japan and, aside from some club dates outside of London, the band had yet to tour the full length of their homeland. They certainly didn't have the backing of the British press. Phil Mogg, not being one for false modesty, later told *Sounds'* Geoff Barton: "There are no bands around in Britain today that I can see doing what we do – and if there are I can't think of any that come up to our standard."[38]

No Heavy Petting, the first UFO album the band made as a five-piece, was recorded at Morgan Studios in London in a fifteen to twenty day period from January to February, 1976. "Well, they [Chrysalis] gave me £1500 and it's £25 an hour," says Lyons. "There wasn't time to spend four days getting a drum sound. We had to go for it. I had to really push it. I remember one time, the end of the evening, I actually fell asleep behind the desk. I woke up and everybody had gone. I lived in Oxfordshire. Most of those records we did at Morgan Studios in Willesden, so you can imagine it's like a two o'clock start and you're home at four in the mornings sometimes. I was driving myself. I remember driving home one night, running off the road and I thought 'Sod this' and I hired a driver in the end."[39]

Lyons was assisted by the car-obsessed engineer Mike Bobak. Bobak could often be found reading a magazine about cars and was more eager to talk about his auto-related hobbies than music.

Lyons offers his thoughts on the band's progression since *Phenomenon*: "When a band does its first record nowadays, things have probably changed because people get thrown into the studio before they're ready because they've won a talent contest or something. In those days you'd do a record after you'd done a bit of road work. The first record is always those songs you've stored up ready to make your record. I know they'd done other stuff before, but this was their first major record deal. All the material was ready to go. You're almost going in and doing the live show. With the second record, O.K, there's a bit leftover and by the third record, you've been on the road all the time and had less time to write, it's always a difficult turning point."[40]

The first batch of sessions was actually held at Wessex Studios before they headed to Morgan Studios. Next door in Morgan Studios, Judas Priest were recording their first proper metal album *Sad Winds Of Destiny* (*Rocka Rolla*, their debut, was more blues rock than metal). By their own admission, UFO became very competitive with Priest, who would go on to have far greater success in the USA than UFO in the following decade.

Leo Lyons had the closest rapport with Way who would also hang out with Lyons on his farm. Way and his wife at the time would stay at Lyons' apartment in London after they tried to crack America, as they had nowhere else to go when they came back to England.

Lyons: "He'd [Way] turn up late saying he was on a bus and he fell off, and there was an old lady being mugged and the police arrived blah blah blah, but eventually he'd turn up and we'd do all the tracks. We'd do the backing tracks first and he didn't have to go in for a few days while we worked on it. Most of my comments, from what I recall, were saying, 'Well, we're getting to the chorus a little too late there ...' or 'What's going to be the chorus? Maybe we should just do half a bridge, we need a solo there, we need an extra verse ... just to sort the arrangements out that way.' They always played my bass on the records."[41]

How did the members of UFO react to each other in the studio? "Yeah, there was tension," Lyons told me. "I think Michael got frustrated when Phil hadn't written his lyrics or what have you. Occasionally, we'd do a track and then we'd go round and do some overdubs and I could see that Michael was getting frustrated by it all."[42]

The album's most notable tracks "Martian Landscape", "Can You Roll Her" and "On With The Action" are famed for Peyronel's harmonies and keyboards. However, Way was not especially fond of keyboards and has always viewed UFO as a hard rock guitar based band. Peyronel remembers that Schenker's dedication to his craft, and his precision and insistence on structuring his melodies accordingly, are some things that stand out. Peyronel also got along with Lyons wonderfully.

Peyronel: "*No Heavy Petting* represents a change in the band's sound because of the use of keyboards. I'd like to think that it wasn't just a question of the keyboards. Naturally, when your songwriting tool is the keyboard, you're bound to write in a different way than a guitarist would. But I'd like to think that it's something less definable than that, more of a feel thing.

'Many have said that I was responsible for this new direction, and although I have never knowingly weighed in on the subject, if one tries to look at it as objectively as possible, the tenor of the material that came after me does seem to bear a resemblance to my input. Songs like "Only You Can Rock Me", for instance. Many have suggested this was a typical Danny song, and hey, I probably might have written it, had I stayed in the band! However, I make no claims in that regard, and if that has, in fact, been the case, then I'm very happy and flattered, and, if not, that's fine too."[43]

While Schenker and Mogg penned a majority of the lyrics on the previously produced Lyons albums, with the odd credit given to Parker and Way, Peyronel added some of his own ideas to *No Heavy Petting*, namely "Highway Lady" and "Martian Landscape" and a co-credit with Schenker and Mogg on "On With The Action", and with Mogg and Parker on "Can You Roll Her". "A Fool In Love" is a cover of the Frankie Miller song, which was co-written by Free's bass player Andy Fraser.

"Highway Lady" appeared to take on a life of its own: it was included alongside "Born To Be Wild" on the compilation *Songs Of The Road Vol 1*

– *The Harley Davidson Story,* Peyronel recorded it for his solo album *Make The Monkey Dance* and X-UFO recorded it for their first CD *Vol 1: The Live Files* [As we'll see, X-UFO are a UFO tribute band comprised of ex-band members].

Peyronel: "... I don't have any memories of having to fight to get my ideas across at all. "Can You Roll Her", for instance, was the result of Andy and I jamming all on our own with the drums and Hammond, one time when the rest of the lads were late to rehearsals. Phil then put those crazy/biker lyrics to it, and it was a great result I think."[44]

No Heavy Petting opens with the unmistakable guitars of "Natural Thing" before the more melodic and mid-paced "I'm A Loser" begins. "Can You Roll Her" is a frantic rocker with some excellent keys and drums. "Belladonna" is a ballad which proves that this incarnation of the band were just as apt at creating a love song as they were a rocker. "Reasons Love" picks up the pace considerably – what a track! It's undoubtedly one of the band's best rock songs from this era despite its relative obscurity. "Highway Lady" is a marvellously melodic song with some superlative keys and a terrific vocal performance. "On With The Action" is a mid-paced song with focused guitars and a lean melody, while "A Fool In Love" is a nifty sing-along number with an indelible chorus. "Martian Landscape" closes the album in an almost eerie, dreamy state.

There is much more of a melodic sensibility on *No Heavy Petting* than the previous two releases, and it doesn't quite gel together as a unifying rock album, though there are some excellent songs. It was something of a minor step backwards for the band, given the harder rock sound of *Phenomenon* and *Force It*. Others would perhaps disagree.

No Heavy Petting was released in May 1976. It reached Number 167 in the USA *Billboard* 200 album charts but failed to chart in the UK. The previous year's *Force It* was the first UFO album to break the US Top 100 yet here the band were, with a new album and they just about made the Top 200! The band issued a couple of singles from the album in Japan: "Can You Roll Her" with "Belladonna" and "Highway Lady" with "A Fool In Love". Unfortunately the record has since been somewhat overlooked in favour of subsequent studio releases. It became something of a lost album. Certainly at the time, the band were upset with the album's poor performance. The fact that Chrysalis had changed distributors probably didn't help matters.

Lyons: "By the third one, they [Chrysalis] started to wake up. You can spend half a million dollars on a record and it'll do nothing. Sometimes the record starts to happen itself. With a hundred thousand dollars it can take it a long way. I think they suffered from that a little bit. By the third record they then decided, right O.K., we've messed up a little bit here as a label. The arguments that I'd had with the record label was that I didn't feel that they were totally expecting the band to do anything. How it works in America in particular, is that if you don't ship enough stock to the stores, the stores sell out and the radio stations don't play the record and the record dies. We had that on a couple of records but it still did very well."[45]

It was reissued in 2007 with a number of previously unreleased bonus tracks: "All Or Nothing", "French Kisses", the Frankie Miller penned "Have You Seen Me Lately Joan", "Do It If You Can" and "All the Strings". "All Or Nothing" was recorded on 15 September 1975 at Morgan Studios while the other tracks were recorded in January 1976 at the same studio.

Critics greeted *No Heavy Petting* with rave reviews. Many fans and critics declared that it was even better than the previous albums Lyons had produced.

Geoff Barton wrote in *Sounds*: "This, UFO's third album to feature guitarist Michael Schenker, is undoubtedly their best so far, being brimful of concise, subtlely dramatic, well executed rock songs." Meanwhile, *Melody Maker* said: "He [Peyronel] succeeds in blending well into the band, broadening their sound while not drastically changing it."

Its place in rock history is evident and while it might lack the hard rock punch of other Schenker era albums, it is highly appreciated by fans and the band itself.

UFO continued to tour heavily and, with a succession of well-received hard rock albums, they were finally getting noticed in the UK and USA. To capitalise on the band's growing success, presumably, Nova Records released *Space Metal* in 1976, a collection of songs from the band's first two albums as well as *Live*.

The band played a run of UK club dates in April with support bands Nutz and Dirty Tricks. Reviewing UFO at the Roundhouse, Geoff Barton wrote in *Sounds* dated May 1, 1976: "Cockiness aside, UFO played an exciting set of oldies interspersed with numbers from their forthcoming, much delayed album *No Heavy Petting*. And whether the audience was familiar with a tune or not, each received the same rapturous reaction."

Lyons: "I saw them live a couple of times. I even did the front of house at the Roundhouse. It was good. The Roundhouse is not the best of places if you're in a band. It's good for atmosphere but the sound was pretty bad. I remember turning up to the gig and them saying, 'Oh, would you mix the sound for us?' I did it. What I remember vividly is someone kicked the door of my Bentley in."[46]

UFO then went over to the USA in May for a heavy bout of touring (with Peter Frampton who was promoting his live album *Frampton Comes Alive!*), where they played a solid set consisting of "Can You Roll Her", "Doctor Doctor", "Oh My", "Out In The Street", "Highway Lady", "I'm A Loser", "Let It Roll", "This Kid's", "Shoot Shoot", "Rock Bottom", "C'mon Everybody" and "Boogie For George".

During some shows they worked in a version of the Billy Preston song "You Are So Beautiful" which included backing vocals from Peyronel, but it was obvious that Way was keen to make the band a more rock-orientated outfit. There was nothing specifically wrong with Peyronel; the band liked him but a more guitar-based sound was wanted. Peyronel's girlfriend Alexandra made the band's onstage attire which they dubbed "Alexandra's Rock Rags".

The band were so used to being onstage, where they displayed an incredible amount of energy, that when they ran into a day off they weren't quite sure what to do with themselves. The days off during the touring schedule disrupted the momentum. The adrenaline and focused intensity and drive that musicians build up on the road is displayed onstage, but when it comes to down time there's nothing to do with that energy except smash up hotel rooms and throw TVs out of the window. Is that what they call rock and roll?

On May 1, UFO performed at the Bill Graham organised Day On The Green Festival in California, which also included Peter Frampton, Fleetwood Mac and Gary Wright. It was a great gig for UFO. Bill Graham was the most powerful promoter in the USA and their inclusion on the festival bill only added further proof that UFO had been making headway on the other side of the Atlantic. UFO were a fantastic live band back then, very raw and edgy. Not only were they a colourful cast of characters themselves, but they were surrounded by interesting people, and their live shows in the States throughout the 1970s would influence a legion of American bands from Pearl Jam to Smashing Pumpkins.

UFO would perhaps find it frustrating that they did not receive the sort of recognition that they deserved in the UK, when they were doing exceedingly well in some other countries. The success of a band in the UK was often down to a hit single, which had eluded UFO despite the staggering success of 'C'mon Everybody' in Germany and Japan. Other British artists such as Peter Frampton and (the post Peter Green incarnation of) Fleetwood Mac would find success in the US before the UK. Elton John was another artist who achieved a significant amount of success in the States before his native Britain. So much so, that when he travelled back to the UK to promote his breakthrough self-titled second album many Brits assumed he was American. UFO would also find greater success in the States in the late 1970s than in the UK.

When asked about touring in UFO, Danny Peyronel said in 2012: "All in all? Great fun, very exciting tours and shows ... enjoyed it. Every band has ups and downs, good days/nights and bad. We wouldn't have been human if we hadn't had our share of that. But nothing was too negative that it should stick out and I harbour nothing but affection for the boys, especially Pete, with whom I had a very emotional reunion recently. He is a good, kind, thoughtful person and I'm honoured to count myself as one of his friends and happy he is one of my best mates."[47]

They stayed on the road through to July. Vancouver saw the band opening for Rick Wakeman who was reportedly not too impressed with UFO's brand of hard rock. UFO was the wrong band to open for the prog rock musician, while in the USA they opened for nine Jethro Tull gigs. "I never actually liked Jethro Tull at all," Mogg admitted to *Goldmine*'s Robert L. Smith in 1980. "Their albums are kind of O.K.: but we did a few gigs with them and they were far, far better than I ever imagined as performers. That was kind of interesting. We opened for them at the time, and the audiences kept yelling, 'Tull, Tull.' And I'd say, 'Hey, we're not dull."[48]

In Chicago, Washington and Boston they opened for the J. Geils Band and received encores each night much to the annoyance of the headlining act. At another Chicago concert, the story goes that headliners Ritchie

Blackmore and Rainbow refused to play after UFO. Although minor details about this story were printed in Michael Schenker's tour diary in the July 1976 issue of the German magazine *Pop*, there may be a certain degree of fabrication about this as there is no other evidence to corroborate Schenker's tale. Two shows with Dave Mason followed.

Al Rudis reviewed UFO supporting Foghat in Chicago with New Yorker Stu Daye, for *Sounds*. He wrote: "But even this type of group suffers when all they can make is noise. The audience wanted to respond, and several numbers got people on their feet. But soon they were sitting again, because the sound was such a blur that even the rhythms couldn't be felt."

Now managed by Dick Jordan Michael, UFO were touring and recording non-stop, which isn't all it is cracked up to be. They had their fair share of substances to keep them entertained, but they were becoming more successful in the US and their aim was to be as big as they possibly could be on the other side of the Atlantic. With all the shows they had performed they had become very confident, but with confidence came arrogance. Nevertheless, the quality of the music spoke for itself and they were selling tickets steadily even without a hit single.

There have been many *This Is Spinal Tap* moments throughout the band's now lengthy history; especially during the 1970s. They played one gig with April Wine, a day before they were scheduled to play on the same bill as Fleetwood Mac in San Bernardino, and they'd had some unknown substances from a bus driver who was on the road with April Wine. During the San Bernardino gig, Mogg was literally rigid onstage from whatever he'd taken. There have also been times when neither the band nor their crew knew how to get to the stage, which was especially true of British bands in the US.

Their tour manager in those days was a Scouser named John "Knowlesy" Knowles who was a rather good bloke. They'd keep all their gig money in a suitcase and after all the gear was packed up and the band and crew were in a hotel, John would get a hooker for the night only to find the next morning she'd ran off with the band's money, so they were often skint. The band would have to phone their agent to send them some cash.

They were funny old days.

Phil Mogg spoke about the band's self-confidence and their rising popularity without major label backing: "We've confidence; it might be confidence in Jim Beam. But really, we have to feel that way. We've gone to places without any publicity machine behind us, and done our show, and drawn twice as many the next time with no one but ourselves having done it."[49]

CHAPTER
THREE

Lights Out –
The Michael Schenker Years Part 2
(1977–1978)

"1977 is going to be our most successful year – I am sure"

Phil Mogg[50]

For *Lights Out*, the band's forthcoming album, UFO had hired keyboardist and rhythm guitarist Paul Raymond from Savoy Brown back in July 1976.

Raymond was born Paul Martin Raymond on November 16, 1945 in St Albans, Hertfordshire. He joined his first band Plastic Penny in 1967 as their keyboardist/singer but the band split up in 1968 and he went on to replace Christine Perfect in the blues rock band Chicken Shack, after she went on to join Fleetwood Mac and marry and later divorce bassist John McVie. After Raymond's stint in Chicken Shack, he joined the British blues band Savoy Brown, originally known as Savoy Brown Blues Band.

Raymond replaced UFO's first keyboardist Danny Peyronel in July after the band's USA dates and would become a vital member of UFO both as a musician and songwriter. Left-handed and nicknamed "Kipper" by the band, Raymond plays the guitar with the strings inverted. "My biggest influences were Bill Evans and Victor Feldman, two extraordinarily talented jazz pianists," Raymond would tell *Get Ready To Rock*'s Jason Ritchie many years later. "As far as rock and blues are concerned it has to be Chuck Berry and Johnny Johnson, the Stones, and the late, great Steve Marriott."[51]

Savoy Brown had parted company with a number of singers throughout the 1970s, leaving Kim Simmonds and Paul Raymond to split lead vocals. They played a show in Saginaw, Michigan with UFO opening and Nazareth headlining. Raymond was blown away by Michael Schenker's guitar playing. Raymond got chatting to Pete Way back at the hotel after the show and Way mentioned that they were thinking of replacing Peyronel. Way said that he'd watched Savoy Brown perform that night and was impressed that Raymond could play guitar and keyboards as well as having the right voice to sing. Way subsequently asked Raymond if he'd be interested in joining UFO.

Back in England, Raymond met the band at The Knoll in Hertfordshire whilst he was still in Savoy Brown. Raymond got the opportunity to chat with the band, jam and have dinner before returning home for the night. The day after, Way called Raymond and offered him the gig. Raymond, who'd done his homework about the band's history and their record deal with Chrysalis, auditioned for the band in London as a formality. The band felt that there was perhaps too much work for Schenker to do onstage, and for the band as a four piece. On the last couple of albums some of the songs had overdubs and keyboards, and for those sounds to transfer to the live setting the band needed a fifth member. Suffice to say the rest of the outfit were impressed with Raymond and he enlisted.

Raymond was the perfect addition to UFO because of his multiple musical talents and strong bluesy voice. Not all of UFO's songs have keyboard parts, but as Raymond played guitar he could add extra meat to Schenker's riffs. In those halcyon days, bands did not use samples of recorded sounds onstage – everything was live.

Schenker is, and always has been since the days of UFO, a solo lead guitarist but Raymond was a nifty rhythm side-kick. The band and their new recruit then went down to a rehearsal studio in Pimlico, London. Leo Lyons – who was loosely managing the band at the time – was there to discuss the next UFO album. Later in the year, the boys had dinner with KISS manager the late Bill Aucoin at trendy eaterie Julie's in Holland Park to discuss his managing UFO (though nothing came from the meeting).

"Paul seems very, very good," Andy Parker said at the time. "As a person we got on really well and, apart from that, he plays keyboards and guitar and sings which is a great boon. Keyboard players are O.K. but you know this band thrives on two guitar work as well, so it's nice if you've got the kind of laid back aspect of the keyboards – because they are basically more of a background thing."[52]

41

What happened to Danny Peyronel? Peyronel remains an important member in the history of UFO having contributed to the band's songwriting, notably on the track "Highway Lady" from *No Heavy Petting*. A live recording featuring Peyronel was released in 1998 as *On With The Action*, which was recorded at the Roundhouse in London in April 1976. The sound that Peyronel brought with him to UFO continued after his departure but with added guitars.

Peyronel recalls his version of events leading to his departure: "Doesn't everyone know this one by now? I didn't 'leave,' I was 'let go.' And, sadly, with a call from the then manager of the band, an *eminence gris* who, oddly, happened to work for the record label too. Talk about conflict of interests. Since then, the reason for my departure has come to the surface quite openly, namely from Pete himself in Martin Popoff's book on the band *Shoot Out The Lights*. The record label had the brilliantly conceived idea of changing distributors in the US right before the release of *No Heavy Petting*.

"The consequence, no great surprise with hindsight, was that after the wild and terrific reception we were getting throughout our strenuous touring in America, the fans would flock to the record stores to buy the album only to find no copies in stock. The end result was also obvious: an album that was expected to better the performance of *Force It* and break the band into the Top 40 charts in the US, barely made it to [Number] 69 or so. The label, and the manager, who ironically were one and the same, were never going to own up to having screwed the band's big opportunity, so they needed a good scapegoat. Who better than 'the new boy?' I was very grateful to Pete for having had the guts to tell things like they were, once and for all ..."[53]

Peyronel went on to form his own rock outfit The Blue Max and wound up in the Spanish bands Banzai and Tarzen, and the Argentinean group Riff. Peyronel is best known for writing the Meat Loaf single "Midnight At The Lost And Found" from Meat Loaf's same titled 1983 album as well as material with the successful UK soul singer Sade. Raymond's live debut with UFO was at three sold out shows at The Marquee Club in London.

After *No Heavy Petting*, the band set to work on a new album. However, it was felt at the time that the band's albums suffered from less than stellar production values, so the band opted to work with the experienced hands of American Ron Nevison, who had engineered The Who's *Quadrophenia* amongst other things. It was hoped this choice would help break the band in the US and set the cash registers rolling. A big name producer would give them the right sound for the all important US radio station playlists. "We decided to make a big change on this album because we weren't happy with the last one," Andy Parker later admitted to Mike Daley of the music magazine *Way Ahead*. "We thought the production lacked a bit, so we thought we'd find ourselves a good producer. I am pleased with it, with one or two reservations."[54]

Lyons: "John Burgess, he was a record producer, a very good record producer, John said to me once: treat every record like your last and every musician like an arsehole and you won't be disappointed. That stuck in my mind at the time. I think I was hurt. By the same token, it's the music business and I've been in it long enough to realise people change. People want to change. From what I understood from the record company, it was their idea. They'd got this idea, 'We want to be big in America, we've got to get American producers to hit this radio thing and get them onboard.' I even had a meeting with them and they said: 'Oh it's very difficult to find American producers.' I knew what their policy was. They introduced it to the band and the band thought it was a good idea. I didn't fall out with them over it."[55]

However, Ron Nevison was much more strong-willed than the band had first assumed. Nevison was best known for his work with, as either producer or engineer for, Led Zeppelin, The Who and Bad Company so he was used to working with big bands with even bigger egos. He was one of the most in-demand studio hands of the decade and would become one of rock's most revered producers.

Born in Philadelphia, Nevison's career stretched back to the late 1960s when he mixed/mastered live recordings for such bands as Derek And The Dominos and Jefferson Airplane, before becoming an in-house producer for Island Studios in Central London from 1970 to 1975. He then returned to Los Angeles where Roger Watson, an A&R executive at the LA office of Chrysalis, contacted Nevison to ask him if he fancied producing UFO. It wasn't a band he was particularly familiar with, but was enticed to work with them after meeting with Watson and label co-founder Terry Ellis. Nevison then sought out the band's albums and was gobsmacked by Schenker's guitar, in particular.

Nevison knew how to handle bands like UFO. He would be the next key ingredient (following on from the addition of Schenker) for the band's sound to travel Stateside. Given Nevison's experience with other high-calibre rock bands he was able to capture the energy and vibe of UFO at their best which, of course, is playing live.

Lights Out was recorded at AIR Studios in London between February and March 1977. AIR Studios, was one of the most popular studios at the time and owned by George Martin. Nevison chose to mix the album at PYE Studios near Marble Arch.

They had a large batch of material to work with having honed much of it at the Pimlico rehearsal studios the previous year. It was Nevison's idea to record a cover version, although it was actually Mogg who chose Love's "Alone Again Or". The album features horn and string arrangements by the Toronto based Allan MacMillan, who had worked with Alice Cooper. Nevison's idea was to incorporate string arrangements into the songs, which was initially met with band resistance. Nevison correctly assumed that the strings would add strength to Schenker's melodies. It took a week to record the string arrangements, which used 24 players.

Nevison had a vision for the band: "I thought they wrote some amazing melodies and I wanted to bring that out. They didn't have anybody in this band that could do anymore than Paul Raymond did which was play the piano and the organ, just the basic stuff. I wanted to add an element to a line-up like that. Using Schenker you have to orchestrate it. They [Chrysalis] allowed me to do that and that's one of the reasons why I think *Lights Out* turned out so well."[56]

Working with Nevison was a tad more difficult than the lads in UFO initially thought. He was strong-minded and intolerant of bad tempers. The band were initially rather scared of their new producer, but Nevison had a sense of humour too. When he let his guard down he knew how to have a laugh and joke with the band, but work always came first. Nevison had lots of ideas and wanted to steer the outfit towards his way of thinking. In due course, Nevison would help the band progress in a way that Leo Lyons was, perhaps, not capable of. Lyons was learning the production ropes at the same time UFO were getting used to working with a producer, whereas Nevison was already a seasoned studio hand. Nevison took the chemistry of the band to a whole new level and helped define a new sound for the band. As a treat, Nevison would take the band out for a meal most nights after the usual twelve hour sessions in the studio.

The one thing which Nevison did not appreciate, was that the band did not write together as a collective. "Schenker wrote these amazing epic riffs," Nevison says. "He didn't write with any sense of a vocalist involved so I had to come in – I didn't rewrite anything but I had to put the verses in where there weren't any. There were these epic themes and sometimes they weren't do-able. I remember in the case of the song 'Try Me' he didn't write a typical verse-chorus-verse-chorus song ... It would have been a hell of a lot easier if Phil or Pete or Paul for that matter would have collaborated with Schenker. It would have made life a lot easier."[57]

Schenker was a loner. Maybe it was because of his personality or maybe it was because he was a stranger in a strange land? "He would do his little demos at home," explains Nevison. "In fact, at the beginning of 'Love To Love' he had this really cool guitar thing. The classic beginning to 'Love To Love' was on cassette and I recorded it, but we couldn't duplicate it – it was too labour intensive. He did a lot of stuff at home. He was guitar riffing. He wasn't thinking at all about vocal breaks."[58]

It was certainly a different experience from the Leo Lyons sessions. The band had become very comfortable working with Lyons after three albums together, so a change in producers was a potentially worrying move for them. Lyons was very laid back and had learned to put up with UFO's kiddy antics. Nevison, on the other hand, was a tough task master and he brought out the best in the band, even using the tensions between Schenker and Mogg to the band's advantage. The response from Chrysalis when Nevison flew back to LA was one of ecstasy, to put it mildly.

Nevison: "With the *Lights Out* album they presented me with a cap and gown like a Headmaster. They appreciated the efforts that I put in. They appreciated that I'm not difficult to work with, just demanding."[59]

Lights Out leads with the stunning "Too Hot To Handle", which is simply one of the greatest rock songs the band have recorded. "Just Another Suicide" is a very creative number with some orchestration and stunning guitar work. "Try Me" opens with some piano before the unmistakable vocals of Mogg begin and it sends a tingle down the listener's spine. It's a wonderful ballad. "Lights Out" is classic rock with a mighty bass line from Pete Way while "Gettin' Ready" is a nifty mid-paced rocker. "Alone Again Or", originally a song by LA hippies Love, sits seamlessly alongside some of the album's more rock orientated numbers. "Electric Phase" is notable for some inventive guitars and a terrific melody, while the closing song, "Love To Love", is perhaps the band's all-time masterpiece ... though it's a tough call with so many to choose from. It's a captivating track with some truly wonderful keys, a strong sense of melody, a taut rhythm section, sturdy vocals and the unmistakeable guitar strings of Mr Schenker. What a way to finish the album!

Lights Out is a masterpiece from start to finish. The production is perfect and the musicianship and vocals are stunning. It remains a glorious release and a testament to the band's enduring legacy. It was unleashed in May 1977 and hit Number 23 in the USA *Billboard* 200 album charts and even charted in the UK, making it to Number 54. It can, quite rightly, claim to be the band's breakthrough release in the USA where it spent half a year in the *Billboard* 200 album charts and went Gold. The album spawned a number of notable singles such as "Too Hot To Handle" (a radio hit in the USA) with "Electric Phase" on red vinyl (coloured vinyl was *de rigueur* in the late 1970s); "Gettin' Ready" with "Too Hot To Handle" and "Alone Again Or" with "Electric Phase" in 1977. "Try Me" with "Gettin' Ready" was issued in 1978 as a single.

The album was reissued in 2008 with several bonus tracks: "Lights Out", "Gettin' Ready", "Love To Love" and "Try Me". These were all live tracks recorded at the Roundhouse in April 1976.

Mogg was pleased with the album and its critical response. "I think this album condenses the better moments from a lot of our other albums," Mogg told Peter Crescenti of *Circus*. "It is more accessible than the other ones. A lot of people have gotten into it who hadn't liked UFO before. The production is a lot crisper."[60]

Lights Out was received by the music media with open arms. It won glowing reviews, even from the *NME* which was more obsessed with punk than anything else in those days.

Geoff Barton wrote in *Sounds*: "The strongest UFO album to date, to be sure – but, as far as I'm concerned, still not quite strong enough ... It's a pity, because *Lights Out* is the album that's going to back up UFO's upcoming weighty UK tour attack, next month's make-it-or-break-it date schedule." Writing in the *NME*, Bob Edmands said: "To anyone who grew up on a diet of Hendrix and Led Zeppelin, it will probably seem tame enough, but compared to many of the more undeserving heirs to their legacies, UFO are classy indeed."

Lights Out has been hailed as the band's finest studio album and is undoubtedly one of rock's greatest albums. It has unquestionably achieved longevity since its original 1977 release. "Lights Out" and "Love To Love" were both featured in the 1999 KISS movie *Detroit Rock City* and "Love To Love" was covered by Djali Zwan for the indie movie *Spun* in 2002. Noted UFO enthusiast Steve Harris of Iron Maiden has declared it one of his favourite UFO songs. *Lights Out* was Number 28 in *Kerrang!*'s "100 Greatest Heavy Metal Albums Of All Time" poll.

With a clutch of new songs from *Lights Out*, such as the title track, "Too Hot To Handle" and "Love To Love", it became more than obvious that UFO was a force to be reckoned with in the UK rock scene. Finally, UFO had become one of the country's most prominent rock bands.

UFO were clearly riding on a wave of success with a series of albums that in many ways set the benchmark for the iconic sound of 1970s British rock. *Phenomenon, Force It, Heavy Petting* and *Lights Out* are cornerstones of the genre and UFO's name had increased in visibility, whilst their audience had grown tenfold. Not only does *Lights Out* remain UFO's finest achievement, their crowning glory, but its initial success brought with it the hedonistic lifestyle that rock 'n' roll has to offer. The band could sell out Odeon and Apollo sized venues and had finally won over the rock critics, but the drugs and drink lifestyle had taken hold of the band and, in many respects, the next few years would become one long blur.

Lights Out also represents the start of a period when many stories were written about UFO; some of them are, no doubt, true but many of them are exaggerated and so it is difficult for a writer to even begin to locate the truth as the memories of those involved have faded for various reasons(!) and accounts cannot be corroborated. One story goes that Way's then wife was fed up of the band's constant touring. One day Way said he was going to post a letter, only to pack a suitcase, go to the airport and disappear to the USA for a few months. One thing is for sure: these wild and crazy stories, whether true or not, have added to the mystery, aura and legend of UFO.

The band toured around Europe to promote the new album, where a typical set included "Lights Out", "Gettin' Ready", "On With The Action", "Doctor Doctor", "Love To Love", "Too Hot To Handle", "I'm A Loser",

"Natural Thing", "Out In The Street", "This Kid's", "Shoot Shoot", "Rock Bottom", "C'mon Everybody" and "Boogie For George".

The band's show in Hannover was reviewed by Tony Stewart for the *NME*. Typical of the über-pretentious *NME*, the review was not entirely generous towards the band or the hard rock genre: "Mogg hauls himself up to the front. A parody of anguish, beads of perspiration streaking his tortured face, he sings not altogether badly but with the forced passion of so many unremarkable rock vocalists." Ouch!

A road jaunt around the UK in April saw the band's performance at the Roundhouse on April 2 heavily bootlegged, which is in itself an indicator that a band's stock is rising. At last the band were making inroads in the place that all of them, except Schenker, called home.

Michael Schenker was obviously the band's golden boy. Some critics have noted that without Schenker, UFO would have been just another average rock band. The guitarist spoke to Germany's *Bravo* magazine about the German-English language barrier: "I still learn English language – there are still some problems during interviews. Many reporters consider me sometimes therefore conceited. Often only the correct words are missing to me. I feel myself much more comfortable onstage – there I can let myself go and rave out."[61]

Prone to stage fright, he was a volatile character despite the reverence he had received, notably in America where he was considered to be one of the greatest hard rock guitarists of the day. Schenker would become known for walking out of the band regardless of their commitments. The growing success of the album would have a profound impact on the lives of each band member.

"Honestly we are all exhausted," Schenker admitted to Germany's *Pop* magazine in July, "We need to go for a holiday after such a tour. But due to sensational sales of our last album *Lights Out*, the management rushes us for another two months USA tour immediately. You can hardly imagine how this bloody travels and the eternal concert stress drives you up the wall."[62]

It was just too hot for Schenker to handle. He was apparently taking a prescription drug at the time called Heminevrin, a muscle relaxant and sedative, which Schenker mixed with alcohol. He just couldn't cope with so many thousands of people staring at him night after night; the pressures and responsibilities of fame. By the way, this is the drug that killed The Who drummer Keith Moon.

As the band were preparing for a tour of the USA, Schenker had reportedly sent a letter to Mogg saying he was leaving the band. Schenker left in June 1977 just six days before an upcoming American tour, while a major tour supporting Rush in September was also on the cards.

Despite the positive reviews and feedback the band was getting from critics and fans alike, Schenker left the UK completely, prompting the band to re-hire former UFO guitarist Paul Chapman – now of Lone Star who were working on their second album, produced by Roy Thomas Baker – to fill the vacant slot on June 20. One other suggestion was Gary Moore, but he was not over the moon at the notion of joining UFO. One rumour was that a young Eddie Van Halen was interested in auditioning to replace Schenker. Eddie read about an audition for the guitar slot in UFO, but didn't travel from Pasadena to LA to audition because he didn't think he would get the gig! He did not pursue the audition because he was too shy. It would have been such a mouthwatering prospect had he joined the band, but I guess some things aren't meant to be.

Having played in UFO for nine months in 1974 on rhythm guitar, it made sense for Chapman to fill the position, albeit on a temporary basis. The band had booked a rehearsal space in LA to prepare for the upcoming American ordeal. Chapman knew the band's music and he'd matured since his 1974 stint. UFO fans were shocked not to see the blond haired German on lead guitar during the opening shows of the USA tour. The band also had dates throughout the summer supporting other artists, including Detroit rocker, Bob Seger. "UFO are at about the point Seger was a year and a half ago," one journalist wrote in *Sounds* at the time. "The band's got everything nearly together for the final push toward superstardom." With UFO though, "nearly" is too often the operative word.

Neither the band nor their manager – Wilf Wright a former Chrysalis executive – were able to contact Schenker despite great efforts and weeks spent doing so, as he was incommunicado. "He just went," Mogg said of Schenker. "He cracked up – we crack a lot of people. Michael is on his own weird astral trip. His threshold of insanity is maybe a bit lower than anyone else's. He walks the line ... "[63] Don't mince your words Phil!

They hadn't a clue what had happened. The band admitted at the time that Schenker had disappeared in the past but always turned up for the gig. This time around they checked his flat in Barnes, London only to discover that he had moved out completely and had sold his car and his personal belongings. The band even tried reaching out to him through various contacts in Germany. Pete Way, along with the band's tour manager Alan, flew to Germany at one point to try to locate Schenker but to no avail. Rumours circulated that Schenker had been abducted by the other sort of UFO, he was camping in Clapham Common and had even joined a religious cult such as the Moonies. Eventually, it came out that Schenker flew back to mainland Europe, spending time with his girlfriend in the south of France and Spain to seek solitude and relaxation. Schenker was in Munich when Way called him to ask him to return the band's gear. Eventually, three months after leaving, Schenker was persuaded by Way to return to the band just in time for the upcoming Rush tour; talk about cutting it fine. Meanwhile, Chapman went back to Lone Star in August.

Former UFO keyboardist Danny Peyronel remembers working with Schenker during *No Heavy Petting*: "Michael and I got along great and he was very warm towards me. I think the fact that I too was a 'furriner', may have been part of it ... perhaps I had more patience with his limited English at the time. Even though I had lived in the US as a child, and spoke like an Anglo (something like an Englishman with a slight American accent, and tinges of whatever you wanted to hear, Dutch, Welsh, I used to get all kinds of guesses from people!), 'technically', English was still my second language, so I maybe had more empathy for his plight. He was, of course, a brilliant guitarist, but his drinking on the road, especially in the US, led to all kinds of mayhem and even cancelled gigs. I remember putting him to bed after picking him up from hotel hallways ... but he was always, at least then, a good natured boy and I enjoyed his company. Hopefully it was reciprocated."[64]

Remaining in the US, UFO (and Max Webster) supported the Canadian progressive rock band Rush on their *A Farewell To Kings* tour in September. Such was the nature of Way and Mogg's personalities that during the tour they would go to the stage shortly before Rush were due to play and nail a pair of fluffy pink slippers to the front of the stage, which remained there while Rush were playing. Apparently Rush were even approached by an American journalist who claimed that the slippers had some sort of mystical meaning; that they were a symbol of some kind. Of course they were a symbol – of UFO's unique sense of humour rather than Rush's deep philosophies.

Despite Schenker's turbulent personality and the tensions that existed in the band at the time between Schenker and Mogg and Way, the band had obviously made the right choice in hiring Ron Nevison. The radio friendly hard rock sound of *Lights Out* was a hit in the US and so the band decamped Stateside in February, 1978 on a near permanent basis. In LA they would create their next masterful opus; their seventh album in total. Schenker had reportedly told the band when he rejoined, that the following release would be his last. However, when it came to pre-recording rehearsals the band did not have any new songs: cocaine, alcohol and the general hedonistic LA lifestyle had put the band members off track. So it was a case of welcome to the Nevison bootcamp, as their no nonsense producer cracked the whip and licked them into shape.

Nevison on Schenker: "... we're not talking about great guitar players; we're talking about great writers and great guitar players. It wasn't just the fact that Schenker was an amazing player, he was an amazing writer. Look what Fleetwood Mac was like before they ran into Lindsey Buckingham. They were just a blues band with a great rhythm section. Things change course when you have talent like that. That's what happened when Schenker joined UFO."[65]

Obsession was recorded with producer Ron Nevison at C.P. McGregor's at the junction of Wilshire Boulevard and Western Avenue, LA. After UFO's stint there, Stevie Wonder purchased the building and named it Wonderland Studios. They also recorded in the famed Record Plant Mobile, which was looked after by Mike Clink, and at West 3rd Carrier Station in Beverly Hills; a former Beverly Hills Post Office which has since become disused. The band managed to get a good sound in the Mobile Studio whilst some backing tracks were recorded at a vacant rehearsals studio in Beverly Hills, which gave the music a rawer vibe. All the overdubs and guitars were recorded at the Mobile Studio and so the recordings sounded different from the studio sound of *Lights Out*. "That was the thing – we wanted the album to sound live, because we feel quite often that the best sound for this band is just that," Way commented at the time, "so that's what we worked towards."[66]

Mike Clink (who would later go on to find great success with Guns N' Roses, Metallica and Heart) acted as the album's assistant engineer while Allan MacMillan returned to provide string arrangements. MacMillan, however, had other commitments and was not as freely available for the recordings as Nevison had hoped.

This release saw the line-up of Phil Mogg, Pete Way, Andy Parker, Michael Schenker and Paul Raymond in full swing. Mogg's late delivery of lyrics frustrated Nevison. Mogg would mumble the words during the recordings until he'd finally written some lyrics.

"No real reason," Mogg told *Sounds*' Geoff Barton at the time about the meaning behind the album's moniker. "It's just that the title seemed pretty apt ... everything we do in the studio gets so involved, so intense, that it becomes, well, an obsession with us. We thought it'd be as good a title as any ..."[67]

Obsession opens with the now iconic "Only You Can Rock Me" which is one of the band's main anthems. "Pack It Up (And Go)" shows off the understated talents of drummer Andy Parker, while Schenker is on fire with a stunning lead riff that ripples through the song. "Arbory Hill" proves that UFO were more than a cut above the average rock band with a strong sense of musicality and a knowledge of their own talents. "Ain't No Baby" is a heavy rocker with an almighty guitar-bass-drums stomp. "Lookin' Out For No.1" opens with some orchestration which is accompanied by a sensitive vocal performance from Mogg before the rest of the band enter the track. "Hot 'N' Ready" screams with some stunning electric guitars and feisty vocals while "Cherry" has a to-die-for guitar solo and staggered melody. "You Don't Fool Me" is a hard as nails song sung with conviction while "Lookin' Out For No. 1 (Reprise)" has Paul Raymond's stamp all over it. "One More For The Rodeo" is a groovy driving rock song while the final song, "Born To Lose", has some tight arrangements but it's Schenker who steals the show.

Whether *Obsession* is better than *Lights Out* is debatable – both albums are hard rock masterpieces, without question. Ron Nevison brought a great deal to the table and turned UFO into a band of considerable worth.

Obsession was released in June 1978. It peaked at Number 41 in the *Billboard* 200 album charts in the USA and fared well in the UK making it to Number 26. A tasty three track EP consisting of "Only You Can Rock Me", "Cherry" and "Rock Bottom" reached Number 50 in the UK in 1978.

Reissued in 2008 with live bonus tracks ("Hot 'N' Ready", "Pack It Up (And Go)" and "Ain't No Baby"), *Obsession* has since become a classic UFO release and a landmark rock album. Metallica front man James Hetfield named his first band Obsession after this seminal rock album.

The album's release was greeted with enthusiastic reviews. Are we seeing a pattern here? It is evident the band were on a creative roll that had begun with *Phenomenon*, while Nevison had raised the bar considerably higher with *Lights Out* and *Obsession*.

Geoff Barton said in *Sounds*: "*Obsession* is a lovingly crafted album. UFO's finest achievement to date. It will easily make the UK album charts and (more notably) will plunge powerfully into the American LP listings, probably rising into the top ten some time later in the year." One journalist wrote in *Melody Maker*: "What UFO do isn't new, but the measured thrust of Schenker's guitar, picking harmonies and runs to mirror and pace Mogg's archetypal hard rock vocals are sufficient to ensure that they do it with enough individuality to keep them in halls full of fans on both sides of the pond."

Over in the USA, Robert Christgau wrote in his *Consumer Guide*: "I've admired their forward motion and facile riffs, so it's my duty to report that they've degenerated into the usual exhibitionism. Theme song: "Lookin' Out For No. 1", a turn of phrase that's becoming as much of a watchword in late '70s rock as 'get together' was in the late '60s." [The Boomtown Rats had a hit single with "Looking After Number One", but if Christgau thought the 1970s were self-serving, then the 1980s must have truly shocked him]

Historically speaking, *Obsession* is up there with *Lights Out* as one of UFO's finest accomplishments. "Arbory Hill", for example, would have a major effect on Pearl Jam guitarist Mike McCready, a well-known UFO fan. The guitarist would even get the chance to discuss the song with Michael Schenker on Eddie Trunk's *The Metal Show* over three decades later. Schenker told McCready how the song was influenced by classical flutes. McCready was in awe of Schenker like so many other guitarists in the rock world.

It was around this time that Chrysalis was plugging a band called The Babys, featuring future Journey keyboardist Jonathan Cain and British AOR singer John Waite. Mogg was not best pleased with the way the company was backing The Babys and felt that Chrysalis should have been treating UFO with similar enthusiasm, so much so that Mogg wrote a song called 'The Babys'.

Nevison: "Phil's wrong about that. He's right and wrong. You see Chrysalis' problem was not the front end; it was the back. They were spending a lot of money on [The] Babys but they didn't have independent distribution. They couldn't put the albums in the stores. Had Blondie and Pat Benatar come before UFO and [The] Babys we'd be talking a whole different conversation. He didn't understand the mechanics of the whole thing. The fact is The Babys weren't selling albums either. [They're a] cult band because they got airplay but they didn't have album sales."[68]

With Blondie and Pat Benatar, Chrysalis had become something of a major label; a far cry from its humble beginnings in 1969 when it was set up initially to promote the talents of Jethro Tull, with Procol Harum, Robin Trower, Ten Years After, Steeleye Span and pop singer Leo Sayer also signing on the dotted line at various times. The name Chrysalis was an amalgamation of the first name of Chris Wright and the surname of Terry Ellis who, between them, founded the company.

It started life as the Ellis-Wright Agency in 1967 but after landing a contract with Island Records the following year, Chrysalis was born. By the mid 1970s, with bands onboard such as UFO, Chrysalis had become a leading independent label despite its perceived marketing flaws. It was a stroke of luck when Ellis – who had moved to the States to strengthen the American side of the label – saw Blondie onstage in a New York club. He was so impressed by them that he took the band out of their contract from a small label because they could not afford to look after the band and signed them to Chrysalis. Their self-titled debut album in 1976 was a hit. The success of Blondie and Benatar – who was also witnessed, initially, by Ellis in a small New York club – and, subsequently in the 1980s, Huey Lewis And The News, a rock band from San Francisco, meant that Chrysalis could have stronger distribution, which, because of the timing, did not benefit UFO. It was simply an unfortunate set of circumstances in many respects for both UFO and The Babys.

Despite the stretches of recording UFO had to commit to in order to make a new studio album, they continued to tour extensively, concentrating their time and energy on the USA and Europe. They were steadily acquiring a reputation as a tremendous live band and Schenker was already lauded as one of the great rock guitarists of the decade, although Ritchie Blackmore of Deep Purple was the hard rock god of the 1970s bar none. Nonetheless, with his trademark black and white Gibson Flying V guitar, Schenker had become a living rock legend.

Throughout 1976 to 1978, UFO hit the road around the USA with a variety of other bands, including Van Halen, Fleetwood Mac, Foghat, Styx, April Wine, Jethro Tull and Nazareth and had acquired a revered reputation in certain States. It was often the case that they'd upstage the headlining act. Touring with so many artists was a fantastic experience for the band, not only to broaden their fanbase on the other side of the Atlantic, but for them to learn a few tricks of the trade such as how to treat an American audience in different cities.

UFO went down especially well in the working class areas of the Midwest which, similarly to the north of England, has a strong and loyal rock following. Audience reactions can be the same the world over because it is the music that ultimately connects the crowd with the band, but there are certainly some fickle cities. Some bands, for example, could find playing to an LA audience far more strenuous than playing to a rock audience in Minnesota. It may be that LA crowds are spoilt for choice, or that in the depths of a Minnesota winter a good rocking band is just what the doctor ordered to warm the cockles of the heart.

During UFO's assault on the American market, punk took the music world by storm in the UK. "The punk thing, well some of that is well cooked up and you can see right through it," Mogg later told *Sounds* writer Pete Makowski. " ... I mean the total crap these people come out with after a certain level of acceptance."[69]

UFO spent most of their time in LA and while punk was mostly (but not entirely) confined to London and New York, it was so shocking because of its nihilistic message that the word spread. Suddenly rock lovin' kids shaved their hair and followed The Sex Pistols and The Clash rather than ELP or even Led Zeppelin. However, some non-punk bands survived and thrived during this period, even if most commentators appeared to have forgotten to reference them. UFO was one of those bands, as was AC/DC fronted by the tough as nails Bon Scott. What these bands had in common was their no-bullshit-taking attitude, their relentlessly energetic stage performances and their crazy backstage antics, which were in many ways aligned with the punk's aggressive attitude. Plus, UFO and their blues rock ilk created mostly snappy three or four minute songs while the punks loudly lambasted the self-indulgent music of Yes and ELP and other prog rock epic songmakers. Punk attempted to take rock 'n' roll back to basics. UFO and AC/DC had been doing it for years. Mogg saw punk as a farce and it had no bearing whatsoever on UFO.

UFO's fanbase was largely in the 16 to 20 age group and pretty male oriented. However, the band found a wider demographic in the States with women and men in almost equal balance. The audiences in the States were certainly much crazier than the Brits. Mogg's favourite places to play in the States were Chicago and San Francisco. The band were earning more money than they ever had before, but they were not in the rich as Croesus league occupied by the likes of Led Zeppelin or Black Sabbath, who spent as much money as they made.

Much of UFO's income went on stage productions, especially in the USA where they could spend up to $500,000 on lighting and stage equipment. $1,000 a night would be spent on the road crew and paying for accommodation.

"Yeah, but you see in American arenas the shows are exciting," Way told *Sounds'* Garry Bushell. "The atmosphere is charged. I've been to see bands in that situation and it's great because bands will spend a lot on their stage shows and, personally, I think as long as you're giving kids a good show and a good sound there's nothing wrong with it."[70]

In the summer of 1978, UFO toured the UK (supported by Marseille) to promote *Obsession* where they performed a terrific set list featuring "Lights Out", "Gettin' Ready", "Love To Love", "On With The Action", "Doctor Doctor", "Try Me", "Too Hot To Handle", "Out In The Street", "This Kid's", "Shoot Shoot", "Rock Bottom", "Let It Roll" and "C'mon Everybody".

The band's gig in Sheffield was reviewed by Andy Gill in *Melody Maker*. He cynically wrote: "Star of the show, of course, is lead guitarist Michael Schenker, who has everything a heavy metal guitarist needs to be successful ... Highlight of the show, for me, was when Schenker, dashing across the stage to 'duel' with the bassist, pulled his lead clean out of its socket: ah, a blissful few seconds of silence in the upper register!"

After the UK, UFO flew across the Atlantic to hit the road in the USA with Blue Öyster Cult and co-headliners Judas Priest. Writing in *Sounds* about the band's performance in LA, Sylvie Simmons wrote: "UFO, though I can't claim to be a fan of their music, were much more dynamic. They came across as real macho kick-out-the-shit rock stars. The applause, together with lit matches and calls for more, make it a safe bet that next time they'll be headlining. UFO specialise in gloriously grandiose heavy metal intros to melodic, even romantic songs building up to dual guitar crashes backed by head-banging drums."

However, it was clear that there were some tensions between Mogg and Schenker. Schenker's famously difficult personality and addictions were getting the better of him and he quit UFO after the band's final show in Palo Alto, California in October, 1978.

Mogg often called Schenker "Michelle" in interviews. When the band were mixing their forthcoming live album *Strangers In The Night*, which was recorded that month, Schenker and Mogg had an altercation which put a nail in the coffin for their professional relationship. Schenker: "He [Mogg] would walk around and fight people. I told him, 'If you ever punch me, I will leave the band.' I guess he wanted to try to find out and he punched me, so I left. And I have no idea what was in his head – but he didn't really get very far afterwards."[71]

Reports at the time suggested he officially quit UFO in December. As reported in *Melody Maker*, being on the road so much caused Schenker to drink excessively. He had become a loner, never hanging out with the band unlike the old days when he first moved to London.

Nevison: "Having a German in an English band that are all taking the piss about who won the war; all of that became too much. In a way they pushed him away a little bit. They went after him, they got him from the Scorpions but I don't know if they ever accepted him as a mate ... If I had a wish I just wish these guys had written more as a band or Schenker would have brought stuff to them and said: 'What do you think?' and worked out stuff."[72]

Frustratingly, UFO would sometimes be referred to as Michael Schenker's band by Americans. UFO now had to move away from that. Schenker allowed his personal demons to get the better of him, although it can be argued that there are more people who are taken over by their own demons than aren't. Members of the band, especially Mogg, found it difficult to talk to Schenker and actually figure out his personality. "I think Michael thought we'd have him back," Way later told Harry Doherty of

Melody Maker. "And now he's realised that that's not so. You see, we knew all the time that you have to tour to make money. He didn't realise that."[73]

Returning home to Germany, Schenker went back to Scorpions for a brief tenure in late 1978. He contributed guitar to three songs on Scorpions' 1979 album *Lovedrive*: "Another Piece Of Meat", "Coast To Coast" and "Lovedrive". In 1979, he toured with Scorpions but left three months later. He was replaced by Matthias Jabs who had actually joined Scorpions prior to Schenker's return. Before auditioning for Aerosmith after Joe Perry left (Schenker's demanding personality wanting to take control of Aerosmith was never going to work with front man Steven Tyler, despite how brilliant Tyler thought Schenker was as a guitarist) and after an aborted attempt to make a new band with Montrose drummer Denny Carmassi and bassist Bill Church, Schenker founded the Michael Schenker Group (MSG) in 1979.

They released their excellent self-titled debut album (produced by Deep Purple bassist Roger Glover) the following year with Gary Barden on vocals. MSG would go on to have great success, but Schenker would continue to battle his personal problems right up to the 2000s. Nevertheless, Schenker would prove to be one of rock and metal's most iconic and innovative guitarists, influencing the likes of Dave Mustaine of Megadeth, James Hetfield and Kirk Hammett of Metallica, Adrian Smith of Iron Maiden and Doug Aldrich of Whitesnake and Dio.

Schenker also influenced the late Randy Rhoads of Quiet Riot and Ozzy's band, The Blizzard Of Oz. When Rhoads tragically died in a plane accident on 19 March 1982, Ozzy Osbourne later called Schenker to ask if he wanted the job. Reports have varied as to why Osbourne and Schenker never collaborated, but with their addictive personalities it would have been a star that burned brightly, but not long.

In 2001, Schenker was asked by the *Chicago Daily Herald*'s Joel Reese how successful UFO would have become had he stayed. "Oh, definitely. Extremely big," Schenker replied. "The thing is, that's not the point. That's not what I'm living for. The point is, we are going to live and die, and I want to find out about something more than making it to the top and becoming rich and famous."[74]

Could UFO continue without Schenker, a musician who had done so much to create the UFO sound? Mogg and Way thought so and set about searching for a replacement. Mogg knew the nature of Schenker's talents as he told the *NME*'s Edmands in 1978: "He's one of the best lead guitarists around. I don't think anyone can touch him."[75]

However, Schenker was not quite so flattering when it came to talking about Mogg. Schenker: "I didn't feel comfortable with Phil Mogg, it was a horror for me. The first time you meet him he seems like a nice guy. After a while though, I changed my mind. He was always hitting people."[76]

Andy Parker was the balanced member of the band, the one who sorted out the difficulties between Schenker and Mogg. He levelled everything out. Rather ironically, they rehired Paul Chapman (again) who brought with him some previously unused song ideas from Lone Star's drummer Dixie Lee. Chapman was at home in Wales, when he got a call from UFO's manager Wilf Wright asking him if he wanted to fly to LA to replace Schenker for the band's upcoming shows. Chapman had been playing clubs in Wales, notably the New Moon in Cardiff, and was not going to turn down another opportunity to join UFO. Chapman, of course, had previously played second guitar to Schenker on tour back in 1974 and had filled in for him in 1977 when he went AWOL. Funnily enough (or maybe not in the small world of heavy rock), Chapman had auditioned for Scorpions in June but his destiny lay with UFO.

"It was a shock when Schenker left," Mogg admitted to *RAW*'s Kirk Blows in 1991. "When Paul [Chapman] came in we had to re-structure everything because his style was so different to Michael's, it was hard. He also used to change in the toilet ... he used to change into his spandex, but he'd still have his spandex on two days later, unbelievable!"[77]

With Chapman back in the fold in December 1978 for some further tour dates in the USA, the band then set to work on their new studio album. Chapman was now a fully-fledged full-time member of UFO. After the tour, Chapman flew to Amsterdam to be with his Dutch wife before he resumed his commitments to the band in the New Year.

UFO had some explaining to do to fans in the USA, because nothing had been publicised about Chapman's arrival. Unsurprisingly, American UFO fans were slightly baffled about the introduction of the band's new guitarist without any word from the band themselves about who he actually was. Chapman was aware of his own talents but not so arrogant to think he could better Schenker's riffs. He knew following in Schenker's wake would not be an easy task and he was aware that the band would lose some fans because of the change over in guitarists.

Chapman focused his thoughts on the task at hand, which was learning all the songs, whilst pushing any negativity and bad thoughts to the back of his mind. The real test for Chapman would be in the studio. They obviously had a great deal to live up to after the stream of classic albums they had recorded with Schenker.

CHAPTER
FOUR

The Wild, The Willing And The Innocent – Moving On With Paul Chapman
(1979 –1981)

*"We look very sexual on stage
and we move better than anyone else"*

Phil Mogg[78]

"The UFO line-up with Michael, Pete, Andy, Paul and myself was quite volatile. It could explode at any time," Mogg explained to Del James at *RIP* magazine. "Everybody had a say in things, and probably the main problem with that band was that I had the biggest mouth."[79]

In January 1979, during a quick-fire UK tour where they played "Electric Phase", "Hot 'N' Ready", "Cherry", "Out In The Street", "Only You Can Rock Me", "Love To Love", "Lights Out", "Rock Bottom", "Too Hot To Handle" and "Shoot Shoot" with "Doctor Doctor" as the one song encore, UFO released their second official live album, *Strangers In The Night*; surely one of the greatest albums of its kind in rock history. Featuring Michael Schenker and giving credit to Chapman, the now classic album was recorded on the band's USA tour during the previous year and boldly illustrates the band in full flight.

Reports at the time circulated a story that ex-guitarist Schenker had flown from Los Angeles to London, rented a car and drove to UFO's gig in Oxford. He didn't go inside the venue but stood outside, listened to two songs, and then drove back to London. Who knows? Schenker is such a character that there were lots of true and false stories and rumours about his activities. He is a mystery; an enigma.

It took the band a few shows to get into shape, but the overall opinion from fans of Paul Chapman was that he was the most capable guitarist to follow in the footsteps of Schenker. The band were especially well-received in the north of England, a stronghold for rock music. "Yeah, from Sheffield onwards things really turned for me ... kids in the audience started shouting for old Lone Star songs, holding up banners that said 'Good luck Paul' ... nice touches, you know, things that gave me an extra boost," Chapman told *Sounds'* Geoff Barton at the time.[80]

Strangers In The Night was produced by Ron Nevison. The famed LA based producer hit the road with the band and a mobile recording studio to capture the excitement of the live shows. Nevison with his assistant engineer Mike Clink joined UFO for six gigs in October: Chicago, Illinois; Kenogha, Wisconsin; Youngstown, Ohio; Columbus, Ohio and Louisville, Kentucky. The songs chosen were specifically culled from the autumn gigs in Chicago and Louisville.

As mentioned, the band had a big following in the Midwest of the USA; playing three nights at the Amphitheatre in Chicago at times. Similarly to KISS and their demographic stronghold Detroit (hence "Detroit Rock City"), Chicago was UFO's adopted American hometown of sorts. In Chicago, UFO could fill a venue with a 15,000 capacity while in other cities audience attendances ranged from 3,000 to almost 6,000. The American market is so big that some bands could have a loyal following in New York or North California, yet at the same time appear to be totally unknown in another part of the country. The audiences during those three Chicago gigs were really up for it – a blessing if you're going for a live recording.

Tension can often bring out the best qualities in a band. Artists can produce outstanding work during times of upheaval and struggle and such was the case with UFO. However, when tension becomes destructive and unpredictable it can often lead to collapse. There were also creative and personal tensions in bands of that era, from The Who to Led Zeppelin by way of The Rolling Stones. Countless books have been written about the unpredictable and hedonistic lifestyles of what are now commonly referred to as classic rock bands. Yet during the wildest periods of their careers they made the finest music; the most ground-breaking and legendary music was crafted when the bands were hooked on various substances. Whatever personal and creative struggles there were between Schenker and Mogg and the rest of the band, obviously helped define UFO's trademark sound, and thus caused them to create some extraordinary music. However, with hindsight, it almost seemed doomed to fail.

There was also a sense of walking the tightrope, especially when it came to live performances, because it was sometimes a case of wondering if Schenker would turn up on time and if he'd finish the gig. Again, such a sense of surprise led to some remarkable live performances, which were perfectly captured by Ron Nevison on *Strangers In The Night*.

As soon as the recording was completed, Nevison hot-footed it back to LA to piece the best songs together to make a live album at Record Plant Studios near Santa Monica Boulevard. Indeed, because of the length of some of the songs and the sheer quality of the tracks, Nevison decided to make the live release a double album.

The recording has been a bone of contention between the band and Schenker, with some suggestions that Schenker refused to overdub his guitar parts having already left the band straight after the USA tour climaxed. Other reports have suggested that Schenker was not happy with the version of "Rock Bottom" and wanted to overdub his lead solo, but Nevison would not allow him to do so. What this does show is that the album authentically represents Schenker's guitar work. However, it has been alleged that Paul Chapman did some overdubbing on parts, although Schenker's guitars came through the drum microphones which would have rendered guitar overdubs impossible.

The debate over the authenticity of *Strangers In The Night* brings to mind the argument that Judas Priest's stunning 1979 *Unleashed In The East* was actually "Unleashed In The Studio" as fans dubbed it. Schenker has since admitted that the band could have chosen better versions of the featured songs. Nevison touched up the mixes in spots and used the crowd noise from Chicago because it was the largest and loudest of the six shows.

However, when Nevison was finalising the release he realised they were a couple of songs short for a full-length double album. To solve this problem the band had regrouped at Record Plant Studios in November 1978 to record "Mother Mary" and "This Kid's" and Nevison mixed those songs with live audience noise. Nobody could tell the difference between those two songs and the rest of the album. Thin Lizzy had recorded "Southbound" at a soundcheck, which they overdubbed with crowd noise and included on their kick-ass live album, *Live And Dangerous*.

To a certain extent, you pays your money you takes your choice. Maybe it wasn't exactly as the punters heard it on the night, but so what?

It is a fantastic celebration of the band's late 1970s line-up of Mogg, Way, Schenker, Raymond and Parker and is one of the best live albums ever released. The sleeve notes also credit Chapman. UFO had already acquired an international reputation but *Strangers In The Night* would cement their status as one of the greatest hard rock bands to come out of Britain in the 1970s.

The release concluded Nevison's three album run with UFO. When asked why UFO were not as big a band as they should have been, he replied: "Well, that's not really their fault or my fault. They had an enormous amount of airplay in the US but they weren't a big band. They were like a medium band. At that point in time they didn't have distribution. Acts like Blondie and Pat Benatar helped get their [Chrysalis] act together. In those days, in the '70s – we're talking '77, '78 and '79 for the albums that I did; when somebody goes into a record store and it's not there they find something else. I had the same problems with albums I did for The Babys. That's a poor effort for Chrysalis ... I have to say even though I trashed Chrysalis for not having distribution and not having records out there they supported me with what I wanted to do with UFO."[81]

He continues: "UFO was a great experience for me on a number of levels. I had done the first three Bad Company albums as an engineer; they were big albums and I later heard that's why they [UFO] wanted me. Even though I wasn't a royalty artist as an engineer; I can tell you I pretty much produced the [Bad Company] albums. I didn't get a credit for it but I do what I do. I built the studio for them. I was the guy that was always telling them [Bad Company] whether it was good or not. When I went on to UFO in '77 I only found out later it was because of the Bad Company albums. I did a nice job with that *Lights Out* album and Chrysalis wanted me to do The Babys, so not only did I end up doing three albums for UFO I ended up doing two Babys albums. That's five albums that I'm really proud of."[82]

Nevison also went on to produce MSG's second album in 1981 and reunited with UFO in the mid 1990s, so UFO was certainly an integral part of his career.

The original version of *Strangers In The Night* opens with "Natural Thing" before moving on to "Out In The Street", "Only You Can Rock Me", "Doctor Doctor", "Mother Mary", "This Kid's", "Love To Love", "Lights Out", "Rock Bottom", "Too Hot To Handle", "I'm A Loser" and "Let It Roll" before it finishes with "Shoot Shoot".

Nevison: "I'll tell you about *Strangers In The Night* as far as the title goes: I was mixing at the Record Plant with my assistant Mike Clink who went on to great fame. He had been out on tour with me to record and we were mixing at the original Record Plant on Seventh Street and I took a break and went next door to have a meal. They played some Sinatra on their sound system. I just sat there and thought what a cool fucking title for an album, Stranger In The Night! I changed it to *Strangers In The Night* and Chrysalis got on board with renting out the Planetarium at Griffith Park for a launch party, which was really cool. Having trashed Chrysalis a little bit in this interview for their lack of back end support, they're front end support was great."[83]

The CD re-issue of *Strangers In The Night* opens with the terrific "Hot 'N' Ready" before the band really gels together with "Cherry". "Let It Roll" offers plenty of thrills while "Love To Love" works just as well onstage as it does on the original studio cut. "Natural Thing" is led by the undeniable guitars of Michael Schenker while "Out In The Street" is much faster than the studio version. "Only You Can Rock Me" is simply awesome and a testament to the band's hard rock credentials. "Mother Mary" is certainly heavy enough to headbang to and "This Kid's" really picks up the pace; it's a fast and raucous song when played live. "Doctor Doctor" is fantastic onstage with a crowd cheering chorus, while "I'm A Loser" shows off a great vocal performance from front man Mogg. "Lights Out" is a sweat-inducing rocker and "Rock Bottom" is just as hard and heavy hitting as anything the band have done before or since. "Too Hot To Handle" is a fist-in-the-air rock anthem while "Shoot Shoot" closes the album in glorious '70s rock style. The fact remains that *Strangers In The Night* is a legendary album and one of the greatest live releases ever issued. It never fails to be hugely entertaining and uplifting.

Strangers In The Night hit Number 7 in the UK album charts in February, a month after its initial 1979 release. Over in the USA it peaked at Number 42. The album was later reissued in 1999 (and 2008) with the bonus tracks "Hot 'N' Ready" and "Cherry". The tracklisting for the 1999 and 2008 versions was reordered to reflect the band's late 1970s set list more accurately. The CD version is a single disc. The 2008 sleeve notes state that "This Kid's" and "Mother Mary" are indeed studio tracks with crowd noise added to make them sound as though they were recorded live. The re-ordered version of the album is currently on CD as part of the band's and EMI's recent reissue campaign [EMI acquired Chrysalis before it was, in turn, bought by Universal].

Critics greeted *Strangers In The Night* with enthusiastic write-ups. Many of the reviews shared the same train of thought: the band sounded much better onstage than they did in the studio. *Strangers In The Night* was as much of a 'best of' album as it was a live release. What the album did – especially to naysayers that branded UFO nothing but a macho testosterone-fuelled rock band – was just how blisteringly brilliant they were onstage. The success of the opus, both commercially and critically, certainly brought UFO a new legion of fans in the USA, UK and elsewhere. With *Strangers In The Night,* UFO now joined the hallowed ranks of other seminal rock bands who have released a double-live vinyl: Queen released *Live Killers*, Rush released *Exit … Stage Left* and Status Quo released *Quo Live.* Go back further in time for Deep Purple's *Made In Japan* and *Uriah Heep Live* to show the canon UFO were following.

Harry Doherty wrote in *Melody Maker*: "The proof comes when the coldness and relative inefficiency of UFO's studio work is placed alongside the roasting live hive of hard rock activity on *Strangers In The Night.* Tracks that sounded mediocre in the studio suddenly come to life in live performance." Bob Edmands in the *NME* penned: "No doubt they'll get disgustingly rich on the strength of *Strangers.* But that's true of all successful rock performances – buy an album, support the wealthy … Inevitably, *Strangers* is an album that will be deeply unfashionable. But if trendies are foolish enough to neglect it, that's their business."

Writing years later in *Kerrang!*, Howard Johnson enthused: "They never quite seemed to capture the intensity of their live performances on record, and the band's studio albums do sound a touch dated these days. No such problem here though, where Ron Nevison allows Schenker's axework to fly clear and free. When the man was on song, believe me, there was no one better!"

Its importance in the rock world is unquestionably cemented, given its status as one of the finest live recordings in rock history. It remains a simply wonderful album and a testament to the band's longevity. *Guitar Player Magazine* would declare "Rock Bottom" from *Strangers In The Night* one of the greatest guitar tunes of all time.

The album has a famous fan in former Guns N' Roses guitarist Slash and regularly appears in lists of great live albums such as *Kerrang!*'s '100

Greatest Heavy Metal Albums Of All Time' where it was placed at Number 47. Joe Elliott of Def Leppard, Mike McCready of Pearl Jam and Metallica have also praised the release. Steve Harris of Iron Maiden – a noted UFO fan – even contributed his thoughts on the album to the 2008 CD reissue.

It is unquestionably a bona-fide masterpiece from start to end. There had been other great live albums to come out of the 1970s that broke some bands into the mainstream – KISS with *Alive!*, AC/DC with *If You Want Blood ... You've Got It*, Thin Lizzy's *Live And Dangerous*, Cheap Trick's *At Budokan*, Peter Frampton with *Frampton Comes Alive!* and Judas Priest with *Unleashed In The East* – and UFO would join the best of them with *Strangers In The Night*.

Despite the reverence that had been bestowed on the band, did they care? Phil Mogg admitted: "We only need to satisfy ourselves. We're one band who wants no regrets. There'll be no saying later that we shouldn't have done this or done that."[84]

The album spawned subsequent EP releases: "Doctor Doctor" with "On With The Action" (recorded on the same 1978 USA tour) and the studio recorded song "Try Me" was released in February and hit Number 35 in the UK singles chart – the first time the band cracked the Top 40. Also released was a live cut of "Shoot Shoot" with "Only You Can Rock Me" and "I'm A Loser" which hit Number 48 in the UK in April, 1979.

This prompted the release of "Doctor Doctor" which led to a live appearance on the BBC TV show, *Top Of The Pops*. "Judas Priest had the nerve to put amplifiers on stage and then mime. We've no amps, no leads," Mogg said of the band's *TOTP* appearance. "We even wanted to use acoustic guitars."[85]

The Schenker era of UFO's career cannot be overstated. Certainly the Ron Nevison produced albums had a major impact on the New Wave Of British Heavy Metal; a period of musical activity in the UK that lasted from around 1979 to 1981 and a little later. The NWOBHM came straight after punk. Young kids all over the UK, in industrial cities such as Newcastle, Sheffield and Birmingham, formed metal bands by adopting the punk do-it-yourself ethos. They started out playing in their garage before they performed in front of audiences. Many of the NWOBHM bands such as Def Leppard, Iron Maiden and Diamond Head were passionate UFO fans and idolised Michael Schenker.

Brian Tatler of Diamond Head recalls: "I first saw UFO in 1978 on the *Obsession* tour at Birmingham Town Hall; I was immediately struck by how cool Michael Schenker looked. His white Flying V, his long blonde hair, dressed in skin-tight black lycra and thigh-length black leather boots. Not only was he an awesome player but he looked amazing too. I thought to myself 'I am having that' so after that one show I pretty much set about trying to copy Schenker's playing style and image."[86]

He continues: "UFO had some great songs and great riffs but it was Schenker's guitar solos that really inspired me. I would study the lead breaks in songs like 'Lights Out', 'Only You Can Rock Me', 'This Kid's' and 'Love To Love', trying to figure out the touch, feel and melody of each one. He never relied on effects either, it seemed like all he used was a wah wah pedal that he would use as a tone control. Michael is one of the all time great lead guitarists. Later in my career our drummer from 1983 to 1985, Robbie France, joined UFO and I got to meet Phil Mogg. He seemed like a nice guy although I did not know what to say to him. I thought he must get this all the time 'I saw you in 1978, etc.' What are you supposed to reply to that?"[87]

While some bands such as Iron Maiden secured major record deals, many of the bands would only self-release music, or at least have it released via small labels. However, the importance of the NWOBHM and the bands that it spawned is long-lasting as it would influence subsequent metal movements such as the Bay Area thrash metal scene on the West Coast of America. UFO may never have made the amount of money that Black Sabbath and Deep Purple earned, but they were surely just as influential.

"It was a shame that we had to split up after *Strangers In The Night*," Schenker reflected to *Hard Roxx*'s Matthew Honey in 1997. "I believe that everything happens for a reason and I accept everything that happened in the past the way it happened ... It is easier to accept what has happened in the past and move on in an enthusiastic and positive way."[88]

As with almost everything surrounding UFO, things were not so clear cut back in 1979. There was always the possibility that UFO would lose much of their fanbase after Schenker's departure. Nevertheless, it was time for Mogg and company to move on. *Strangers In The Night* brought about the end of an era and a new one had dawned.

To promote the release of *Strangers In The Night* and to showcase Paul Chapman's noticeable skills on the fretboard, UFO hit the road in the USA in 1979. They had become a popular touring act across the Atlantic, where they could sell out big arenas in some States just on the strength of their name. They toured for the second time as guests of Rush, who presumably forgave them the pink slippers prank, and even played at the World Music Festival in California. They toured the summer of 1979 with Judas Priest as support; they too were supporting their own live album – *Unleashed In The East*. In Chicago, UFO became the support band to Judas Priest as a one-off. Another leg of the band's USA tour followed with Aussie rockers AC/DC as support. AC/DC provided UFO with their toughest act to follow; it was very competitive, but in a healthy and positively challenging way.

The tour with AC/DC was a typically rock 'n' roll affair. When they hit Tennessee, they stayed at the Hyatt Regency in Knoxville. At 2 a.m., with members of both bands in the hotel bar, Andy Parker encouraged Paul Raymond to play the hotel piano and despite several warnings from hotel security to "keep the darn noise down", the police were called.

Paul Raymond: "I was frogmarched away by the police in handcuffs with Angus Young's words 'that's right, take 'im away and hang the little fucker!' ringing in my ears. Later at the police station, on complaining that I had never been arrested for playing a piano before, the officer replied in his Southern drawl, 'You just played it too damn long, boy! ...'"[89]

UFO had now cracked the USA – so much so that they made some high-profile TV appearances, even guesting on *Hollywood Squares* [better known in the UK as *Celebrity Squares*]. They spent so much time in the States that they had by now bought a house in LA which they used as a temporary base. "England is still our home," Chapman said to David Fricke at *Circus* in 1979, "but having a house in LA is really convenient for us work-wise. I'm not there much because of all the touring, but if you're on the road and you've got three days off, you go home to your own bed sheets and get your socks washed."[90]

Chapman was especially fond of Texas, where they had an FM station that played nothing but rock music. They spent so much time in the States that it was easier for them to live there. The whole point of the band living in the USA was for them to broaden their sound by identifying with American bands and also growing their US fanbase. Mogg and Way adjusted to life in LA and enjoyed over-indulgence in various substances. Mogg had a Pontiac Trans Am while Way drove a Chevrolet Camaro and they'd race each other like maniacs around Laurel Canyon.

Phil Mogg was asked by one *NME* journalist about why UFO's music was different from other blues rock bands such as Led Zeppelin. He replied: "I feel that we're more current. We're more happening now. Zeppelin was then. And they've remained in that period. They haven't moved. We've moved. We've moved each year and each album. That's it."[91]

Mogg has never been shy when it comes to voicing his own opinions and causing controversy. It was a ballsy comment to make about one of the world's biggest acts. Nevertheless, UFO had developed an identifiable sound of their own, which would definitely stand the test of time.

With their tour of the USA out of the way, the band set to work on a new studio album. *No Place To Run* was produced by the revered former Beatles producer George Martin at his AIR Studios on the luxurious Caribbean island of Montserrat and AIR Studios in London from July to August, 1979.

"Initially, we wanted Ted Templeman to produce the album," Mogg admitted to Steve Gett of *Melody Maker* at the time, "but because he's a house producer for Warner Brothers he's only allowed one outside project a year. We had to get out of America for visa problems, and, in fact, we've been so busy touring that we hadn't had a break for 14 months, so we asked about the studio charges at Montserrat."[92]

How did the legendary Beatles producer end up working with a band such as UFO? The generally reported story is that UFO had spent some studio time at AIR Studios in Central London which George Martin had founded in 1969. Martin, who was having trouble convincing bands to use his Montserrat studio, was in the London studio when UFO were there. He told UFO that if they used his studio in Montserrat he'd produce their album. It's an offer you can't refuse, isn't it?

George Martin had first visited the island in 1977 and, by 1979, he had built a studio there. The Montserrat based AIR Studios would become a recording haven for many high-profile artists such as Paul McCartney, Elton John, The Rolling Stones and The Police, but was destroyed by Hurricane Hugo in 1989. UFO faced their own squall in the summer of 1979: they spent two months on the island, but after about six weeks working there Hurricane David hit on August 25. Thankfully, they were unharmed.

Steve Churchyard joined them as assistant engineer with mixer/engineer Geoff Emerick. The line-up for this album features Phil Mogg,

Pete Way, Andy Parker, Paul Raymond and the newly recruited Paul Chapman on guitar. It was Chapman's first studio release with UFO, so he had a great deal to live up to when comparing the forthcoming album with the band's past work with Schenker. How could they possibly top the likes of *Lights Out*? The Ron Nevison albums would be tough to follow.

With Paul Chapman, the band's dynamics had changed, as had their style of writing. Despite George Martin's pedigree, perhaps he was not the best producer to capture UFO's driving hard rock sound, and he was horrified that Mogg didn't turn in the lyrics on time. Due to the slight change in the band's line-up they opted for a more guitar orientated album, with less keyboard input from Raymond, which would allow Chapman to take lead. However, not all fans would appreciate it. An integral part of UFO's sound had been the keyboard atmospherics.

It was around this time that Mogg discovered Bruce Springsteen, whose best known and appreciated songs are epics such as "Born To Run" and "Jungleland"; both tracks, to a degree, had an impact on UFO's front man. Certainly the title track "No Place To Run" became something of a mini-epic in the studio. The press later made a great deal out of Mogg's supposed infatuation with Springsteen, but it really wasn't anything more than listening to the odd song by The Boss. Most of Mogg's personal record collection was, in fact, made up of old blues albums.

When the band first started out, Mogg listened to Bob Dylan and was influenced by Dylan's verse writing. However, Mogg soon moved on from Dylan as he would from Springsteen. Mogg would later criticise Springsteen's songs for sounding the same and mulling over the same tried and tested topics of American life; it had become a tired style with repetitive substance.

Such a seemingly lightweight melodic rock direction wasn't on the agenda for Messrs Way and Mogg: " ... we felt that the combination of the two [UFO and George Martin] was strange enough to get something that sounded a bit different but was still a strong rock album. The funny thing is that he's always known for his orchestrations and that is his strongest point, but we said when we went in that we wanted a straight rock album with no strings or fancy bits."[93]

Mogg wasn't entirely happy with the end mix of the album, as the band were on a European road jaunt during the final stages of recording. Martin has all but blotted the album – and the experience of working with

UFO – from his consciousness. He has rarely, if ever, spoken about UFO in specific terms.

No Place To Run opens with the spacey "Alpha Centauri" which recalls the band's beginnings, while "Lettin' Go" is a strong enough rocker. "Mystery Train" is a suitably bluesy cover of the famed Elvis song. "This Fire Burns Tonight" is an oddly effective ballad that deserves more credit, while "Gone In The Night" is a somewhat below par number though the keys are suitably melodic. "Young Blood" has a gritty Rolling Stones feel to it and is perhaps the album's standout rock number. "No Place To Run" is an excellent song, appropriately dark and edgy. "Take It Or Leave It" is a bit of a come down after the terrific previous two songs. It has an accomplished melody, but it doesn't feel like UFO. "Money, Money" opens with a killer guitar riff before the rest of the band join in on the fun. The closing track, "Anyday", is an average rock number, though Chapman shines with a mid-song riff.

No Place To Run has some worthwhile tunes, but overall it's let down by a distinctly modest production. It's hardly the best album to follow such a run of rock classics from UFO, but it does have some merits.

Released in January 1980, *No Place To Run* hit Number 11 in the UK and eventually went silver, making it their most successful album to date. Meanwhile, over in the USA, where it was released a little earlier than in the band's homeland, it peaked at Number 51 in the *Billboard* 200 album charts. The album was released with various covers in the UK with the only difference from each one being the colouring – presumably the record company had taken a leaf from Stiff Records' book of clever marketing ploys. "Lettin' Go" and "Young Blood" (Number 41 in the UK singles chart) were both released as singles. The 2009 reissue includes several bonus tracks: an alternate studio version of "Gone In The Night" and live versions of "Lettin' Go", "Mystery Train" and "No Place To Run", which were recorded at The Marquee Club in London in November 1980.

Upon the album's release there was a general feeling amongst fans that the band had made an album aimed at the US FM stations – a more radio friendly feeling animal. "I think it's a valid attempt to try and do a few things differently," Mogg explained to Garry Bushell at *Sounds* in 1980. "It'd be easy to cliché ourselves, or write the standard HM album ... We intended it to be different, I'm not saying it's worked necessarily, but it's what we wanted."[94]

Would *No Place To Run* be strong enough to follow the brilliance of *Strangers In The Night*? Critics gave *No Place To Run* lukewarm reviews in the main; much of the criticism was aimed at the production and choice of songs.

Robin Smith wrote in *Record Mirror*: "I didn't like his [George Martin's] efforts on the single 'Young Blood' but the rest of the album is a near masterpiece of controlled bludgeoning." Long time UFO fan Geoff Barton said in *Sounds*: "But overall, like I say, a rather unspectacular offering. Listening to the LP once again I find what I miss most of all is Paul Raymond's wondrously atmospheric keyboard work. On *No Place To Run* he's given few chances to shine and ends up supplying some 'honky tonk' piano backups which, if they weren't all but lost in the mix, would have had me making unfavourable REO Speedwagon comparisons."

On the other hand, Steve Gett wrote in *Melody Maker*: "UFO have set an extremely high standard of hard rock with *No Place To Run*, and quite clearly it will be enormously successful. Run, don't walk to buy it – unless you feel your nervous system may be frayed by UFO's sound and fury."

Its place in the band's canon is hardly vital. *No Place To Run* is not a bad album but given the strength of the albums that came immediately before it, *No Place To Run* was something of a disappointment, yet there is a section of the band's fanbase that hold the Paul Chapman albums in high regard. However, *No Place To Run* does not feature in any polls of all time great rock albums and so forth. It sounds somewhat dated in comparison to the band's previous work. However, better albums would be released by the band in due course. It's largely remembered for being Paul Raymond's sabbatical sign-off from UFO before he rejoined in the 1990s.

The band had done a run of British dates in December before the release of *No Place To Run*, but a fully-fledged UK tour was scheduled for early 1980 during the time of the album's release. The road jaunt kicked off at the Liverpool Empire on January 13. In the past, Mogg had written a majority of the band's material with music written by Schenker, Way and Raymond, but this dynamic was set to change again with yet more line-up changes that would ultimately slow the band down.

Paul Raymond left after the *No Place To Run* tour (with Girl as support), which ended with five (the original flyer for the tour states three) sold out nights at the Hammersmith Odeon in London in early February. They played "Lettin' Go", "No Place To Run", "Out In The Street", "Cherry", "Only You Can Rock Me", "Love To Love", a cover of the Little Junior's Blue Flames number "Mystery Train" and the classic "Lights Out". It was a staggering achievement for the band. They were used to residencies at The Marquee Club and the Roundhouse but the Hammersmith Odeon was a different kettle of fish. Not only had UFO built up a loyal following around the UK, but in their hometown of London too.

Geoff Barton praised the band in his review of one of the London gigs in *Sounds*: "I left the gig in no doubt that UFO are currently Britain's finest, and I want to see 'em again real soon. And in any case, who is Michael Schenker?"

Raymond had become an even more crucial band member after the departure of Schenker and would even go on to join MSG in 1981 in time for their first world tour, which included opening for Molly Hatchet on some dates in the USA. At the time, Schenker and MSG were managed by Peter Mensch who contacted Raymond about joining MSG when Denny Carmassi and Billy Sheehan were in the band. Schenker was in bad shape in those days, so Raymond did not think the relationship would work out. However, by 1981 Schenker has cleaned up his act and Raymond felt that UFO was on the slide. So with top notch drummer Cozy Powell in MSG, Raymond decided to leave UFO and join up with Schenker.

In the UFO camp, Raymond was briefly replaced by Cardiff born musician John Sloman (known for his stints in Lone Star and Uriah Heep) for just a couple of months or so. During the summer of 1980, Sloman was working on some new material with Uriah Heep at Nomis Rehearsal room near Olympia Studios in London. UFO were rehearsing in a nearby room and Paul Raymond would call in on Uriah Heep and talk to them and listen to their new songs. Phil Mogg also made an appearance.

Sloman: "A while after, their manager called to ask me if I'd stand in for their keyboard player/guitar player in a rehearsal because he was in LA. I went down there. It was just Phil and Paul. We jammed on some of their stuff. Sometimes I played keyboards, other times guitar. I remember at some point in the proceedings Paul turns to me, winks and says: 'There's more to this than meets the eye.' I just nodded and smiled because I'd already figured out I was being auditioned by stealth."[95]

Shortly thereafter, but still in the summer of 1980, Sloman was asked to join UFO. He declined. Sloman was actually a fan of the band

and regarded *Force It* as one of his all time favourite albums. He simply preferred to be a keyboard player rather than a singer/keyboardist and so he had little inclination to take up the seat previously occupied by Paul Raymond. However, Sloman was happy to take up the invitation of contributing Springsteen style piano keys to some tentative sessions for the band's forthcoming album, which would be titled *The Wild, The Willing And The Innocent.*

"Around this time, a piece appeared in *Sounds* with the headline HEEP MAN TO JOIN UFO?," Sloman recalls. "It certainly stirred things up within the Heep camp for me, even though I'd had nothing whatsoever to do with it [It was later revealed to be UFO manager Wilf Wright who'd leaked the story to the press]. This culminated in me having a rather brief phone conversation with Gerry Bron one night, where he forbade me to do the UFO album (an inappropriate demand as I was never ever signed to Uriah Heep). Anyway, I told Gerry that if that was the case I was leaving Heep (not, I hasten to add, to join UFO). Soon afterwards Gerry relented about the UFO album."[96]

Sloman enjoyed working with the band and Mogg and Way were especially fun to be around. The sessions went well and they had some very powerful songs laid down.

Sloman: "Two tracks stuck in my mind: one with a single guitar chug intro which I added some piano to, and a really tender acoustic guitar and piano ballad. There were no titles at this point. In the end I contributed piano to about four or five tracks. I wasn't even sure if they were going to use what I'd played, given that they might eventually find a permanent keyboard player/guitar player who might want to do his own thing. Anyway, I wished the guys well and went back to the new Heep material."

Sloman was also asked to join the band onstage for the Reading Festival and other live dates that were looming, but he declined. He remembers: "... I was writing and recording new Heep material with Trevor [Bolder] and wouldn't have had the time to do justice to both. Most days I was leaving the UFO session at Wessex Studios in North London and travelling to Shepperton where we were demoing the new Heep material. Mick [Box] had injured his hand in a car crash so I was doing guitar parts as well as vocals."[97]

Sloman also went on to work with Gary Moore and Praying Mantis. Meantime, former Wild Horses and future Gary Moore collaborator, guitarist and keyboardist Neil Carter stepped in to replace Raymond permanently in the role which Sloman had declined. Carter was friends with Phil Collen of the British glam metal band Girl (he later joined Def Leppard) who was friends with UFO, and Collen mentioned Carter to Mogg. Mogg thought that if Carter could cope with working with Wild Horses cohorts Brian Robertson and Jimmy Bain then he could survive working in UFO. Carter had an instant rapport with the band.

As quoted in the *NME* at the time, Phil Mogg said in a press release: "Paul is no longer with us because his ideas no longer fitted in with what we wanted to do, but despite rumours that we would play Reading as a four-piece, UFO is a five-piece band and, as far as we're concerned, always will be."[98]

With a classically trained background, Carter also helped the band with songwriting after the departure of Schenker. Until Carter joined UFO, his primary instrument was the guitar and he never actually played keyboards live onstage, aside from a brief stint with Gilbert O'Sullivan.

Carter's first live appearance with UFO came with two warm-up gigs prior to the Reading Festival at Taunton Odeon on 21 August and St Austell New Cornish Riviera the day after. The band then headlined Saturday night's shenanigans at the three day long Reading Festival on 23 August 1980, which also included Iron Maiden and Pat Travers Band.

Asked about the Reading Festival performance, Carter says: "Bit daunting having so much new material to remember, but very exciting at the same time. It felt so right for me and I liked what they did, although before joining I only had a scant knowledge of their songs so the set was pretty fresh to me. I was also quite young still (22) so it was a tremendous break but I never felt nervous playing large crowds so it was mostly all pleasure! I smile when I think Iron Maiden were then second on the bill to us. Our chaplain at my school [Carter later became a teacher] told me he was in the audience at Reading as a young student and remembered the three big balloons spelling U. F. O. He told me that just before we went on 'U' sailed off into the sunset just leaving 'F O'! That is pure UFO!"[99]

On September 20 in Colmar, France, UFO performed at a festival with Wishbone Ash. On October 29, they performed at the Westfalenhalle in Dortmund, Germany playing a set list of "Chains Chains", "Lettin' Go", "Long Gone", "Cherry", "Only You Can Rock Me", "No Place To Run", "Makin' Moves", "Love To Love", "Mystery Train", "Too Hot To Handle", "Lights Out", "Rock Bottom" and "Doctor Doctor".

UFO closed 1980 with a run of British dates, taking Fist on tour with them as support, before touring around mainland Europe finishing on December 14 in Portugal. The band opened 1981 with gigs in places they had not visited for some time, such as Bradford and Carlisle. "I tend to keep myself to myself on tours," Carter admitted to the *Melody Maker*'s Brian Harrigan. "I suppose I'm a quiet sort of bloke really. Don't get me wrong, though, I'm enjoying playing with this band so much I couldn't explain it. The thing is they're so good at winding people up it becomes a bit overwhelming at times."[100]

With Carter joining Mogg, Way, Chapman and Parker in the camp, UFO set to work in earnest on their next studio release: album number nine. After living in LA for about two years, UFO's working visas had come to an end. The band had already decamped to England. Self-produced for the first time after firing a producer, *The Wild, The Willing And The Innocent* was recorded at AIR Studios in London with additional spots of recording completed at Wessex Sound Studios, Utopia, Maison Rouge and Red Barn with engineers Steve Churchyard, Gary Edwards and Jeremy Green. Churchyard and Chapman both lived in Kingston, Surrey at the time and used to commute to the studio together.

"The bulk of the backing tracks were recorded and they were at the stage of guitar solos and Phil's vocals by the time I got involved," recalls Carter. "We then added other stuff, backing vocals and the sax solo. Then it was mixing, all done at AIR London in Oxford Street. It was weird having people like George Martin and Linda McCartney wandering in while you were in the studio, but it was their domain. My favourite bit of that album is still the string arrangements; they are so good."[101]

The band wanted a rawer sound unlike the previous album which they felt lacked edge. Conductor Paul Buckmaster, perhaps best known for his work with Elton John, arranged the orchestral sound of the album, which was an experimental approach for the band. However, the use of the saxophone by Neil Carter would be one step beyond for one particular longstanding member of the fold ... more of that later!

The work includes some uncredited keyboards by John Sloman. After the summer sessions of 1980, Sloman had moved on with his career but he still remembers the music he had helped craft with UFO.

Sloman: "Sometime later I was at home with my girlfriend watching TV. *Top Of The Pops* comes on. And there's UFO playing their latest single 'Lonely Heart', with that guitar chug intro that I contributed those piano chords to. 'That's my piano playing.' 'Are you sure?', my girlfriend said. 'Absolutely sure.' My girlfriend (who was in the business and knew Wilf Wright) talked to Wilf on my behalf. Wilf, feeling a tug on his wallet-strings, said that all my parts, including those on 'Lonely Heart' had been replaced. To this day I've never heard the album other than the night I stumbled into 'Lonely Heart' on *TOTP*. People tell me I'm credited on the sleeve for playing parts Wilf said were no longer there, but I've never so much as set eyes on the sleeve in order to see for myself. I'd like to hear 'Lonely Heart' again, as well as that acoustic guitar and piano ballad that I laid down with Paul back in the summer of 1980."[102]

Returning to the Springsteen influence, it had clearly crept in and flowed throughout the album: note how the title tips its hat to Springsteen's 1973 album *The Wild, The Innocent And The E Street Shuffle*. The idea of calling the album 'Jungleland' after the Springsteen epic from *Born To Run* was even thrown around at one point.

Carter: "Phil was always the dominant force and I think still is. The singer is the sound of any band and he 'is' UFO. Without Phil it wouldn't sound like UFO whoever was playing and he has been the 'constant' so I can say that without hesitation. Pete and Phil made a good 'team' as the central core and their humour has played a part in the story."[103]

Carter had eased into the band well enough. He was more than happy to be playing in a band as successful as UFO even though they were arguably on the wane. With Carter in the band UFO were more than willing to explore new musical territories, even if some of their fans would not be open to the idea of experimentation. Their aim was to find the right balance between guitars and keyboards.

The band knew they really had to up their game after the mixed reviews of *No Place To Run*, which was largely attacked for being too lightweight and lacking in standout rock songs. Many fans thought that it was a mistake to have hired George Martin despite his enviable credentials. If the forthcoming album failed it would do so because the band produced it themselves – the buck stopped with them.

"There's no concept to it at all," Mogg said about the forthcoming album. "All we tried to do was make the record more melodic, more meaningful to us than the ones before."[104]

The Wild, The Willing And The Innocent opens with the gritty guitar-led rocker, "Chains Chains" while "Long Gone" proves just what an accomplished guitarist Paul Chapman is in his own right. "The Wild, The Willing And The Innocent" is a wonderfully melodic song with some Springsteen-style keys and, once it gets going, a stomping melody. "It's Killing Me" is an all-but-forgotten yet minor gem from the band, while "Makin' Moves" is a speedy number with some excellent guitars and drums. "Lonely Heart" is Mogg's nod to Springsteen; the intro was straight out of *Born To Run*. "Couldn't Get It Right" opens with a gritty riff from Chapman, while "Profession Of Violence", which was released as 'Profession Of' in the USA – ironically a far more violent country than the UK – closes proceedings. It's an odd choice to finish the album; it would have been better suited as a middle song. It's simply not lively enough though it is musically accomplished.

More rock-centric than its predecessor, *The Wild, The Willing And The Innocent* has some fine moments and a suitable strong sense of melody and gusto. UFO still had something to say despite some criticisms from the naysayers.

The Wild, The Willing And The Innocent was released in January 1981. It peaked at Number 77 in the USA and Number 19 in the UK. Again, the original album cover was designed by Hipgnosis and was typically controversial with a man stabbing a naked woman in the back with a drill. "Couldn't Get It Right" with a live version of "Hot 'N' Ready" (recorded at the 1980 Reading Festival) was released as a single as was "Lonely Heart" with "Long Gone", which hit Number 41 in the UK singles chart. The 2009 reissue includes live versions of "Long Gone", "Lonely Heart" and "Makin' Moves" that were recorded at the Hammersmith Odeon in January 1981 and November 1980, respectively.

The Wild, The Willing And The Innocent received much better reviews than *No Place To Run*. It is a stronger, more rounded rock album and the critics took note.

Writing in *Record Mirror*, Robin Smith said: "Grittier than the last album, *The Wild, The Willing And The Innocent* will leave you with mud on your palm and grit in your eye."

Its role in the band's back catalogue is understated. There are many UFO fans that have since praised the Paul Chapman era albums and, similarly to *No Place To Run*, *The Wild, The Willing And The Innocent* has an eager following of fans. Sadly, it remains somewhat overlooked by everyone else. It's a robust rock album which deserves more mainstream attention.

Less hard rock and more light pop, the group did receive a minor hit with "Lonely Heart" but it was obvious the band's sound missed Schenker's fierce Flying V attack, which left some fans worried that UFO's glory days were behind them. Would they ever be able to recapture the hard rock halcyon era of the late 1970s?

To promote their new album, they toured the USA, supporting Cheap Trick, from February. In fact, much of 1981 was spent touring the States. The American road jaunt included a spot on the Iowa Jam in Des Moines on May 24, which also saw performances from The Outlaws, 38. Special, April Wine, Luxury and Crosby, Stills And Nash. From July 3 to July 30, UFO played a series of gigs in Spain and the USA, supporting the likes of Def Leppard and Rainbow. Rainbow were touring in support of their album *Difficult To Cure*.

Former Deep Purple and Rainbow roadie Colin Hart recalls: "We were in San Sebastian, Spain, and the dressing room areas were kinda sparse, with curtains separating each area. UFO were scheduled to perform next, and just before they were due to hit the stage, Ian Broad, who worked exclusively for Ritchie as his personal roadie, decided to toss a huge bowl of salad over the divider into UFO's area. Well, they were dressed and ready for the stage and Phil Mogg was not amused at all. He came out fuming and Ian, urged on by Ritchie, confronted Phil and decided to throw a punch. That was a bad move at best, as Phil had been a bit of a boxer in his day. He dodged the punch and returned a right hook that should have been enough to stop it ..."[105]

Hart continues: "However, Ritchie encouraged a dizzy Ian to have another go and in he went. There was a very brief and bloody bar room style fight, with Ian suffering almost all the damage. I stepped in to stop it, as Ian was getting hurt, but Ritchie grabbed me around the neck from behind and insisted I leave them alone. Down went all the dressing room dividers and crap was flying everywhere. Ian gave up, thankfully, before suffering more. He was bleeding from one ear and his nose was swollen and bloody, cuts everywhere. Phil, on the other hand, had barely a scratch and calmly continued on his way to the stage to do their set. Later in the hotel, Ritchie was in his room trying to get to sleep and there was a party going on a couple of doors away. Ritchie came out of his room dressed in his PJ's, which he always wore, and banged on the door shouting for them to shut the [fuck] up. The door opened and who was there – Mr Mogg, who said something like, 'Can I help you?' and Ritchie just said: 'Can you keep the noise down?' and quietly retreated to his room. I watched this unfold with Eric Thompsen from near Eric's room. We could hardly contain our laughter!"[106]

On August 2, UFO performed at the Day On The Green Festival at Oakland Stadium in California that also included REO Speedwagon and Kansas before supporting Iron Maiden at Long Beach Arena on August 4.

The band soon began the next phase of their career.

CHAPTER
FIVE

Mechanix –
The Departure Of Pete Way
And The Break Up Of The Band
(1982 –1983)

*"As a band, we've never really placed
a great amount of emphasis on Britain."*

Phil Mogg[107]

After some heavy touring throughout 1981, songwriting sessions for the next album were held and UFO began work on *Mechanix*, which was recorded at Mountain Studios in Attalens, Switzerland, The Manor Studio in Shipton-On-Cherwell, Oxfordshire and London's Scorpio Sound and Maison Rouge Studios. " ... we were in Switzerland staying in houses belonging to Queen," says Carter. "There was a lot of 'wood stealing' and Pete's dodgy cooking. Going into the casino after recording and losing big bucks and everything costing a fortune."[108]

They hooked up with producer Gary Lyons, who had worked with Queen and Foreigner, and engineer Peter Thea to help them gain a new perspective on the hard rock sound which they appeared to have distanced themselves from. The band were looking for a named producer who would give them a more polished commercial vibe and thus an American angle. The band needed a radio hit.

They did not have a clear vision of what they wanted from Lyons. "We virtually told him to do what he wanted and we think it's come out very well," Mogg said at the time. "We think the album has a more commercial feel, if that's not a dirty word. Producing ourselves was a bit of a strain in some ways. Maybe we don't have enough self-discipline ... What we wanted this time was someone to come in, get hold of the material, take a completely different look at it and get the whole thing moving."[109]

This album represented the line-up of Phil Mogg, Pete Way, Andy Parker, Paul Chapman and Neil Carter. The band had also teamed up with a new manager by the name of Carl Leighton-Pope, after parting ways with Wilf Wright who went on to manage Cockney Rejects.

Switzerland was an excellent place for the band to record, although it was expensive. They certainly hadn't earned the sort of money Queen had made in their career. "There was a lot of experimenting with things, not everything worked, but if you don't try, you don't know," says Carter about working in Switzerland. "I had a cringe-worthy experience doing the string arrangement for 'Terri' as it hadn't occurred to me that actual session string players were going to play it and my attempt was rudimentary at best. I think I could do it 1000 times better these days. I was always there with Gary Lyons at ridiculous hours of the day, as he liked to keep going on and on and on, but I am quite proud of many of the tracks on that album. 'Let It Rain', 'Dreaming' and 'The Writer' are my favourites."[110]

They spent a significant amount of time in the studio trying to recapture the energy and sound of the band as if they were live onstage. In terms of the lyrics, it was always Mogg who wrote the lyrics and melody, but for this album, he had some help from Carter, and Lyons managed to get Mogg to re-write a couple of the songs, as the premise was not clear. The band's tenth album was something of a welcome return to form.

Carter: "It would always be individuals coming up with riffs, ideas, etc., and them being moulded together to make a song structure, generally without a vocal line or lyrics. Then that would be worked on in the studio and then Phil would do his bit. It is a bit of a haphazard way of doing things but somehow over the years it generally worked O.K. I had some input on vocal lines as time went on, as and when required."[111]

"Actually, for a change, we had more than enough material for the album" explained Andy Parker to the *Melody Maker*'s Brian Harrigan. "We usually have about nine songs and then we start worrying whether there's enough there and start to think about, you know, maybe stretching some of them so there won't be any embarrassing gaps. But this time we have a couple of tracks to spare."[112]

When the band recorded at The Manor in Oxfordshire, owned by Richard Branson, Steve Marriott would pop by to say hello and listen to the band's new material. With the multi-talented Carter in the group and Paul Chapman fully accepted by the fans, UFO were about to deliver their best album since *Obsession*.

Mechanix opens strongly with "The Writer" before the raucous "Somethin' Else", the band's second Eddie Cochran cover, following in the footsteps of "C'mon Everybody", kicks into action. "Back Into My Life" is a mid-paced ballad with a sensitive vocal performance from Mr Mogg. "You'll Get Love" could fit on a Foreigner album and not sound out of place; UFO's attempt at commercial melodic rock did shine on some songs. "Doing It All For You" opens with Parker's drums before Chapman lets rip with a gritty guitar lead. It's a stodgy, feisty song. "We Belong To The Night" picks up the pace considerably, while "Let It Rain" is perhaps the album's standout track; it's an absolute gem. "Terri" is a slow-ish song which Mogg sings with soul while "Feel It" sees the band back on rock form. Finally, "Dreaming" is a terrific little rocker with some wailing guitars and is the sort of song UFO should finish most, if not all, of their albums with.

An excellent album with some terrific songs, *Mechanix* saw the band back to their hard rocking best and Chapman had become a force to be reckoned with by this point. It remains the best of the Paul Chapman era albums. However, the release does sound too American; it lacks the British rock stomp of the 1970s.

Mechanix was released in February 1982. It hit Number 82 in the USA, while in the UK it peaked at a respectable Number 8; the band's highest ever UK charting album. To market the album, the accompanying press release at the time said "Mechanix: It will tighten your nuts." "The Writer" was released as a single in 1982 and hit Number 23 in the mainstream Rock charts in the USA, while "Let It Rain" was also released the same year and climbed only to Number 62 in the UK.

Maybe the album was not the hit they had hoped for but they remained satisfied with its quality, as Pete Way told *Sounds*' Garry Bushell: "Maybe it is too American for England and maybe there are certain things I would have changed personally, but I'm still pleased with it. Don't forget there are a lot of tracks on *Mechanix* and we're getting knocked for two ballads which are after all bonus tracks."[113]

The 2009 reissue includes an extra three live tracks: "We Belong To The Night" (Oxford, 25 November 1983), "Let It Rain" (Oxford, 24 November 1983), and "Doing It All For You" (Birmingham Odeon soundcheck).

Critics greeted *Mechanix* with mostly keen reviews. Writing in *Sounds*, Philip Bell enthused: "*Mechanix* should secure their place in the earwaxworks for a while yet, for the bottom line is that without fail, UFO always deliver." Meanwhile, Jason Ritchie of *Get Ready To Rock* praised the reissue of *Mechanix* in 2009. He enthused: "One of the band's best albums for me and this re-release/re-master is worthy of a place in your collection."

Mechanix was the album the band were desperate for after the departure of Schenker back in 1978. If only this had been the album to follow *Strangers In The Night*, rather than *No Place To Run,* then who knows what might have happened. Positively received by critics, and the band's biggest chart hit in the UK, UFO also received mainstream prominence in the US with the hit single "Back Into My Life".

Its significance in the band's history is rather understated, similar to the other two Chapman releases. It will never win any greatest albums of all time polls or acquire any prominence as a revered album, but it is something of a lost gem. Serious UFO fans, however, rate it as one of the band's best releases.

Andy Parker: "We'd always used Hipgnosis for our covers, but by then [management] didn't want to pay Hipgnosis. So, we had in-house people do the cover and a lot of people complained because it was really kind of cheesy. So, you're already noticing, from the late seventies, we weren't really getting support."[114] It had been that way since Schenker left. Hell, if George Martin couldn't produce a major record for them, who could? The answer was obviously Ron Nevison, but he would not re-enter the picture for quite some time to come.

The band had already begun touring the UK in support of the album from January 6 to January 28. The tour also included a gig at the Victoria Hall in Stoke on January 7, which was reviewed by the *Record Mirror*'s Andy Hughes. He wrote: "What was needed was a real crowd stormer like 'Doctor Doctor', now sadly dropped from the live set. 'Lights Out' did the job fairly well, but by now it was apparent that the band were less delighted with the show."

The UK tour was undoubtedly a success. A famous bootleg that surfaced in the 1990s called *UFO Landed London* was recorded on 28 January 1982 at the Hammersmith Odeon during the band's second and final of two sold out gigs at the venue. BBC sound engineers were at the show to record a robust sounding performance for posterity. The line-up of Mogg, Way, Chapman, Carter and Parker are on fire. It was officially released as *Regenerator – Live 1982* in November 2001 and as part of the excellent 2009 *Official Bootleg Box Set 1975-1982*. The band then drove up north to Manchester to perform on TV for the *Oxford Road Show* on January 29, although some reports have suggested the band played a third night at Hammersmith, which could either have taken place on January 29 or on January 27 after they travelled from playing a gig the previous night in Gloucester.

Although UFO fans may have craved the Schenker era material, Mogg and company were more enthusiastic about playing material from the latest album and the past two releases. The band blitzed through "We Belong To The Night", "Let It Rain", "Long Gone" "The Wild, The Willing And The Innocent", "Only You Can Rock Me", "No Place To Run", "Love To Love", "Doing It All For You", "Makin' Moves", "Too Hot To Handle" and "Mystery Train".

Reviewing the band's show from the Manchester Apollo, Brian Harrigan wrote in *Melody Maker*: "They've tightened up considerably since *The Wild, The Willing And The Innocent* tour when I thought that they'd lost their way. With newish member Neil Carter making his presence felt more forcibly, they've expanded their musical horizons."

UFO then supported Ozzy on his *Diary Of A Madman* tour in February through to March with Starfighters and Saxon joining them (separately) on select dates.

Carter talks about life on the road with UFO: "Crazy train time as we were with Ozzy in the States and doing some big shows of our own. The band was pretty good then and the set list was a strong crowd pleaser. I also had a lot more to contribute as I had started to write more, and playing songs you had a hand in writing is always rewarding. It was a typical 'band on the road in US in the early '80s scenario' with all that went with it! A lot of fun ... at times!"[115]

Due to the untimely death of Ozzy's guitarist Randy Rhoads in an air accident on March 19, Foreigner replaced Ozzy as headliners at the Tangerine Bowl in Orlando on March 20. UFO stayed on the road in the

USA with Ozzy returning (accompanied by Bernie Tormé on guitar) in April. On May 3, Magnum joined UFO and Ozzy for a show at the Nassau Coliseum in New York. UFO also performed some headlining shows of their own through to the end of May before they played with their old sparring partner Rainbow on June 2 and June 4, and with Iron Maiden and Rainbow on June 5 in Wisconsin. It was at one of those shows in support of *Mechanix* that Pearl Jam guitarist Mike McCready first saw UFO live. Even though his hero Michael Schenker was no longer in the band he was still hugely impressed by UFO's onstage abilities.

Carter had become accustomed to the band's wacky sense of humour. Way and Mogg were very much the Peter Cook and Dudley Moore type British comedy duo of the band, always winding each other, and everyone else, up. Even Chapman knew how to have a laugh too. He wasn't afraid of making digs at his UFO cohorts. Humour has always been a central ingredient in the band's daily make-up even when darker forces have been at play. "We have to keep an eye on Neil," Chapman joked to *Kerrang!*'s Karen Harvey, "because we never know what he's going to wear next. You should see one thing he's got – talk about *Star Trek*! It's covered in ruffles and things."[116]

Back in England, a two day festival was held at the 30,000 capacity Peterborough football ground on June 12 and 13; headlined by UFO and Saxon with Molly Hatchet, Tygers Of Pan Tang, Budgie, Girlschool and Y&T (making their British debut) also on the bill.

Despite the success and reverence that had been bestowed upon the band over the years, and the acclaim they'd been given in the States, they had never been considered a major league band. Asked why this was the case, Neil Carter told music journalist Jill Eckersley: "We're not businessmen at all, how many musicians are? Basically, we only care about the music and the kids in the audience, but we've had to learn to care about the other stuff as well. If we were the cut-throat type we would probably be a lot richer but ... we're just too nice!"[117]

However, frustrated with the more melodic and ultimately commercial direction that UFO was taking, such as the use of saxophones on *Mechanix*, founding member Pete Way left the band after UFO opened for Rainbow in the USA on June 5. He formed Fastway with Motörhead guitarist Eddie Clarke. "We started rehearsing down in Sussex and he just never turned up," Mogg explained to *Kerrang!*'s Dave Dickson. "He was rehearsing up here [London] with 'Slow' Eddie. When I rang him up he said: 'Oh, I'll be down tomorrow,' but he never came, But if you know what Pete's like it's to be expected."[118]

Way was very critical of *Mechanix* and the musical direction the band had taken, calling it "wheelchair music". It was more experimental than past releases and certainly more melodic in parts. The focus on Bruce Springsteen style arrangements did not sit well with UFO fans who craved a return to the hard rock sound of the late 1970s.

"It was always fairly even really and didn't seem different when he left, he just didn't turn up one day," says Carter when asked about the relationship between Mogg and Way. "I later found out that he didn't like the direction he felt UFO were heading and I feel a bit responsible. Maybe I had something to do with that. But then my time in the band was so small and, at a distance, those albums are good but not classic UFO ones. I don't think they have done any damage to the heritage. Pete actually left while we were starting *Making Contact* so we had finished all the *Mechanix* gigs. I suppose the timing was right, but it must have affected Phil as they had worked together for so long."[119]

There were some contract complications for Fastway. Chrysalis wanted to sign the band, as did CBS who made a bigger offer, so naturally Way said yes to CBS without a second's thought. "I didn't know what my contract with Chrysalis was. I was a key member of the band, so they were gonna sue CBS and me," Way admitted, "so I couldn't play with Fastway unless Fastway signed with Chrysalis. So Chrysalis said they'd give me my own record deal if I stayed with them and I said to Eddie and the management that I'm not going to hold everything up because of the legal things."[120]

Indeed, because of the legal shenanigans it was better for the label to bring in another bass player so they could hit the road. Mick Feat played bass on the album even though Way is credited, but he'd already left Fastway by the time of the recording sessions. Feat was replaced by former Taste bassist Charlie McCracken by the time the band had begun touring.

Way then went on to play bass for Ozzy Osbourne (who called Way Mr Medinite on account of his fondness for the patent cough syrup he drank to get to sleep) on his *Back At The Moon* Tour in 1983 before he was let go. Way spoke to *Rock Power*'s Mark Day in 1991 about leaving

UFO and joining Ozzy's band: "Ozzy's like a mate but I was pretty fucked up at the time. It's difficult when you leave something you helped create and watched it grow. It works well then suddenly you think 'shit, I'm on my own, you're not used to it.'"[121]

The reports in the rock press at the time suggested that Way was out of Ozzy's band because drummer Tommy Aldridge complained that Way couldn't play. " ...Tommy Aldridge is very, very good; Pete isn't very, very good," Mogg told *Metal Fury*'s Mick Wall at the time. "But then with us that was Pete's forte, the sort of shambolic hit or miss attitude. That's his niche. But in Ozzy's band you're talking about paid session musicians. I mean it's obvious to me that Pete wouldn't fit in terribly well."[122]

Way continued to keep himself out of mischief by working with The Cockney Rejects (on 1982's *The Wild Ones*) and Twisted Sister (on 1982's *Under The Blade*). He founded his own band Waysted in 1982, which also featured ex-UFO keyboardist/guitarist Paul Raymond, Fin Muir, Frank Noon and Ronnie Kayfield in its initial line-up. They released their debut album *Vices* in 1983, which hit Number 78 in the UK charts. Further albums continued throughout the 1980s, including a self-titled EP in 1984 and *The Good The Bad And The Waysted* in 1985, which saw the inclusion of Paul Chapman. Their third album *Save Your Prayers* made it to Number 185 in the US *Billboard* 200 album charts in 1986; the band's most successful album in the USA. Waysted then went on the backburner until the end of the 1990s.

Way's argument that he was not satisfied with the melodic direction UFO were taking rang true with fans of many other bands, and even some of Mogg's heroes such as Eric Clapton, whose 1980s work – some of which was produced by Phil Collins – was almost entirely devoid of the blues. Metal gods Judas Priest began the decade with *British Steel*, a remarkable metal album that started the band's pop-metal commercial era. ZZ Top would also make some commercial rock albums aided by – gasp – synthesizers; David Coverdale would transform Whitesnake from a blues rock band into a Transatlantic hard rock MTV style outfit. Many of the once towering rock bands of the 1980s were lured by the great Yankee dollar and the emergence of MTV.

UFO would sadly not make the sort of money that some of their contemporaries earned throughout the decade, nor clock up a succession of hit albums on both sides of the Atlantic, which proved more than anything else that UFO are better off making hard rock albums with blues influences rather than straightforward AOR.

Hard blues rock is what they do best. In fact, the blues had seemingly disappeared from mainstream rock music all together. Hard rockers Deep Purple would reunite in 1984 with the classic Mark II line-up and release *Perfect Strangers*; an excellent hard rock album but one that lacks the heavy blues of the 1970s work. Black Sabbath were another band that had lost touch with the blues; the band was fronted by American metal singer, the late Ronnie James Dio and while they made some excellent material, it was hardly bluesy. Some have argued that Judas Priest's *British Steel* album was the last hard rock/heavy metal album to truly embrace the blues despite its commercial angle.

UFO would also lose touch with the blues. Nevertheless in the post-Schenker years with Paul Chapman on guitar, UFO had begun to explore other musical avenues. Had they cemented and then followed one musical identity, it could be argued that they'd be criticised for making the same album over and over again. Such criticisms have plagued the likes of AC/DC, Status Quo and Motörhead. If a band forms an identity and follows such musical blueprints for their whole career they are chastised for it, yet if they try something new they are attacked for selling out.

Controversy appeared to follow UFO seemingly everywhere during the release of *Mechanix*. During the first night at the Hammersmith Clarendon Ballroom in November, Mogg was so hammered he forgot the words and even sat down between some songs for up to five minutes. The gig went down in rock history for all the wrong reasons. Was UFO on the way out? Much was happening to them personally during this period: Mogg and Way had fallen off the wagon, Way had fallen out of the band, while Parker had settled in California, far from the band's London base.

Making Contact, the band's follow-up to the hit album *Mechanix*, was recorded at The Manor Studio in Shipton-On-Cherwell in Oxfordshire and London's Townhouse Studios, White House and Maison Rouge Studios from August to December, 1982. With Pete Way out of the fold and with no permanent bassist replacement in sight, Paul Chapman played bass and guitars in the studio with Carter adding bass, guitars, keyboards and vocals joining singer Mogg and drummer Parker. Produced by Mick Glossop, the album was also engineered by Peter Thea and Richard Manwaring. Mogg explained how Glossop came into the equation: "Well, we had to sack Gary Lyons after about four weeks when we realised we were paying him a lot of money and he wasn't doing very much."[123]

The band were dismayed by Lyons' apparent lack of work ethic at The Manor in Oxford, but more than pleased with how Glossop would work through lunch and be the first in and the last out every day. Glossop moved the band to the Townhouse Studios in Shepherd's Bush, which was also owned by Richard Branson, before they relocated to Maison Rouge Studios in Fulham Road.

"They went through various contacts and a call came through that they want me to do it," remarks Glossop. "I went up to the Manor and listened to what they'd done and had a chat with the band; I just picked up the baton as it were. They'd recorded all the rhythm tracks so I didn't get to work with Andy, the drummer, until the next project which was the *Headstone* project. I worked on some live recordings on that."[124]

Glossop worked well with the band. "Excellent, a gentleman, and very much on my level," Carter says of Glossop. "He found us a bit frustrating at times but his heart was totally in what we were doing. He was bought in after an initial hiatus with Gary Lyons who seemed to want to produce the album from his bed most of the time! Mick was a breath of fresh air."[125]

It was not an especially intensive period, nor did Glossop have to struggle with members of UFO in the way previous producers had. Glossop did not socialise with the band either, as it was simply a case of working twelve hour days. "I'd heard stories about falling out with Gary and they wanted to make the record," he says. "They were keen about it being good and that's all really that they were concerned about. I came in and wanted the same thing so there wasn't any kind of conflict about it. There wasn't any problem in that respect. They wanted to make a great record. There was a blueprint for the sound already there. I knew what the band was about and they'd recorded these tracks already, anyway. I wasn't going to come in and take all the guitars off and replace them with synthesizers. That wasn't the point of what I was doing. I never approach records with the view of transforming the band into something which they're not. The start is to always see them live to get an idea of what the essence of the band is, but I was aware of what UFO were about anyway.

I wanted to make it as contemporary as possible but still with respect for the legacy of the band."[126]

Mogg actually wrote much of the album when he was on tour, rather than getting drunk or getting embroiled in other shenanigans. By the time the band entered the studio, Mogg had over twenty songs prepared. They went to the White House and Maison Rouge studios in London to do a significant amount of overdubbing. Parker had flown in from California but after he recorded his tracks he flew right back.

Glossop: "They'd recorded rhythm tracks and a few overdubs but no vocals. They had to do the instrumental backing tracks with no vocals on, so the first thing I did was find out what the songs were about. I asked Phil to go and record some guide vocals, some of which ended up being live, master vocals on the album. The performances were pretty good, actually, particularly on the first day. Sometimes with a guide vocal, actually often with a guide vocal, the lyrics are sometimes not finished or the melody's not finalised so those vocals are references for people working on the song. Quite often they don't perform to the best of what's needed that's why they're called guides, but Phil did pretty well. That was a good start. From there we did guitar, keyboards, overdubs and other vocal overdubs as well and Neil did some harmony vocals."[127]

Glossop remembers that the band were in a diplomatic mood, although old tensions did surface at times. "Onstage Phil is fairly static," comments Glossop, "whereas Pete is a complete lunatic and he used to get more attention, so I think there was a bit of tension there but he worked for it. Onstage you've got to get that attention."[128]

The bass was split almost evenly by Carter (who played on four songs) and Chapman (who played on six). "It was a bit odd at first," Chapman admitted, "since we really didn't know how to go about recording it, whether we should put all the guitars on first or what. In the end we just let it take its natural course and we had a lot of fun doing it."[129]

Carter had lost his 'new boy' status and had been fully accepted as a member of the band, especially on the songwriting front. *Making Contact* is the album that Carter has the most input on in terms of songwriting. Carter had many ideas and he had a strong working relationship with Mogg. Carter was a quick learner and knew how to express his ideas. He was very keen and wanted to contribute as much as possible. "I think we missed Pete's spirit and crazy humour but we just got on with it and did the best we could," he says now. "It was a very carefully made album and a lot of hard work went into it. Paul and I shared the bass playing, he was better than me, although I couldn't tell you who plays on what now. I like some of the songs on that and the production is pretty authentic sounding."[130]

Glossop: "Neil was a very large contributor and extremely enthusiastic as well, being the new boy in the band, I suppose. Paul was great. We worked on his solos quite a lot and he worked very hard. He came up with lots of ideas. The vocals were Phil's but Neil and Paul were very committed to the arrangements of the songs and put a lot of work in. I got on great with both of them."[131]

The label and their A&R representative, Roy Eldridge, were pleased with the album, as was manager Carl Leighton-Pope. Glossop did not run into any problems whatsoever with either Chrysalis or Leighton-Pope.

Overall, it was a positive experience for the producer, despite the band's problematic reputation. "I've heard all of this. I've had a lot worse issues with other people," Glossop says now. "Not showing up, or wanting to go down to the club or something before it's finished and that sort of thing. This is why although it wasn't an intentionally shrewd move on my part, because I just wanted to hear what the song was about, it was obvious to me that I need guide vocals on the tracks but it wasn't until later that I learned how reluctant Phil was to go and do any work. They didn't want to rebuild the project but pick up and get the album going again in the best possible way. The idea of Phil being uncooperative at that stage wasn't really going to happen, so he had to go and sing the songs."[132]

Making Contact opens with "Blinded By A Lie", which is not unlike a rock song by Journey, Foreigner or any American/Transatlantic band of that ilk. "Diesel In The Dust" starts with some gritty guitars, a plodding bass and some steady drums before Mogg joins in on the action. "A Fool For Love" begins as a seemingly average ballad, though the pace picks up and it becomes far more enjoyable. "You And Me" sounds very much like mid 1980s Whitesnake and, while it has a strong melody, it lacks an aggressive touch to elevate it to a higher level of acceptance. "When It's Time To Rock" is a speedy rocker and the perfect song to move the album forward after a sleepy fourth track. "The Way The Wild Wind Blows" opens with an awesome guitar riff and some suitable catchy keys; it's a terrific number and one of the album's standout songs. "Call My Name" is nothing special though it does have a curiously alluring melody. "All Over You" brings some much needed grit and mud to the album, while "No Getaway" is toe-tapping fun. The final song, "Push, It's Love", opens with some pounding tracks and a meaty bass line which propels the song to a fiery climax.

An energetic release, *Making Contact* saw UFO making further attempts at capturing a commercial melodic rock sound and, for the most part, it works, though some fans would prefer a grittier sounding UFO. Needless to say, there are some excellent songs on the album. The mix isn't perfect by any means but the songs are of worth.

Indeed, the label wanted the band to deliver a commercial album with hit singles as AOR bands such as Journey, Foreigner and Styx churned out on a regular basis. Carter explained the influence Journey had on his songwriting at that point: "I think Journey were in my consciousness, but also touring the States a lot had made me very aware of the sound of those sort of American acts. Radio was such a big thing in the US then and it was very new to me as our sort of music wasn't played much in England at the time on the mainstream radio, only in recent years have we had specific rock radio stations."[133]

He continues: "I really did like the sound of their [Journey's] albums but my favourite, *Frontiers*, wasn't issued until after we released *Making Contact*. In fact [future one-time UFO bassist] Billy Sheehan played me an advance copy he had on a bus journey in Poland [in 1983!] I can remember loving it immediately. So although I did like the band it was mainly a general awareness of the big US sound that had an influence."[134]

Making Contact was released in February 1983; one year after *Mechanix*. The band's eleventh studio offering got to Number 153 in the USA *Billboard* 200 album charts and Number 32 in the UK. "When It's Time To Rock" was released as a single but stalled at Number 70 in the UK. The 2009 reissue includes the bonus tracks "Everybody Knows" and live versions (recorded in Oxford) of "When It's Time To Rock" and "Blinded By A Lie".

Glossop: "Good songs, good arrangements, good playing, it sounds good. I like it. If I was approached by a rock band that wanted to listen to that type of '70s/'80s rock then I wouldn't have any hesitation playing that album to say, well, here's an example of something I've done."[135]

Critics greeted *Making Contact* with mostly strong reviews and noted the achievements of Paul Chapman who had fitted comfortably into the band.

Dave Dickson wrote in *Kerrang!*: "Mick Glossop should be commended for capturing a rawer, more compelling sound from UFO ... Whatever happens UFO have emerged with a powerful slab of vinyl of which they can be justifiably proud. Isn't that enough?" Writing in *Sounds: Guitar Heroes*, Steve Gett said: "A lot of people still believe UFO were never the same after Michael Schenker left, but over the past three years Chapman has proven he's not a man to be ignored."

Similarly to the other Paul Chapman albums, only UFO zealots refer to these releases in conversation while others, who are perhaps not overly acquainted with UFO, tend to only speak about Michael Schenker's contributions to UFO's arsenal.

1983 was not too kind to UFO. New York born Talas bassist Billy Sheehan entered the UFO camp to replace Way on the live front on a non-permanent basis from January to February 1983. Mogg said at the time: "We'll use him when we can, but when he's not available we'll find someone else for stage work."[136]

Why did the band choose Sheehan? In 1978, UFO played a gig in New York with AC/DC and Talas. Members of UFO went to the gig early for the soundcheck and they heard a massive sounding bass emanating from a dressing room. It was Billy Sheehan. After the gig they hit a local bar with Sheehan and members of Talas for a jam session. Sheehan gave Mogg his number if he ever needed a bassist. However, Mogg lost his number but UFO shared the bill with Talas around the time Way left, and Mogg took the opportunity to ask Sheehan if he wanted to tour with UFO. Talas had just released *High Speed On Ice* and Sheehan was unsure about what to do: either stay with Talas or fly to England to be with UFO. Given the open nature of the opportunity, Sheehan hit the road with UFO. Sheehan was very talented, always professional and excellent onstage even if his style was not totally suited to UFO.

The first night of the tour was in Poland on January 28. The band covered much of Europe, including Germany, Holland, Spain and France as well as Eastern territories such as Poland and Yugoslavia. There were not many bands who toured Eastern Europe at that time because of the Cold War, but Budgie had been there in 1982 and Burke Shelley – a Cardiff born musician and a friend of Paul Chapman's – recommended the trip. When UFO arrived in Europe they were pleased to discover that there was a strong fanbase for rock and heavy metal music. The band had not toured Europe properly – aside from the odd gig – since 1980 so they were thrilled to be on the road again. UFO's credibility has always stemmed from their prowess as a live band.

Kerrang! reviewed the Sheehan-UFO collaboration at the Bataclan in Paris on February 7: "Sheehan has made it clear that he will not be staying too long, but he cavorts around the stage in a whirl of headbanging and flying fingers. UFO look more live and alive than a year or so ago."

During the European leg of the tour at a gig in Athens, Greece on February 26 (some reports have suggested February 27) Mogg collapsed onstage. This prompted the 5,000 strong audience at the Sporting Arena to go crazy and cause a near riot with one audience member throwing an object at Sheehan, which found its target. Mogg was hospitalised and the support band Spider finished the last three dates of the tour on their own.

Neil Carter spoke to Jill Eckersley in 1983: "Looking back now, we can see it had been building for some time. Phil did get very tense, but on this tour he seemed to go further than before till it all got too much for him. I'm sure the various events of the past two years hit him harder than he realised."[137]

The band headed home to rest before an upcoming British tour but, still suffering from the injury received in Athens, Sheehan went back to New York. It was obvious he was not going to stay in UFO even before the incident. He was perhaps too professional and polished for a band such as UFO. Mogg was drinking too much and the band had internal troubles so Sheehan did not return.

Sheehan spoke about this period many years later: "I wasn't asked to join. They needed a bass player for an upcoming tour and I agreed to do it. Talas opened for UFO (hence the Schenker connection) and they knew who I was. It was supremely un-together. Very sad – I loved that band, and Schenker. Seeing it up close as a dysfunctional, drug infested catastrophe was very disappointing. It broke my heart actually."[138]

The future of UFO seemed unclear and Chrysalis released a press statement to that effect. A tour was already arranged for March and the funding had been supplied by Adrian Hopkins but Mogg needed time to recover. Nobody appeared to know what would happen to UFO once the tour was completed. After the critical and commercial failure of *Making Contact*, and the personnel changes, UFO decided to call it a day. After a tour of the UK in March (beginning at the Ipswich Gaumont on March 21) through to April, which included former Eddie And The Hot Rods and The Damned bassist Paul Gray, the band officially split up.

The Essex born bassist Paul Gray scored several hit singles with pub rock/new wave band Eddie And The Hot Rods before he was enticed to join The Damned to replace Algy Ward. Having contributed to two albums by The Damned – *The Black Album* and *Strawberries* – Gray left the band in February 1983 due to creative differences and took up the gig with UFO. Interestingly, UFO fans at the time noticed the similarities between Way and Gray both in looks and musical ability. Gray actually handed in his notice not long after he joined UFO and was looking out for another band. This, and other factors, promoted Mogg to call time on the band.

The invitation to join UFO was fortuitous. He says now: "I'd met Paul Chapman a few times (who lived in Cardiff as did I), we had mutual friends ... we sort of played each other our records and got pissed together on a few occasions as far as I can remember. I got a call from him when they were in Spain a couple of weeks into a world tour, saying that Billy Sheehan was about to fuck off back to the US and did I fancy the gig?"[139]

He continues: "Next day I went up to London to meet their manager Carl Leighton-Pope (Blatant-Joke was their name for him as I remember). Nice chap – we had a bit of a waffle and he got on the phone to Phil. 'Your new bass player is lying on the floor completely out of it on drink and drugs, he'll fit in really well,' quoth he. I imagine Mogg chuckled on the other end. Easiest audition I ever had. In fact, apart from my first band Eddie And The Hot Rods, I never auditioned for anyone but that's another story.

"Carl handed me a bunch of UFO albums with crosses by song titles and simply said: 'Here you go, learn these, your plane leaves for Madrid tomorrow.' And that was it."[140]

The record company politics had also worn down the band's enthusiasm. First they got dropped by Chrysalis after the poor sales of *Misdemeanor*, they were frustrated that their publishing contract with EMI was not renewed and were not having much luck securing a new record deal. Phil Mogg: "UFO are on the shelf, the band is there to be re-activated if and when required. If anything comes up we'll be ready to take it. But for the moment that's all I can say. We were pushed into a corner and this position was made very difficult for us ..."[141]

Offering his own thoughts, Carter spoke about the breakup of the band: "Well, and this is quite well documented, it was the three of us that said to Phil we didn't want to carry on. The tour of Europe that ended abruptly in Greece was the final straw and the band were going downhill rapidly, both in musical terms and personally, so we were very concerned that it would get ugly. There were many factors involved but I feel that nowadays it's pointless bringing all that up. I see Phil in Brighton occasionally and he is such a different man and great company. I think, from what I've read, that both he and Pete have fond memories of me which is really nice and they are always very positive. But at the time the situation had become impossible, the band were basically worn down from constant work and seemingly no financial reward. Mismanagement played a big part in the story over the years so I am not surprised, in hindsight, how that period in the band's history turned out."[142]

Prior to the tour, there was some talk about how confidently Mogg would handle the ordeal given the nature of recent events. The band needed to go out on a high note and obviously the fans wanted them to deliver the goods. They felt it was time to end the band's career by playing fairly extensive sized venues of several thousand capacities rather than playing in front of dwindling audiences. UFO did not want to be one of those bands that play in venues of increasingly smaller sizes with each subsequent tour. The enthusiasm had to be there and in 1983 it obviously was not. What Mogg found difficult, and which ultimately led to him having, some said, a nervous breakdown in Athens, was not only did he have to cope with the touring but the recording and business end of the band too. It perhaps got too much for him to take, but there is little value in us playing amateur psychologists.

Mogg admitted to *Sounds* that the previous year had not been an especially enjoyable time for him, although he was over the moon about how *Making Contact* turned out. " ... the strain of keeping it all going was too much in the end," he said. "But we've already started rehearsing and I can promise all the fans who've supported us over the years that this will be the last UFO tour ever."[143]

The band played two farewell gigs in London, and Chippenham Golddiggers on April 6, though a second show was added at the

Hammersmith Odeon on April 15. The road jaunt consisted of 24 dates in total. However, proposed dates for South East Asia and the USA did not go ahead. It was not such a great climax to the career of one of Britain's most brilliant rock bands.

"It was O.K. surprisingly, given that we all knew that it would be the last of that era," says Carter about the tour. "The shows were a good standard and we recorded a few, the atmosphere was civil between the three of us and Phil, and having Paul [Gray] onboard freshened it up a bit. He was very able and his style suited what we did."[144]

Offering his own thoughts on the tour, Gray says: "... it wasn't the happiest band in the world at that time. Obviously the cracks had widened, but personally I got on with everyone really well. They were all fabulous musicians, no matter what state they may have been in ... professional to the end as I recall when it came down to it. There was a fair amount of stuff flying about at the time: stage left for a bit of this, stage right for those, copious amounts of booze. I remember one gig where Tonka was a bit the worse for wear; he disappeared from the stage to chuck up behind the amps still playing and didn't miss a note. I loved playing with them – it did me a lot of good as a bassist. They always had a great stage sound and were pretty note perfect. Great road crew too, very much a family affair, and no rock star egos – unlike some bands I could mention ..."[145]

UFO had basically self-destructed due to internal tensions and substance abuse. It seemed that nobody in the band was happy with the current situation. "I had a lot of personal problems," Parker confessed in 2011. "We worked ourselves to death. We spent so much time on the road. For ten years, virtually, we never had a break. We'd do tour, studio, rehearse, studio, tour ... and we never had any time. I was going through a divorce and was trying to get custody of my kid."[146]

The band's farewell set list featured "When It's Time To Rock", "Blinded By A Lie", "We Belong To The Night", "Let It Rain", "No Place To Run", "Only You Can Rock Me", "Love To Love", "Couldn't Get It Right", "Long Gone", "Diesel In The Dust", "Too Hot To Handle" and "Lights Out" before a double-whammy encore of "Rock Bottom" and "Doctor Doctor". The band played shows all over the UK, hitting Ipswich, Sheffield, Nottingham, Oxford, Birmingham and London. *Sounds* scribe Mark Putterford attended the Oxford Apollo gig and enthused: "If I were you, I'd get a glimpse of this rare rock species before it becomes extinct."

UFO released the compilation *Headstone* (its complete title was *Headstone: The Best Of UFO*), which also included songs by other bands that feature former UFO members (namely, Whitesnake, Scorpions, Lonestar, MSG and Wild Horses) while the artwork depicts a headstone showing the band's formation date but a non-specific end date, which some fans thought was the band's way of indicating that they might actually reform at some point. It was produced and engineered by Mick Glossop. "I didn't really have any problems with Phil to be honest because we repaired some of the vocals on the live album [*Headstone*] and that was no problem either. We had to work at it because some of them had fairly high notes in them which was hard for him to get. They were a bit out of his range or at the peak of his range. He didn't run up and say, 'Oh, I'm not doing that.' He came in and worked at it."[147]

The original eighteen track double vinyl also included five UFO live tracks that were recorded at the Hammersmith Odeon on 15 April 1983.

Glossop: "I thought they were pretty good, a tight rock band. They're a very '70s orientated band in terms of the style of rock that they were doing. Not that that was a bad thing. I remember at the time there was lots of discussions about how rock bands should sound. A lot of bands were criticised for being American sounding, i.e. melodic, not hard enough. Keyboards were often a part of this whole thing. Guitars give it the edge but keyboards make everything smooth and bland. That was the completely generalised attitude towards it. Bands like Whitesnake and Rainbow had had commercial success because they were performing material that was much more melodic and had a lot less hard edged rock. It was a lot different from Motörhead; a more extreme, hard edged rock band with virtually no melody at all. I generally had a lot of opinions from musicians and there was a feeling from a lot of musicians that that was being too soft and bland."[148]

Headstone was released in August, 1983. It stuck at Number 39 in the UK Top 40 and was later reissued in 2009 with a different tracklisting, without the songs by associated acts and including eleven live UFO recordings; six live songs that were previously unreleased from the same Hammersmith show.

Mark Putterford reviewed the original collection in *Sounds*. He ended his positive review by saying: "Let's hope UFO are laid to rest now and not subjected to the kind of 'cashing in' rip-offs that have marred the name of other bands. Amen."

What was Mogg going to do now? He told *Kerrang!*'s Steve Gett: "I've got a paper round. No, I'm joining the dole queue. To be serious, I've got a few ideas and I'm sure everyone else [in the band] has, too. But I'll just wait till it evolves."[149]

One would think that with Mogg's songwriting credits on UFO's back catalogue and their near week long stint at the Hammersmith Odeon that Mogg had a wedge of dosh, but this was far from the truth.

Phil Mogg spoke about his lack of royalties and the band's ignorance when it came to money to Michael Hann of *The Guardian* over twenty years later: "I ended up having to go to the dole office. I'd never been before. There was a bloke in front of me in the queue. He looked and said: 'Aren't you with UFO?' I said: 'Yeah.' I was already very embarrassed going there. He said: 'What are you doing here?' I said: 'Same as you. I need some money.' I was absolutely borassic. At the same point I ended up sleeping round a friend of mine's because I was so skint."[150]

What money the band did make did not go in their pockets, but rather to pay for studio time which they thought the label paid for. The money also went on various substances. Being on tour was like one long hangover especially when they toured with bands of equal thirst for the wilder side of rock 'n' roll. However, the band members were in healthy shape, physically.

The 1978 to 1983 period, and from *The Wild, The Willing And The Innocent* to *Making Contact*, has become known as the 'Paul Chapman era' and is looked upon fondly by fans of the band. Certainly on the live front they remained an incredibly energetic and powerful unit despite the commercial nature of the music they made during that period. Chapman was an excellent addition to the band and a worthy successor to Michael Schenker, whose personality was always going to be at odds with Phil Mogg; an equally hot-headed and difficult man at times, especially when armed with some tins of Special Brew. But alas, all was not well within the band's camp and it was time to end this particular era.

Mogg may have chosen to stay out of music for a while but Chapman, Carter and Parker had other ideas. The trio decided to record some demos with Chapman on vocals. The idea was to attempt to entice a record company to hand them a contract. They also had notions of hiring Cheap Trick's Robin Zander to sing lead vocals but the trio left it alone. Carter went on to have a successful career with the late Gary Moore replacing John Sloman. He is now a music teacher based in Brighton; one of his former pupils included Gary Moore's son.

Carter talks about touring with the band: "Memory tends to dull the pain ... but it could be amazing and hell in varying degrees. The early days with them, when Pete was in the band, are the best memories as the dynamic within UFO was better then and the 'bad side' was less to the fore. But there were some times of utter madness where you would have to pinch yourself to believe what was happening around you. I am sure some of the members won't remember too much detail however! Musically it could be brilliant and playing those 'enormadomes' in the States for the first time was incredible. I can still picture the vast crowds and lighters!"[151]

Carter offers his final thoughts on his period in UFO: "I think it was always a bit of a rollercoaster but I wouldn't have missed it for the world. I had some amazing experiences, got to tour the USA in the heyday of stadium rock, met some crazy people and did some crazy things. I have 30 years plus to look back on it now, but I am proud to have been part of the history of UFO."[152]

Chapman, on the other hand, moved to Florida to form D.O.A. with singer David Edwards, guitarist Robert Journey, drummer Paul Barron and bassist Steve Chikitus. D.O.A. really was Dead On Arrival and Chapman then formed Ghost with singer Carl Sentance, previously of Persian Risk before Chapman moved to join Waysted in late 1983.

Parker moved to LA where he joined Scarlett. He later wound up working with Way in Waysted before joining the American bands Dr Wish and Rexx And Johnson. Paul Gray, meanwhile, formed a new band called Sing Sing with guitarist Nigel Bennett and drummer Steve Nicol. Gray later joined Eddie Clarke in Fastway.

Michael Schenker released the live album *Rock Will Never Die* as MSG in 1984, featuring a guest appearance from Rudolf Schenker and Scorpions front man Klaus Meine on a cover of "Doctor Doctor". The album hit Number 24 in the UK; certainly a healthy position for a live release.

Although with UFO seemingly laid to rest and the former members of the band working on other projects, it was obvious from what Mogg had hinted at on the cover of *Headstone* that the band – perhaps a different incarnation – was going to return at some point. It was just a question of when. Despite the frustrations Mogg faced in UFO, it was his band and to a lesser extent it was Pete Way's too, but Mogg – like Tony Iommi with Black Sabbath – was never going to let the band die.

CHAPTER
SIX

Ain't Misbehavin' –
The Turbulent Return Of UFO
(1984 –1989)

*"There is nothing, and I mean nothing,
preconceived about UFO ... not even our name."*

Phil Mogg[153]

Over a year after UFO's UK farewell tour and the failure of the *Making Contact* album, UFO reformed with a new line-up. In 1984, Phil Mogg spent some time in Los Angeles as a sort of reprieve after the sticky end to UFO's previous incarnation. It was the first time Mogg had been without a record deal since his mid-twenties. He didn't know what he wanted to do and had lost interest in music. However, it was in LA that he decided to get a new version of the band together in early 1984.

Rumours abounded that Mogg was going to team up with George Lynch of Dokken, but they were unfounded. Mogg met Swedish guitarist and UFO fan Yngwie Malmsteen who had recently moved to California. Malmsteen was set to leave the band Steeler but ended up joining Alcatrazz, a new project devised by former Rainbow singer Graham Bonnet. Mogg and Malmsteen spoke about a collaboration under the UFO moniker but thankfully (given their temperamental natures) the collaboration did not come to fruition. Mogg also met guitar wiz-kid Steve Vai in LA but, again, nothing came of it.

Mogg knew he wanted an American guitarist, his view being that there were no unique sounding lead guitar players in the UK. However, Mogg was wary of American players too. "In America they all go to guitar school, but they do tend to come out playing scales," the singer said to *Metal Hammer*'s Chris Welch. "They forget about feeling because they learn so mechanically. Two notes from Eric Clapton is worth a thousand from anybody else."[154]

On the lookout for a guitar player of worth, it was in LA that Mogg met Mike Varney. Through Varney, founder of Shrapnel Records and a contributor to *Guitar Player* magazine where he edited a column, Mogg contacted guitarist Tommy McClendon (later nicknamed "Atomik Tommy M") best known for his tenures in Boy Wonder, Loudness and Thunderwing.

UFO had previously had a German guitarist in the band, a Brit and now an American. Throughout the band's history they have always had creativity coming in from all different angles. With the previous line-ups it can be argued that they'd become stale because they'd known each other and had played together for so long. The band had become too comfortable and safe. Mogg now wanted something fresh and different. Certainly the nationalities had an impact on the band's overall guitar sound. McClendon brought with him a very distinctive West Coast guitar feel.

With McClendon onboard, Mogg re-recruited Paul Gray (though Dokken's Jeff Pilson was in line for the gig at one point) and, for a short time, keyboards player Barbara Schenker (sister of Michael and from a band called Viva) may have joined Mogg and his cohorts for some rehearsals, before Paul Raymond re-entered the camp in time for a batch of upcoming live shows. The original drummer for this line-up was Miles Baggs but for reasons unknown it never worked out. Mogg subsequently brought in drummer Robbie France, a one-time member of Diamond Head who contributed to their third album *Canterbury*.

One little known factual nugget is that Mogg considered not calling this band UFO but rather The Great Outdoors, named after an off licence in Edgbaston in the Midlands, around the corner from a flat Mogg was sharing with Way and his then girlfriend.

Mogg: "This band is worlds apart from the old UFO, there's a different attitude altogether. I mean, I'm quite prepared for all the flak we're going to get from the English press ... I was going to say it's better. But it's a different thing, it's not the same as the old UFO."[155]

The new line-up of the band rehearsed for two months in Birmingham in late 1984. McClendon, a teetotaller, found the experience of working in Birmingham very odd. Had it been an international city such as London, perhaps he would had been more comfortable, but Birmingham was too much of a stark contrast to LA. The Midlands-based live music staging company LSD put together some money for an upcoming tour and studio time.

UFO committed themselves to a thirteen date tour of the UK with support band Tobruk, in order to debut some new songs and show off the new line-up before they went to record a new album. The tour began at Nottingham Rock City on December 12 and finished in London at the Lyceum on December 18. The tour was completely self-financed. "Very nervous," Mogg admitted to *Kerrang!*'s Mark Putterford when asked how he felt before the tour. "I felt nervous because we'd had a major disaster the last time the band toured – especially the episode in Greece ... But the guys who play in this band are reliable."[156]

The new line-up of UFO set to work on writing fresh material for a proposed album, having signed a new deal back in April with Chrysalis. "The problem with Chrysalis is that I don't think they ever knew how to promote us in the past," Mogg admitted at the time to *Rock Scene*. "The situation this time around is totally different. There was a whole company change and now the attitude is different. Plus, we've got new management so everything is more responsible and how it should be, rather than pissing out the window."[157]

However, the band suffered a blow to the new line-up prior to recording, after France decided to leave during preproduction at Stanbridge Studios (a stunning 14th century house in Sussex). France, who was born in Sheffield and raised in Australia, died on January 12, 2012. He never fully explained his reasons behind leaving UFO and went on to join Wishbone Ash and Skunk Anansie. France was soon replaced by former Magnum drummer Jim Simpson in early 1985. Simpson would feature on the band's upcoming album. For the band's twelfth studio release, UFO consisted of singer Phil Mogg, lead guitarist Tommy McClendon, keyboards player Paul Raymond, bassist Paul Gray and drummer Jim Simpson.

"Lovely bloke, I wouldn't have a bad word to say about him," Gray says about Mogg. "Straight down the line. A lot of fun to be around. We got on very well. He used to spend a lot of time with me in Cardiff in the subsequent [post-*Headstone*] reincarnation; we'd be writing songs on my 4-track and knocking back the bevies. But we got stuff done, and his melodies were great. One of my three favourite singers in the world: him,

Steve Marriott and Robin Zander. Usually the initial lyrical ideas he came up with were the ones that ended up on the albums."[158]

At Chrysalis' suggestion, UFO initially hooked up with famed American producer Kevin Elson – best known for his work with such American melodic rock bands as Journey and Lynyrd Skynyrd – at The Manor Studios, but for various reasons the collaboration did not work out. "... played around for a few days and that was it. They were not ready to make an album material wise," Elson said in an email to me. "Wasn't around Phil much other than talking about the material."[159]

John Burgess and Stuart Slater at Chrysalis began talks with Thin Lizzy producer Nick Tauber about rescuing the project.

Tauber: "... apparently he'd [Elson] taken three days to get a drum sound and Phil just lost his temper and screamed at him, and asked him why the fuck he'd taken so long. It scared the shit out of him because Phil can be quite tough. He packed his bags and came straight back to London and went home. I got this call and went down there and got on really well with them. I had a little word with Phil about being patient and said you can't do that to people. It only took me a day to get a drum sound. The Manor Studios had one of the best drum rooms in existence. It was an amazing drum room so I don't know why it took someone so long to get a drum sound. Maybe it wasn't what the guy was looking for? I don't know. I don't like to say things about other producers. All I know is it didn't take me long to get a drum sound."[160]

Gray corroborates: "... he [Elson] spent the best part of the next week trying to get a drum sound. I went to bed with the sound of Jim's snare drum echoing through the fields, and woke up in the morning to the poor fucker still bashing it. Eventually Mogg flipped – marched into the control room and said something like, 'May I suggest you return from whence you came and stop wasting any more of our time and money' or words to that effect, which he duly did. Thing is, we were then stuck in a stupidly expensive studio with no producer; not many available at short notice. Know what I mean?"[161]

Tauber then routined the band for a couple of weeks at The Manor, which was certainly not cheap at around £1,200 per day. The famed recording studio included a luxury swimming pool which Ozzy Osbourne had once driven a car into. They were ready to record the album but time was of the essence, so they moved to Wisseloord Studios in Hilversum, Holland where Meat Loaf and Def Leppard had previously recorded. Tauber was accompanied by engineer Jon Jacobs. Hilversum, was dubbed "the Beverly Hills of Holland" by Raymond. Given the relaxed laws over there, the band and producer took every opportunity to party.

Tauber: "I wouldn't start recording until we'd done a proper routine. I refuse to record until I routine the tracks. I always routine everything. If you're a rock band, first of all, you've gotta have good songs and then you've got to have a great performance. Good rock is all about good performance. It plays well and it's put together well. There's no way bands can put anything together or play well if they don't know it. A producer's job is to get the arrangements right, to make sure the choruses are right, to get the speed right. I don't do records without routining, ever. I don't think it's the right way it make records ... before you go and make a record you've got to have some songs because it's expensive. Why would you sit in a studio with all that gear and all that money and make things up? I like to have an idea of where the record's going before I go in."[162]

Mogg was more than pleased that the new line-up of the band had the same approach when it came to writing and recording new songs. It many ways *Misdemeanor* is the album Mogg wanted *Making Contact* to be. They had more time to work on the new songs and plan the direction of their comeback release. There are also more keyboards on *Misdemeanor* as Mogg wanted to try and shift the balance between keyboards and guitars. However, Mogg was more than aware that the true sound of UFO was one of guitars.

On the subject of the new line-up, Tauber remembers: "It took Tommy a little time to get into the English humour because English bands are merciless piss-takers ... he was an incredible guitarist. Very much in that Van Halen mode but very good technique, very precise. Very good musician, Tommy. He had that American feel. Americans do a lot of practice. English rock bands are very feel driven."[163]

The producer rubbed along well with Mogg: whenever Tauber asked the singer to do something, he would do it. They had a friendly rapport and good relations in the studio.

Tauber: "I had to push him. I said: 'Come on Phil, you've got to get on with it because we're gonna be finished with the backing tracks and we haven't even got the lyrics.' That's him. He's never changed. That's what he is. After all these years I can't imagine somehow him changing even now. He was good with his vocals. The only thing is, we'd get a vocal down which I thought was really good and I said to Phil: 'Are you happy with that?' because I want everyone to be happy. He said: 'Yeah, it's pretty cool,' and then he'd come back the next day and say 'I'm not really sure'. But that is very common with singers. People make Phil Mogg out in some ways to be a bit of a monster. I never found that."[164]

He continues: "I like Phil Mogg. He had all the problems that all the lead singers have. They've all got egos the size of houses. I think Phil, in some ways, just because they'd had this massive drug phase going on, has been maligned a bit and I think it's really unfair. It's no worse than loads of lead singers that I've worked with in my time, except for Phil Lynott [who] was always on time. He ran that band. He was incredible. I never had a problem with them [UFO]; they were nice kids. Even though we all had too much to drink, including me, because we were under pressure but I can't say I have a bad word to say about any of them. Nice people ... The quiet one was Jim, the drummer. Tommy – everybody took him as the little Japanese guy that'd come from America. I think there was a minor bit of friction between Paul and Phil, but when you've been working with someone for that long they're always going to get on your nerves. It's like a marriage. They still work together. I can't see it being that bad."[165]

"Wreckless", "Heaven's Gate" and "This Time", for example, are very melodic and were co-written by McClendon and Mogg, with the exception of "This Time" which Gray wrote with Mogg. Gray also co-wrote "One Heart", "Night Run" and "Blue". Gray had significant input with the album's lyrics. At the time he wrote on keyboards and some of the more melodic end of the album was down to his talents. Gray says now: "The songs of mine that ended up on the album I'd actually written for The Damned but were never used or put forward. Mogg preferred those to the stuff I wrote specifically with UFO in mind. 'Hhmm ... got any more of the old punk rock stuff?', he'd enquire. The melodies he sang and scatted over the top were of course very different to what I'd originally had in mind, and took the songs to another place. Just goes to show, it's all rock 'n' roll at the end of the day, no matter what box music journalists wanna put you in."[166]

The band and producer were both pleased with the album despite the stress and pressure of delivering it on time after a false start. A tour had also been planned, so there was extra stress in getting it finished and ready for delivery. They were working sixteen hour days to deliver the album. It would have been preferable to have had a week off before mixing rather than going straight from recording the songs to mixing them.

"I think they [Chrysalis] just wanted to get the thing out," affirms Tauber. "... I wouldn't book a tour until the album's been recorded. It's silly to book a tour with the band until the mixing stage, then you know when the record's going to be done. They had this big false start. It had some great solos, some great vocal performances and some great songs. There's nothing wrong with it. I like that record. I think it's a good record. I've always liked it. It's one of the best records they made in that period."[167]

The aim with the album was to make a commercial sounding radio-friendly work that would travel across to the States and gain radio and chart success over there. Tauber wanted more backing vocals to give the songs an American AOR feel, but Mogg was not enthusiastic about the notion. "I would have loved to have worked with them [again]," Tauber says now. "I know Phil had his moments that everybody goes on about but so what? I've always worked with people that are hard work. As long as it's professional hard work and professional arguments. Everyone does it. You shouldn't take it personally; it's business. I think people paint a bad picture. They like that rock 'n' roll thing – the history and all the drugs and the drink. They love that."[168]

The musicians got on well with each other; they liked to drink as most bands do, although McClendon was not much of a drinker. Sharing his own thoughts on the overall experience of working with Tauber and the outcome of the recording sessions, Gray explains: "Lovely bloke, very jolly, liked a joke, bit like your favourite uncle when you were a kid. Very good at vibing everyone up and all of that. Liked a bit of a party."[169]

He continues: "I have to be a bit diplomatic here. It all started off great – the backing tracks were really tough and rocking – but he gradually lost the plot with excessive amounts of overdubs, in my opinion anyway, and the end result was something of an aural murk and not to my liking. I think the guitars sounded particularly horrible. Maybe he was under pressure from the record company to make it fit the American market at the time, who knows, all that bollocks goes on. And then we relocated to Hilversum in Holland to get it mixed: it was party central, really. Not really conducive to knuckling down to the task at hand. It didn't sound much like us in the end, which I think was a real shame. I've still got tapes of rough board mixes of the rhythm guitar, bass and drum tracks, and they rocked like fuck."[170]

Misdemeanor opens with the lightweight keyboard-laden melodic rock feel of "This Time" and, while fans of harder rock may baulk at UFO trying to sound like Foreigner, it has to be said that "This Time" is a catchy AOR number. "One Heart" has a heavier stomp than the first track, due mostly to some pounding drums, though it is soaked in glorious melodic rock keys. "Night Run" is just a tad too commercial and radio-friendly; it lacks a more aggressive guitar attack. "The Only Ones" is an average track, better suited to an AOR singer such as John Waite than Phil Mogg. "Meanstreets" picks up the pace considerably and sees UFO putting their rock shoes back on. "Name Of Love" has a wailing metal guitar while "Blue" lacks a clearer mix to bring out the guitars. It sounds suffocated. "Dream The Dream" is a dreamy, dulcet ballad with slightly too pronounced drums, while "Heaven's Gate" is an unfocused mess of guitars and keyboards though it has a standout chorus. "Wreckless" closes the album suitably enough.

Misdemeanor could not have been made in any other decade but the 1980s. The band appeared to have lost the dirt and grind of the previous decade in favour of a much more commercial and fluffy sound, though it has to be said there are some great songs to be found on the album. *Misdemeanor* deserves to be rediscovered, though it is a far cry even from the Chapman releases of the early 1980s. Indeed, due to the final mix, the vocals do swallow up the guitars leaving an unbalanced sounding album.

Misdemeanor was released in February 1985 in the UK and March 1986 in the USA, where it was remixed. It reached Number 106 in the USA and Number 74 in the UK. "Night Run" was released as a single in 1986 and reached Number 94 in the UK. Interestingly, the American release contained three songs ("Night Run", "This Time" and "Heaven's Gate") which, at the behest of Chrysalis, were remixed by Dave Wittman of Foreigner and Billy Idol fame.

The 2009 reissue of *Misdemeanor* includes several US remixes as bonus tracks: "Night Run", "This Time", "Heaven's Gate", "Name Of Love", "One Heart" and "Blue".

Music journalists greeted *Misdemeanor* with admirable write-ups; some reviewers even hailed it as the band's finest release in a decade. Overall, however, sales and reviews were thin on the ground.

Dave Dickson wrote in *Kerrang!*: "The good news is that I have absolutely no hesitation in proclaiming this as the finest LP UFO have issued since *Lights Out*, besting even their death-throes release, *Making Contact*, which in itself was hugely impressive."

The album was criticised for its lightweight production, which caused the guitars to sound very shallow, although it does feature a strong set of songs. It's sadly faded into the mists of time as with most of UFO's 1980s output.

Tauber offers his own thoughts: "If we'd got the mix absolutely right it would have been a classic. That's the only regret I have, otherwise the playing was great, good songs. It did bring them back a bit because it got some good reviews. They did start again after that. It did revive their career again and I'm very proud of that. I think I could have done a better job, but I thought they were really good."[171]

Misdemeanor was not the hit the band had hoped for and, in truth, needed. Mogg's aim with the new line-up, album and live shows was to re-establish UFO. Was it working? Since the departure of Schenker all those years ago, it seemed that the band's line-up was simply nothing more than a stream of peripatetic musicians coming and going. The 1980s did not produce bands with as much staying power as bands that had formed in the previous decade. The record company mentality had an impact: if bands didn't shift enough copies of an album they'd get dropped. Did this affect the quality of the music? It certainly made 1980s rock more commercial and mainstream. The industry had become more cut-throat and bands of UFO's type were struggling. The only way UFO could survive was to do what they'd always done: hit the road, Jack.

UFO played some high-profile gigs in 1985. They performed at the Poperinge Festival in Belgium before they headed back to the UK to strut their stuff at the Knebworth Fayre on June 22, marking the UK debut of the latest incarnation: Mogg, McClendon, Raymond, Gray and Simpson. Also on the bill was a reunited Deep Purple as headliners, while other acts on the bill included Scorpions, Meat Loaf, Mountain, Blackfoot, Mama's Boys and Alaska. UFO played "Blinded By A Lie", "Heaven's Gate", "Wreckless", "Love To Love", "Night Run", "Only You Can Rock Me", "Lights Out" and

"Doctor Doctor". UFO's acclaimed performance was broadcast on Radio 1's *Friday Rock Show*.

Mogg was more than pleased with the latest line-up of the band and they worked well together. Mogg's aim was to make everything much easier this time around and, with new management (Neil Levine) and everything seemingly content at the label, Mogg was in high spirits. However, they were faced with the dilemma that all longstanding bands face when they reform with a new line-up: how do you live up to past glories? Mogg appeared to shrug off such comparisons with his usual wit and soldier on. He was far keener to talk about the new band, whereas critics and interviewers were constantly asking him about comparisons between the new UFO and the old.

Let's be honest, UFO were never the most disciplined of rock bands and they never exercised much will power or foresight. With Mogg's old drinking buddy Way out of the picture, he could focus on the music.

Mogg: "I'm not saying I'm drinking tea all the time, but I'm not going to go onstage drunk anymore either. There's a fine line between what rock and roll is, and what acting unprofessionally is. I owe it to the band, the fans, and myself to make sure I can give my best every night, and I'm determined to do that."[172]

UFO also toured the UK with support bands Pallas and Shy in late 1985. The tour ran from November 13 (Bristol) to November 30 (London).

Kerrang!'s Derek Oliver was at the Manchester Apollo show on November 24. He observed: "The crowd had been hostile, even openly aggressive during the opening numbers – but, by the time Mogg's marauders reached the end of the set, victory had been secured. It was the end of a battle between the past and the present; UFO then and UFO now."

Shy's front man Tony Mills recalls playing at the Bristol Dome on November 14: "Phil Mogg had run out of cough medicine again, and he sent his bouncer to our dressing room door, not so much for, 'Is it O.K. if Phil borrows some of your cough medicine?' as 'Phil wants to talk to you now!' I fully consented to the meeting and followed the bruiser down the corridor. Anyway, as soon as he took charge of my fifty quid bottle of sauce that I imported from Australia they booted me out of the dressing room. 'Charming,' I thought, some people have no decorum ..."[173]

Mills remembers November 22: "Landing at the Barrowlands in Glasgow on the UFO *Misdemeanor* tour I couldn't believe how bloody huge the venue was. I actually thought that it would be too big for UFO with Shy as a support act, but nevertheless, it seemed to fill up anyway. There was nothing surprising going on, apart from the fact that it was dark, cold and pissing down outside."[174]

He continues: "I'll never forget being very thirsty onstage and seeing what I thought was a pint of water by the monitor desk. I took a hefty swig, but it was not meant for me. It was Phil's glass. My thirst was never quenched. If I'd have swallowed, I think the gig would have been out of the question. The audience were bloody wonderful, but only a couple of pints of 'heavy' (when I actually figured out what 'heavy' meant), and a Bridie from Forfar put the memory where it belongs."[175]

Concluding his thoughts on the tour, Mills says: "Most of the band were sort of, well, generally pissed quite a lot. But specifically, I remember Jim Simpson being the great communicator and the happy face. We had to pull Oxford through serious illness, but the tour really gave me the desire for live performance and gave me the feel of what touring should really be all about. '85 was a good time. Neil Levine, from Light And Sound Design, became Shy's manager until 1990 after this tour."[176]

After journeying around the UK, a European tour dubbed Metal Battle was arranged in March 1986, which saw UFO support Accept on a three band bill that had Dokken as openers. UFO were incredibly tight and well-rehearsed onstage. "They were great fun ...," says Gray of the live shows. "Lots of lovely young ladies around who kept us entertained, except the Accept gigs where it was all blokes, well, we had a lot of fun, it would be rude not to. Personally, I had the time of my life. Imagine being a kid in a sweet shop, and being told 'Fill yer boots, Sonny ...' I certainly filled mine!"[177]

There was yet more touring as the band committed themselves to some headlining shows of their own around Europe, as well as some gigs in Scandinavia in April supporting Twisted Sister, before some further headlining solo shows on the continent. Dave Dickson saw UFO at the Hungexpo in Budapest and wrote in *Kerrang!*: "It's difficult for a band who've ploughed so much into a gig to get so little back, so Mogg tries a foray into the photo-pit during the encore and the kids at the front go crazy and the photographers even more so ..."

The band then headed to the USA, where they could no longer headline major venues. In May 1986, during UFO's USA club tour, Paul Raymond, whose heart was no longer in it, quit after just one gig and headed back home. His seemingly sudden departure was sparked just prior to their second gig in Phoenix. Raymond reportedly made some sort of ultimatum to Mogg and tour manager Ted Gardner. Raymond did not turn up at the soundcheck and once the band returned to their hotel, there was a handwritten note from Raymond stating that he'd quit the band. Paul Gray partly filled Raymond's role at the Phoenix gig. McClendon's old friend and colleague David Jacobson, better known for his stint in the Eric Martin Band, joined as the band's new keyboard player, with his tenure ending in August.

1986 also saw the release of the UFO collection, *Anthology*, issued by Chrysalis subsidiary Castle, who owned the band's back catalogue from 1973 onwards. The collection is made up of songs from *Phenomenon*, *Force It*, *No Heavy Petting*, *Lights Out*, *Mechanix* and *Making Contact*. UFO also released the official concert video *The Misdemeanor Tour – Live*.

After the USA tour and the underwhelming reaction to *Misdemeanor*, the band basically split up, although it was not announced officially.

Nick Tauber: "I think that band needed two more albums together and one more tour and they could have been amazing. They didn't persist with that line-up. They changed it too quickly. They should have been more patient. They should have thought – how long did it take that original line-up to be really cool? Quite a few years. When I worked with Lizzy it wasn't until that third record [1973's *Vagabonds Of The Western World*] that they really started to peak. On every record a band makes there's always two or three fantastic tracks but as a whole piece of music ... Understanding how to write a great rock song is hard, understanding how to perform in the studio is hard and finding the right producer that clicks with you is hard and performing onstage and building up a following ... it takes time."[178]

After the lengthy US and European tours, the band were knackered and needed a break. There wasn't much time to write on the road. "... as soon as we were back in Blighty, Chrysalis wanted a new album," explains Gray. "But we didn't really have any songs ready, or even written, so we had to go pretty much straight away into this horrible dark rehearsal room in Birmingham to write and rehearse. None of us wanted to be there, we could have done with a break. We had lots of visits to the pub, for Guinness, I recall."[179]

Before UFO subsequently called it a day, they set to work on their first batch of new material since 1985 with the seven-track EP/mini-album, *Ain't Misbehavin'*, which was recorded at the Abattoir and S.S.E. Studios in 1986 with producer/manager Neil Levine. The songs were recorded using eight and four track equipment while Mogg's vocals were recorded in his living room, of all places. The line-up for this particular album included Mogg, McClendon, Gray and Simpson.

Recording the album was more of a hobby for Mogg because of the low budget that he had to work with. The album certainly did not represent a rebirth of the band; it was something of a fans-only release that represented the sort of material Mogg was writing after they toured the USA with *Misdemeanor*. If anything, the new material was supposed to revive interest in the band from Chrysalis with the intention of convincing the label to keep UFO on their books. The EP was a demo tape more than anything.

Indeed, because of the budget, Mogg found it difficult to record it. "I think we could be a lot bigger that we are," Mogg admitted to Merryl Lentz of *Hit Parader*, "but that's something that doesn't really bother us. We're happy; we just really enjoy what we're doing ... This is a damned good way not to do anything – it's better than working!"[180]

The six-track EP, or mini album as some would call it, was hardly going to reignite the band's career. However, while fans look back at *Ain't Misbehavin'* as a stutter in UFO's career, it does have its admirers.

Gray: "... I think the end result is far preferable to *Misdemeanor*. It sounded raw, and still does, much more how we were live. There are some great songs on there. 'Another Saturday Night', I particularly love; I had the keyboard parts and chords for it, and Tommy came up with a terrific syncopated guitar part. I prefer Tommy's playing on this album. Phil's lyrics were so sympathetic to the music, always were, really. 'Rock Boyz Rock' is another great one. We recorded them ourselves at UB40's studio in Birmingham as demos for Chrysalis, who clearly thought otherwise as they declined to renew their option and dropped us. But I like it: raw and emotive, as it should've been."[181]

Ain't Misbehavin' opens with "Between A Rock And A Hard Place", which furthers Mogg's apparent thirst for a more commercial radio-

Left: Phil Mogg: To quote producer Kit Woolven "That is what you call a rock singer" (see page 132). © Rich Galbraith

Below: Messrs Way and Schenker rock out in Norman, OK, August 1978. © Rich Galbraith

Left top: Mogg and Schenker: rock gods. August 1978, two months before Schenker checked out for the first time. © Rich Galbraith

Far left below: The legend that is Andy Parker. © Rich Galbraith

Left below: Pete Way animated, as ever, on stage. That's one reason fans love him so much. © Rich Galbraith

Right: Music Press Advert from 1978. © Unknown

Below right: Not a bad evening's entertainment! 1976 gig. © Rich Galbraith

Above: Paul "Tonka" Chapman is still fondly remembered. SITN Tour, 1979. © Ian Parry

Right: Bassist Paul Gray, formerly employed by Eddie & The Hot Rods and The Damned. © Ian Parry

...ove: Multi-instrumentalist
...l Carter, who went on
...work with the late Gary
...ore and even taught
...y's son guitar.
...an Parry

...ht: Phil Mogg 1983
...king Contact Tour.
...an Parry

Paul Loasby Productions
132 Liverpool Road, London N1 1LA. Telephone: (01) 609 8471. Telex: 261507

Entertainments Department
– 5 DEC 1984

MEMO

TO: ALL VENUES
RE :   UFO
DATE :   3rd DECEMBER 1984

1.   GET IN: is set for 9am.

2.   ELECTRICIAN: Could we please have the electrician from the get-in time, to be on call all day and during the show.

3.   SECURITY: Please supply adequate security to cover all exits and entrances to the venue and auditorium, dressing rooms stage, and mixer. Please advise us how many security in your estimation this will require and a quote on same.

4.   PARKING: We will require parking for 2 articulated lorries and 1 coach.

5.   STAGE CREW: Could you please supply 10 stage crew for the get-in and get-out, to be there from 9.00am.

6.   POWER REQUIREMENTS: We will need a single phase at 120amps and 3 phase at 200 amps.

7.   CATERING: The band will be bringing in their own caterers who will need space to set up as usual.

8.   SUPPORT: The support group will be TOBRUK., who will play for 45 mins.

9.   TIMES: As follows: 7.30 – 8.15   TOBRUK
                                8.45 – 10.15 UFO

10. MERCHANDISING: The band will be supplying merchandising but no programmes.

Above left: UFO's requests were surprisingly modest, as can be seen from this rider in 1984. © Unknown

Above: Joining UFO wasn't even a pipedream for Vinnie Moore at this 1987 instore demo in Enid, OK. © Rich Galbraith

Below: Shy's Tony Mills toured with UFO in 1984. Mr Mogg requisitioned Tony's expensive cough medicine (see page 113). © Tony Mills

Opposite left: Phil Mogg from 1998. The tour where he and Michael Schenker got back out on the road together ... temporarily. © Andy Brailsford

Opposite centre: A dark haired Michael Schenker in 1998. You may not recognise him, but the Flying V is a dead giveaway. © Andy Brailsford

Opposite right: Pete Way from 2004. A massive Aston Villa fan, he has the club badge on his bass guitar. © Andy Brailsford

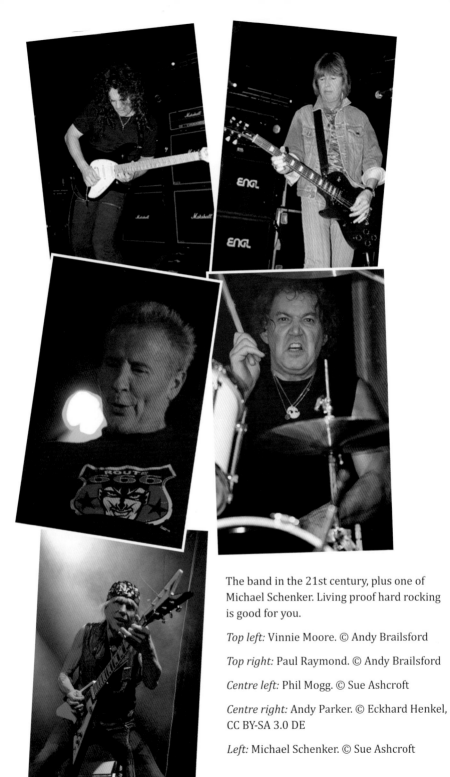

The band in the 21st century, plus one of Michael Schenker. Living proof hard rocking is good for you.

Top left: Vinnie Moore. © Andy Brailsford

Top right: Paul Raymond. © Andy Brailsford

Centre left: Phil Mogg. © Sue Ashcroft

Centre right: Andy Parker. © Eckhard Henkel, CC BY-SA 3.0 DE

Left: Michael Schenker. © Sue Ashcroft

friendly hard rock sound. UFO fans would no doubt have preferred a return to the grittier, harder sound of the Schenker years. Hair Metal was in full swing at this point with its dominance on the LA music scene, and UFO were seemingly heading toward that direction with songs such as "Another Saturday Night". It's a distinctly unoriginal and ineffective ballad, though the melody is fairly catchy. "At War With The World" does have the rough edges of a demo and Mogg does not sound especially enthusiastic, although there is a wailing central guitar solo. "Hunger In The Night" is, again, another AOR sounding track, while "Easy Money" has some likeable guitars. "Rock Boyz, Rock" closes the album and leaves the impression that perhaps Mogg's heart was not fully in it. "Lonely Cities (Of The Heart)" was included on the Japanese release as an exclusive bonus track.

Ain't Misbehavin' has seemingly faded into the mists of time. It is no longer available to buy, though it is going for higher prices than your average album on Amazon and eBay. Many UFO fans were unmoved by it and those who had bought the LP version were not enthusiastic enough to buy the CD release. It remains doubtful if it will get a reissue, though from an historical and completist perspective it would be worthwhile seeing a new edition complete with detailed sleeve notes. Perhaps a reissue label would consider buying the rights? Only time will tell at this stage.

Eventually released in February 1988, *Ain't Misbehavin'* failed to chart in the USA (where it was released via Metal Blade) and in the UK (through the independent label FM/Revolver).

Brian Slagel, Metal Blade's founder and CEO, remembers: "I had the extreme pleasure as a massive UFO fan to be able to release one of their records here in North America. We did *Ain't Misbehavin'* which was not a landmark album for the band, but still a very good one. We flew Phil over for a weekend of press and we really enjoyed having him here. Great guy, and very professional when it came to everything. The album did really well for us actually and it was truly an honour for us to have worked with them, even for such a short time."[182]

Ain't Misbehavin' was greeted with mostly unenthusiastic reviews. It was hardly the band's greatest effort and critics took the opportunity to bash it.

Mark Putterford in *Metal Hammer*: "On evidence of *Ain't Misbehavin'* I couldn't go as far as saying it's *Lights Out* for Phil Mogg, but I would suggest it's about time he changed a few bulbs."

How does it fit into the band's back catalogue? It is a release that has been almost entirely forgotten. It was not exactly a fine return to the studio for UFO. Given that the mini-album/EP was created with the intention of attracting record label interest, Mogg can be forgiven for such a lacklustre release.

Pete Way was asked by *Metal Rules'* Marko Syrjala in 2007 for his opinions on those last three recordings, which he does not appear on. He replied: "I think the direction wasn't really particularly special. I'm not so critical if I listen to some of it, which I never really do, but there are some good songs there. At that time, if you think back, record companies tried to get you to make a single, so what happens is you're not really being true to the music if you're changing your music to have a single ..."[183]

Given the topsy-turvy nature of the band's recent history and Mogg's reputation as something of a hell raiser after a few drinks, plus the lukewarm response to their new material, it's hard to imagine that in the late 1970s UFO were selling two or even three consecutive nights in US 15,000 seater venues. What had gone wrong? With a voice like Mogg's he should have been a rock star of Steven Tyler proportions and UFO should have been much bigger.

It was obvious that both Mogg and UFO fans missed Pete Way, as the songs were considerably below par. 1987 to 1988 was a period of inactivity for UFO. Mogg kept busy by managing The Quireboys for about five months, which featured his nephew Nigel Mogg on bass. Managing The Quireboys was an experience for Mogg; it reminded him of UFO back in the old days – the struggle and heartache, trying to get gigs, the daily routines and so on.

Mogg reformed UFO for a one-off special performance at the *Metal Hammer* (*MH*) magazine party in December 1987, with ex-Jagged Edge guitarist Myke Gray and bassist Paul Gray, with drummer Jim Simpson and Eddie George on keyboards.

Myke Gray: "I can't actually remember how I came to be involved but expect it was done through my manager. I was, and still am, a massive Michael Schenker fan so still consider it an honour to of been part of the band even for a day. I was only 17 so the gravity of what I was being asked to do didn't really enter my mind, I would be more nervous now to step into the very big shoes of one of the greatest guitar players of all time.

The only thing I truly remember was getting ready to play the encore of 'Rock Bottom' and thinking I'd better not fuck this up!"[184]

The *MH* gig was held at London's Astoria on Charing Cross Road and was in aid of Great Ormond Street Children's Hospital's Wishing Well appeal. The band played "We Belong To The Night", "Between A Rock And A Hard Place", "Too Hot To Handle", "Blinded By A Lie", "Heaven's Gate", "Lonely Heart", "At War With The World", "Chains Chains", "Only You Can Rock Me", "Lights Out", "Rock Bottom" and "Doctor Doctor".

"I'm my own worst enemy and I admit that it was a mistake," Mogg told *Kerrang!*'s Derek Oliver in 1988. "The problem is that I'm a sucker for playing and when it was suggested we do a one-off charity show I thought yeah, let's do it. But once I had committed myself it became increasingly difficult to alter things – there really wasn't much I could do without upsetting a lot of people. It was definitely a case of only having myself to blame."[185]

What happened to the *Misdemeanor* line-up? McClendon had been out of the picture since the recording sessions of 1986, after which he played guitar on Winter Reign's album *The Beginning* before moving back to the USA. Meanwhile, Simpson had joined U.S.I. before touring with Bonnie Tyler. He joined Budgie in 1988 and then the Newcastle band Red Dogs. Paul Gray, on the other hand, had rejoined his first love, Eddie And The Hot Rods, and then a Swedish metal band called Heavy Load before reuniting with The Damned. Many years later, Simpson and Gray would team up with The Damned guitarist Alan Lee Shaw in a band called Mischief.

Speaking about the end of his tenure in UFO, Paul Gray recalls: "It was really sad. Tommy had had enough and fucked off back to America; there was no money left, the band was broke. We did a gig [1987 *MH* Xmas party) with a guitarist called Myke Gray (no relation) in London, and it just sort of fizzled away …"[186]

The various line-up changes of UFO throughout the post-Way years are hardly remembered by even the most enthusiastic of fans. *The Best Of The Rest*, a compilation focusing on the post-Schenker years, was released in 1988 via Chrysalis. It focuses on material from *No Place To Run* and *The Wild, The Willing And The Innocent* as well as *Mechanix, Making*

Contact and *Misdemeanor*. Neither *Misdemeanor* nor *Ain't Misbehavin'* were critically or commercially successful and, with the seemingly never ending line-up changes, the band folded officially for the second time in the decade and their career in 1989.

Meanwhile, Michael Schenker collaborated with singer Robin McAuley which saw MSG morph into the McAuley Schenker Group with the release of 1987's *Perfect Timing.* However, this would only last for three studio albums and two live releases before MSG was reborn yet again with new members (ex-Yngwie Malmsteen bassist Barry Sparks, former Great King Rat singer Leif Sundin and drummer Shane Gaalaas) in the mid 1990s. In 1990, Schenker even replaced the late Robbin Crosby in Ratt and appeared on their 1990 MTV *Unplugged* performance, but his tenure was only brief and now largely forgotten.

Towards the end of the decade, Pete Way bought a house near Phil Mogg in Bearwood, Birmingham. The pair rekindled their friendship but they didn't plan to restart UFO. They simply began writing songs and rehearsing. The break appeared to have done them some good because they enjoyed working together once again. In May, Mogg told *Kerrang!*'s Derek Oliver that they'd "started mucking around, writing songs and jamming. We've already written about 12 songs and we're still steaming on."[187]

It was obvious that Mogg needed Way if UFO were to ever be taken seriously again. Once they had compiled a set of songs they must have posed the question: What is the point in having new songs without a band to play them? They didn't want to be Chas & Dave, so they started looking for musicians. Indeed, the duo recorded some new tracks in mid-1988 through to the new year with a series of musicians, notably, guitarist and UFO old boy Myke Gray – who was by now in Skin – local guitarists Rik Sanford and Tony Glidewell (both of Starfighters), Eric Gammans and drummer Fabio Del Rio.

There was so much indulgence in alcohol that Gray found the sessions to be somewhat lacklustre, although there is no doubt he remains pleased to be part of UFO's legacy. Gray also wanted to form his own band and so after some demos and showcases he moved on. He says now: "I remember it being very unproductive and a lot of time wasting. I was very young, didn't drink and played guitar for ten hours a day, and Pete and Phil were seasoned rock stars who had different life agendas, but I am glad I did it and I learnt a lot. I still consider it a huge honour to have been involved in it even if it was for just a very short period. Pete and Phil are legends, and I grew up with, and still listen to, UFO."[188]

However, it was Sanford with whom Mogg and Way established a connection. The material the pair were writing had very much blues based origins and Sanford's playing fitted the direction of the new material, which the duo felt was harder hitting than *Misdemeanor*. They wanted a guitarist they could write strong and memorable songs with, rather than somebody who could merely follow the motions. "Well, when you work on songs you need someone who's sympathetic with that style and Rik's style leans towards playing in that manner," Mogg explained to *Metal Forces* Garry Sharpe-Young.[189]

It was with Rik Sanford that the duo recorded some of their best material from this era, which would be archived for later use. The material they recorded with Sanford was different from what they had crafted with Schenker, Chapman or McClendon.

There were other possibilities in the new line-up. Mogg and Way even discussed the notion of working with Chris Caffery of Savatage but sadly nothing came of this. Mogg and Way also proposed the idea of reuniting with Schenker and Chapman but it was a complicated procedure. One other option was to head over to LA to reunite with Andy Parker as well as Schenker. Mogg had even spoken to Parker about the possibility of reuniting. Having Schenker back in the band would certainly have been lucrative from both a musical and commercial viewpoint but, given Mogg's past relationship with him, the idea was not all together feasible.

Despite the changes in UFO's line-up throughout the 1980s, Mogg did not want a Deep Purple situation with musicians coming in and out of the band. The core members of the original line-up of UFO – Mogg, Way and Parker – knew each other from when they left school and they played well together, but in the 1980s Mogg found it difficult to find a new set of musicians that had the same sort of chemistry. The original UFO band was very tight as well as fiery, but Mogg had chopped and changed the various line-ups since Schenker departed. Of course, the stress of keeping the band together and the exhausting way of life – touring, rehearsals, recording and then back on tour again – wore everyone down in the end, especially Mogg. It is like a continuous cycle and one that seemingly never ends. Yet UFO had always been a touring band. They were of that 1960s and 1970s ilk of bands that built a fanbase through constant gigging. It was the old fashioned way of how a band progressed: they'd get an audience for a gig and that audience would tell a few friends who'd go to the band's next gig and so on. Very different from the 'let's stick a video on You Tube and see if it goes viral' approach of today.

However, despite the various musicians that the original duo had collaborated with over the previous year or so, UFO remained distinctly Mogg and Way by April 1989. The new songs represented the latter period of UFO's career with more of an emphasis on the blues which Mogg adored. Asked more specifically about the new material, Mogg told *RIP*'s Del James in 1988, with typical offbeat humour: "We've got just over an album's worth of material. Some songs are 'It's A Shame', 'Electra Glide In Blue', 'Border Line', and the other ones are called 'Untitled', 'Don't Know' and 'Haven't Got A Clue'."[190]

The 1980s had evidently been a difficult period for the band and, while many fans maintain that the Paul Chapman era is of worth, others would claim UFO had become a pale shadow of itself. However, UFO, or rather more specifically the Michael Schenker era of UFO, continued to be as influential as any other British hard rock band that had originated in the 1970s. Their influence was especially prominent on American bands.

American rock and metal dominated the airwaves in the 1980s and bands such as Metallica, Megadeth and Guns N' Roses were huge fans of UFO. UFO may have lost the mass popularity that they had achieved by the end of the previous decade, but the quality of their music speaks for itself and there's no doubt that albums such as *Lights Out* and *Strangers In The Night* are as influential as anything by Black Sabbath or Deep Purple. UFO were true survivors and, to an extent (as with guitarist Tony Iommi and his band Black Sabbath), Phil Mogg had never given up and, even when he seemingly had laid the band to rest, he always knew UFO would reinvent itself again at some point in the future.

Talking about the most dominant member of UFO, former keyboardist Danny Peyronel attests: "In a 'power' sense, undoubtedly and unquestionably, Phil. Michael was very dominant musically, in that most of the material (except my contributions!), came from riffs he would come up with. However, Phil's lyrics and singing were fundamental to the identity of the band. This is obvious from the fact that the band survived the many non-Michael periods and did so fine. Pete too was entirely fundamental! He was very much 'the image' and the stage presence of UFO. And he was a major contributor to the music of many songs as well. So, I repeat, overall it would have to be Phil. His present singing and writing is superb, having only grown and matured in a wonderful way, so Kudos to him!"[191]

Mogg had seen UFO survive the punk era; they had influenced the NWOBHM bands and they had inspired many American metal bands from Van Halen to Metallica. UFO have never gained the sort of prominence they truly deserve and such comments can be made about many other bands from Diamond Head to Thin Lizzy.

Would fans ever see Schenker and UFO perform together again? That, said Hamlet, is the question.

CHAPTER
SEVEN

High Stakes & Dangerous Men –
Mogg and Way Reunite
(1990 –1994)

"I don't think any of us realised the band would go on that long. It's been up and down, up and down, on / off, on / off and quite a wiry relationship. Maybe, it's the diversity of the people involved."

Phil Mogg[192]

After almost three years of inactivity, UFO was brought back together in 1991 by Phil Mogg and Pete Way, with guitarist Laurence Archer (well known for his stints in Stampede, Phil Lynott's Grand Slam and Rhode Island Red) and drummer Clive Edwards. Edwards knew his onions having played with a wide variety of hard rock bands prior to joining UFO, including Screaming Lord Sutch, Pat Travers Band, Uli Roth's Electric Sun, Wild Horses, Bernie Marsden's SOS and Lionheart.

However, while rumours of a reunion with Schenker circulated amongst the rock press and UFO's fanbase, Way was quick to quash the idea during an interview with Neil Jeffries at *Kerrang!*. Way stated that the band did not approach Schenker, "but through Chrysalis, Michael said he would like to work with us, He wanted £100,000 up front then he would do a tour and an album."[193]

Way and Mogg obviously assumed that Schenker was only in it for the money and not the music. Schenker's reported financial demands certainly tainted Mogg and Way's view of the German guitarist. The reunion was never pursued on the band's part.

Way: "Paul Chapman was the same, he found out what was going on and offered his services for £800 a week and then we found out he was playing clubs in Florida billing himself as *UFO featuring Paul Chapman*."[194]

If Mogg and Way wanted to make UFO about the money they would have signed with a major label, but they never wanted the involvement of an A&R man. As long as they could get enough money to make an album they were more than pleased to work independently. They also had their own vision about how UFO should sound. It was always the music that mattered for UFO; that and Aston Villa as far as Way was considered. He is a lifelong Villa fan and even gave his Villa shirt to Tesla's Brian Wheat (goodness only knows what he made of it!).

The band, specifically Mogg and Way, never felt any pressure because they were not sure if they were going to go through with creating a revised version of UFO. It was not until Archer joined the camp that they seriously began to think that a new formation of the band could exist on its own terms. Way was Archer's initial contact because Way had wanted him to join Waysted in the early years of the band. Way had found a guitarist whom both he and Mogg admired and, though having the right guitarist was not the main reason behind forming the band, it was certainly one of the most fundamental factors.

The original UFO duo were more than pleased with Archer, whom they considered to be one of the most distinctive rock guitarists working in England. Edwards had a deserved reputation as a rock drummer of worth. It was Archer who recommended Edwards; the guitarist gave the drummer a call and said they were working on some new material and he should come and check it out.

The band were eager to explain to the press that it was not a UFO reunion *per se* but rather a new beginning. It was different from previous versions of the band. "It might sound funny to say it, but having been in bands that change their line-up, it's like being in a soccer team, where you change this guy and that guy. But this is brand new and it's very exciting," Way discussed with *Riff Raff*'s Lyn Guy.[195]

Both Archer and Edwards' style of playing suited the new rock-based direction of the band. Archer's fluid and focused style of playing was certainly more in line with Schenker and Chapman than Tommy McClendon's. Mogg and Way wanted to shift the new version of the band towards UFO's classic mid to late 1970s rock origins. Mogg was not interested in looking for a Yngwie Malmsteen or an Eddie Van Halen, because it would not have suited UFO as it stood in 1991 (not that either one of those would have joined!); nor would it have suited the style of rock music that was being played at the time, in an era of grunge and American alternative rock.

However, with the success of British rock bands such as Thunder, there was certainly a market for a newly revised version of UFO. "Y'know we could have come back years ago, but with Myke Gray it would have been naff and UFO set such standards, well, except when I left for Waysted, that we've got to be good," Way admitted to *Metal Forces* writer Garry Sharpe-Young at the time.[196]

The newly rejuvenated band set to work on a brand new studio album. Expressing his thoughts on the new line-up of UFO, Phil Mogg spoke to *RAW*: "Now when I get up in the morning, I don't feel like I'm going into two rounds [of boxing]. There are no big fights anymore. If you start the day and you've got to fight Schenker, then [drummer Andy] Parker, then you've got to fight Way, it gets exhausting and you end up not singing anything."[197]

Named after the Western novel, *High Stakes And Desperate Men*, which Mogg had been reading at the time, *High Stakes & Dangerous Men*, UFO's thirteenth album, was recorded between summer and Christmas of 1991 at the Livehouse Studios in Launceston, Cornwall, Studio 125 in Burgess Hill, Black Barn Studios in Woking and London's Wessex Studios and EZ Studios.

The band hooked up with producer Kit Woolven, famed for his work with Thin Lizzy and Magnum. Edwards knew Woolven from years ago when Woolven produced the 1981 Wild Horses album *Stand Your Ground*. Woolven's name came up in conversation as soon as the band began discussing producers. Woolven was also an experienced engineer and used to working with different personalities. Had the band brought in a big-named producer he'd more than likely want full control of the album but Mogg was very particular about how the band should sound on record.

Way: "It's very important to be able to relate to the producer and he [Kit] has a great deal of experience. Kit knows exactly what he's doing and gives off good vibes."[198]

Initial rehearsals, which were rather lengthy, were done in London before pre-production in South Wales, while the bulk of the recording was done in Launceston. A great deal of work was done during rehearsals, and Archer had a few ideas of his own which he threw around, such as

"Back Door Man", but nothing had been written. It was all music with no lyrics. "Now our rehearsals are what's giving us the buzz," admitted Way. "In some ways, recording isn't that much fun because there's a lot of hard work in making it sound like it does at rehearsals."[199]

The rehearsals went smoothly though it was more akin to a group of strangers working on new material than a group of seasoned musicians churning out some classic songs. After the rehearsals, the band got round to working on some demos.

Clive Edwards remembers: "Phil's attitude was that he didn't wanna know the old stuff. To get a record company interested you had to do something to move forward. It wasn't just going out and playing live and playing all the old stuff. Right from the very start we were working on a couple of ideas that turned out to be 'One Of Those Nights', 'Borderline' and 'Burning Fire'. Those were the first three tracks that we recorded. It was from there that a record deal came along. There was a lot of talk about whether they were committed to actually going out there and bringing UFO back or whether they needed a few quid for the next six months – let's do this and walk away again."[200]

He continues: "Most of the time we did the album virtually karaoke as well. We did have words for those three songs, 'Borderline', 'One Of Those Nights' and 'Burning Fire', because they'd already been recorded, but when we recorded the rest of the album we had very few words. He [Mogg] kept singing the same old words for different songs. It was very funny."[201]

After rehearsals in London, the band decamped to a big studio rehearsal complex called Bluestone Studios in South Wales for an intensive two to three week period of pre-production, before moving to Launceston to record. Wales was idyllic, but there was little for them to do but work.

Woolven brought with him a portable studio and various provisions. Woolven would work well into the night, primarily with Archer and Edwards, in order to get the guide tracks to the point where all they needed was Mogg's vocals. Woolven collaborated tightly with Archer and Edwards. They would put down the drums and guitars as a guide and then spend a day or so on each song laying down the bass work with Way.

Woolven: "We recorded the drums in a rather unusual way. Clive is a really good drummer, brilliant: great timing, inventive skills, technical skills. When we were doing pre-production out in Wales, for one reason or another, sometimes Pete wouldn't be in the rehearsal room and I'd pick up his bass and start playing. Clive is just one of those drummers when he's playing he makes it easy. I'm no great bass player – I'm not a bass player – but I pick up the bass, and Clive made it so easy."[202]

It took around four days to put down the backing tracks and guide guitars, yet it was taking a day (if they were lucky) working on the bass. "What would happen is after Pete had gone to bed I would then sit there and repair all the basslines," Woolven recalls. "It was unbelievable."[203]

However, they didn't get any vocals until after they recorded the album. They had frivolous names for songs because Mogg had yet to write any lyrics or come up with a title. Working with Mogg was akin to completing a giant jigsaw, because the band and producer had to wait for little pieces from him to assemble the whole thing. Slowly but surely the band and producer would find out what the song was. "Back Door Man", for example, was written in such a way.

Edwards has a damning verdict on Messrs Mogg and Way "... the thing is they [Mogg and Way] got pissed really quick. They were like alcoholics. Basically they had four tins of Special Brew – the first one would wake them up, the second one they were at their best, the third one was kind of tipsy, the fourth one it was all downhill. By the time they had a fifth one it was bedtime. When Phil was really drunk he was awful; he was terrible. It was nice really when he'd just bugger off. Pete would last a bit longer, but Pete was pretty much the same. It doesn't take much to get them drunk, because I think they've got so much alcohol in their system anyway. There wouldn't be mega drinking sessions. The others had gone to bed and we would spend time working on the songs."[204]

Woolven remembers that during the backing track stages he made a personal policy not to drink booze; instead he opted for watered lemon juice which also acts as a form of detox, ridding the body of chemicals. Mogg and Way also tried it and they did well for a time, however, old habits came back to haunt them by the time they moved to Cornwall.

Woolven: "It took bloody ages doing mainly Pete's bass parts. I know Pete was starting to drink, but sneakily. There's a place called the Lighthouse in Launceston: accommodation, a big old hotel next to the studio and my room was right at the top of the house and Phil's room was, in fact, the room right by the front door on the bottom of the house.

I came down one morning and [Phil] stuck his head around a corner, and he went 'Kit' [and I] went 'Phil, What?' [and he said:] 'I think I've started drinking again.' I went 'Why's that? Why've you started drinking again?' He said: 'Because I can't explain this?' and he opened the door and the room – there wasn't a stick of furniture that wasn't smashed to pieces. Matchstick sized pieces of woods. The wardrobe was trashed, the bed was trashed, the table was trashed. He said: 'I can't explain it; I must've started drinking again.

'I remember a few days later I was looking for Phil and I said to Laurence Archer. I said, 'Have you seen Phil? I need to put a guide vocal on this track.' He said: 'The last time I saw him he was lying in the gutter outsider Woolworth's in Launceston.' He was lying in a gutter outside Woolworth's throwing abuse at old ladies (laughs)."[205]

Had the band worked full-time in London there's no doubt that Mogg and Way would have had far more distractions, but in Launceston there was nothing to do except work on the music or go to the pub and play pool. In Launceston, the band had to work closely together and spend a great deal of time in each other's company so, in that sense, the environment helped them become closer, to gel together.

Edwards: "It was incredibly frustrating working, first of all in dribs and drabs, but working also in that period between the second tin of Special Brew and onto the third when you had the best, because afterwards it's gone. But sometimes it was nice just to work with Laurence and Kit. It was frustrating, but that's a part of the gig. It's not gonna be any different. Apparently, he's [Mogg] done that lots of times previously, writing the words later on. You can't make people work completely differently to how they are. That was one of the reasons why a big producer wouldn't have worked, because there'd have to be a bit of discipline there. You had to work with somebody like Kit who was very, very good at working with characters. He'd worked with Phil Lynott. He'd worked with Brian Robertson and people like that so he knew how to coach the best out of people."[206]

Kit Woolven spoke about the different working methods of producers: "I spoke to Phil sometime after that album [*High Stakes ...*] and he said: 'I wanna get Ron Nevison to do it [the next album].' I said: 'Yeah sure, why's that?' and he said: 'Because he [Ron] won't take any shit from me. He will make me finish the album quickly.' I must admit I didn't do that. He had a system which I thought was the way he worked and, to be honest, I had no backup whatsoever. I just had to wait till he had his little window in the day where he could sing and that's the way I dealt with it. Be it right or wrong that's the way I dealt with it at the time. I think Phil probably needs somebody to give him hell. Like really go at him. To be honest, I don't feel right enough to do that, really. I mean, if you can't be fucking adult...[207]

"Phil was always alright with me. Phil was always absolutely fine with me. We seemed to have quite a rapport. The thing is with somebody who drinks like that, what are you gonna do? Tell them to stop drinking? With Phil, it got to a stage where I knew and he knew that when he was doing vocals he would start drinking first thing in the morning and get himself to a point where he was singing really well. He'd be fantastic for an hour and a half and then he'd get to a point where he'd go: 'You know it's over, don't you?' I said 'Yeah.' He said: 'What I'm gonna do now is get more and more drunk.' You had to persevere. Love him (laughs)."[208]

Pete Way, on the other hand, would last a bit longer. He was a happy drunk yet he'd cause more damage. He'd fall through windows or go flying through the kitchen and land head first on the kitchen worktop. He would create chaos and damage but he was a laugh-a-minute guy; very much a comedian. In many respects Mogg was Yin to Way's Yang.

Archer: "When we did the *High Stakes* album, 90% of it was – I would say – myself, Clive and with a bit of input from Pete. We wrote and arranged without too much of an idea what was happening vocally because Phil wasn't being very creative at that point. He was throwing ideas in. He had very small ideas but, in the end, we had to arrange it without having an idea of what vocal we were going to get. We got all the backing tracks down without hearing a note of what Phil was doing. Phil would hide himself away and come out at the end of it. Drink is the demon for him and he wasn't so much difficult to work with, he would just not be there. He'd be somewhere else in the studio, locked in a room or he'd be out of it for a certain time in the day. There was a small working period with Phil. We started rehearsals at 10 o'clock in the morning and get till about two and he'd be all over really. When Phil's not drinking and he's lucid everything's really good."[209]

UFO – Mogg, Archer, Way and Edwards – were joined in the studio by Deep Purple's Don Airey on keyboards and backing singers Terry Reid and ex-Night singer Stevie Lange, former wife of top rock producer

Robert "Mutt" Lange. The vibe was positive when Stevie Lange was in the studio, but with Terry Reid, it was something else entirely. Reid liked to drink. He'd come into the studio after a few drinks, and though he was friendly and an amazing singer, there was little opportunity for him to sing because he was so intoxicated. The band would have liked more vocal contributions from him; it didn't work out in the end. What they did get from Reid, however, was outstanding.

Woolven: "He [Reid] did, for my liking, spend far too much time in the studio because he annoyed the fuck out of me. He couldn't remember the lines and I think he only had to sing 'Oh she's the one', and he couldn't remember it! He kept twiddling around and I had to go in and untangle the leads to the headphones about three times because he got himself so knotted up because he was spinning around and not remembering 'Oh she's the one'. Eventually he did sing it, but he sang it in the wrong place. This was in the early days of sampling so I cut the sample and put it in the right place. Phil said: 'You can't do that. It's Terry Reid.' To be honest, I didn't know much about him at the time. Certainly he was a big hero for Phil."[210]

In terms of keyboard contributions, Don Airey was numero uno. Probably the most famous and successful keyboard player in rock, Airey instinctively knows how much to play and when to play it. He always comes up with the right notes and while some keyboard players tend to overplay and want to try different things, Airey is quite the opposite.

The album took months to finish and even by the time the songs had been completed, the band and producer were still waiting for Mogg to get his act together. However, it was pointless attempting to rush Mogg because he worked at his own speed. "While I was mixing, he was still writing the lyrics for songs that we hadn't got vocals on," recalls Woolven in 2012. "Listening to the album this morning I made a note to myself; on the second song there's some dodgy lyrics on there. There's a reference to Arnold Schwarzenegger and there's something about lemonade and Courvoisier, and they're lines that I came up with because Phil couldn't. It got to the stage – I think it must have been the last song that we were waiting for lyrics for – I said for Christ sakes sing that. It was hard but I do have a lot of time for Phil. He's a survivor. In Launceston, we're putting down the backing tracks, and there's the in-house engineer that I used as an assistant down there, and I wanted Phil to get some guide vocals down so I knew what we were dealing with. Phil started singing and as soon as he opened his mouth the assistant engineer at Launceston looked at me in utter amazement. That is what you **call** a rock singer!"[211]

UFO had become something of a British rock institution, albeit on a cult level – they weren't a household name like Whitesnake. They did not have any preconceived notions of making an album that sounded like the UFO of old. They knew that merely copying the past sound was not the right way forward for this version of the band, and Mogg had always tried to stay clear of emulating the past in the various incarnations of UFO throughout the 1980s. New material – the sound and style – just came naturally. There were certainly no plans to change the band's sound to an entirely different direction. The band wanted to capture the vibe of the rehearsals in the studio. They did not want an album's worth of songs that sounded too clean cut and polished; instead they opted for a rawer sound.

Certainly Archer and Edwards learned more than they already knew about how to structure songs, bridges and choruses and how to put together an arrangement that works. By the time the album was recorded, all the backing tracks had been completed so it was essentially an expansion of what they had done at Bluestones in Wales, but without too much of Mogg's presence. Mogg came in at the end and began assembling vocals. The album was completed at Burgess Hill.

Asked if there was a feeling within the band that the album would never get finished, Archer says: "I think he [Mogg] knew and that's why we put more pressure on him. It was up and down, going on a few tangents here and there. He was getting better and he actually was sober for quite a long time when we started. After we finished the album he was actually a lot more together."[212]

The band and producer had creative and artistic freedom and were pleased that the label essentially left them alone to work. They did not have visits from A&R men, although Robin Greatrex of Razor Records was growing impatient with how long it took. Recording was slowed down when the band hit the road.

Woolven: "It was one of those never-ending things. Started it in the summer in 1991, early summer, and we didn't get finished till Christmas. I know in November they had a European tour to do and Phil said to me: 'What are you doing while we're away doing this tour?' And I said: 'Twiddling my thumbs waiting for you to get back to get the fucking thing finished.' He said: 'Why don't you come with us and do front of house sound?' and I went 'Allright'. It was one of the funniest three weeks in my life. I don't think I've ever laughed so much. It was actually hilarious. But the album took forever."[213]

The new look UFO with keyboardist Jem Davis, who went on to join FM, made their live debut for six UK dates in November, 1991. The band could not afford to hire Don Airey for the tour, and this was no reflection on Davis, who is an excellent keyboard player in his own right. Archer was not keen on having a second guitarist, as in a Paul Raymond figure, so the idea of having a guitarist and keyboardist was never pursued.

It was a low profile tour to see how the band worked onstage and in front of an audience. There was the possibility that they would not be doing it for long so they wanted to test the waters, as it were. They had much to prove because of the band's legacy and the amount of people that liked UFO. They also used the tour as an opportunity to build up a new fanbase.

Way had been out of the band for several years and, with the music industry becoming increasingly fickle, they did have a great deal to prove to themselves and their fans. UFO enthusiasts were not only keen to hear the classic Schenker material, they also wanted to learn how the new material fitted in with the vintage songs. The tour also included four dates in Spain with Magnum initially planned as support, but they could not make it in the end.

UFO have always been a relatively down to earth band throughout the various incarnations, while Mogg and Way are perfect for interviewers. Similar to Francis Rossi and Rick Parfitt of Status Quo, they have a rapport, bouncing jokes off each other like an old married couple. Yet there is an integrity to them and their music which is not always highlighted as interviewers have tended to concentrate on the wilder aspects of the band's history. Certainly, they have treated each gig like a party in the past and in 1991 they had an incredible amount of energy, both onstage and off. Mogg was in fantastic physical shape, while his voice was as raw, bluesy and powerful as ever. Way was playing well, and Edwards and Archer had brought some life and much needed drive back into the band. The challenge for UFO was to make the audiences happy night after night, because expectations were high. Aside from Pete Way suffering from a bout of flu, the tour was a success and went smoothly.

Woolven: "To be honest, I don't really remember any sort of real rapport between them. Only time I ever saw any rapport between them that I remember – and I could be totally wrong – is when I went out to do front of house for them and they were very, very funny. Pete fell over one time on stage and Phil pretended not to notice and stomped across the stage with a mic on a microphone stand – a tripod stand rather than a round based stand – and he had the microphone at an angle and planted two of the prongs either side of Pete's neck. It got to the end of the song and Pete looks up sort of 'Let me out now' and Phil just goes 'Doctor Doctor' and they go into that for the whole song."[214]

The band aired some new material and generally received a welcome reception from longstanding fans. The homecoming London show was held at the Town & Country Club on November 13. UFO sailed through "Born For The Good Life", "Borderline", "Only You Can Rock Me", "Long Gone", "One Of Those Nights", "Back Door Man", "Too Hot To Handle", "Love To Love", "Shoot Shoot" and "Lights Out" and an encore of "Doctor Doctor", "Rock Bottom" and "Mystery Train".

The set list reflected both the past and the present in an attempt to appease the longstanding UFO fans who had stayed with the band through thick and thin. Writing in *Kerrang!* Chris Watts said of the gig: "The 'old shit' is magnificent. 'Love To Love' crashes out with mood and drama intact. 'Lights Out' still sounds thunderous. Even 'Shoot Shoot' kicks like a bastard after all these years."

During the tour, much songwriting was still going on behind the scenes. "We wanted to do quite a bit of writing and we wanted to pick and choose material," Archer stated in 2012. "The ironic thing is Phil didn't want to do what I would call classic material. If he had his way he would have done none of the classics. It would have been all new material you'd never heard of, which was fine. I never had a problem with that. I concentrated on writing stuff and getting bits and pieces to him. Due to his fragile state at the time, it would have taken a long time to get things nailed down. We had gigs lined up and took a long time rehearsing and a long time throwing ideas about. It got to a point where we had to start putting a set together because we were going to be out on the road very soon. He [Mogg] hated doing anything like that [*Strangers In The Night*]. He was just fed up of doing all that which seems a bit weird because I went to see them not long ago and they did all the back catalogue."[215]

The band's aim was to return to UFO's trademark guitar sound, specifically that of the late 1970s and early 1980s. Much of the material was brand new, although they did use some songs from very early demos that Mogg and Way recorded when they rekindled their songwriting partnership a few years earlier.

High Stakes & Dangerous Men opens with the terrific hard rock stomp of "Borderline" while "Primed For Time" ups the grit and aggression even further. The band are simply on fire by the third track, "She's The One". "Ain't Life Sweet" is a speedy rocker with some excellent drums and an awesome lead riff. "Don't Want To Lose You" is a shout-it-out-loud ballad with some effective backing vocals, while "Burnin' Fire" is a fantastic little song with a feisty vocal performance. "Running Up The Highway" is led by Archer's superb guitars and "Back Door Man" is an intoxicating blues soaked track. "One Of Those Nights" has an indelible chorus perfect for the live stage; it's the album's standout ballad.

"Revolution" is a mid-paced number which sees Mogg's vocal shine in all its glory while "Love Deadly Love" is a raucous rock 'n' roller with some nifty keys. "Let The Good Times Roll" is a more than an appropriate way to close the band's glorious return to form.

High Stakes & Dangerous Men was UFO's strongest release since *Mechanix* or possibly even *Strangers In The Night*. It was a fine return to form and a big leap forward from the commercial rock of the mid to late 1980s. It remains a shame that this particular line-up did not make any more studio albums.

Inevitably there was going to be a fair amount of naysayers; people who thought UFO would not be able to deliver and that their best years where behind them. There is, however, an element of danger in rock 'n' roll and UFO wanted to prove that they still had something to say that was worth listening to and, more importantly, that they could still make music that rocked.

"We were very pleased with the new material but we want to be careful about the choice of singles, in case they project the wrong image," Way explained to *Metal Hammer*'s Chris Welch. "It's years since Phil Mogg and I worked together and quite a few years since the last UFO record. The new music is very rocky, and the songs are pretty basic, but we have taken into account the changes in record technology since we first started."[216]

High Stakes & Dangerous Men was released in April 1992 via Razor Records in the UK, but failed to chart there or in the USA, just like the previous EP/mini-album *Ain't Misbehavin'*. Its American release was held back in hopes of a reunion of the Schenker era line-up.

"I actually think our new record is the best we've ever made. It's had that much thought put in it," Way told *RAW*'s Kirk Blows at the time."[217]

High Stakes & Dangerous Men was unleashed to excellent reviews; the best write-ups the band had received since *Mechanix*. UFO were back!

Writing in *Metal Forces*, Jerry Ewing enthused: "No old boys trying to recapture lost glory here, just the sort of solid, quality British hard rock we've been looking for. We've all been moaning about where did classy British rock go. UFO have provided the answer." Meanwhile, Paul Henderson wrote in *Kerrang!*: "... *High Stakes & Dangerous Men* turns out to be a long way from being the kind of limp, half-hearted, half-cocked affair that re-grouping after a lengthy 'sabbatical' often throws up." And *RAW* stated: "The band's history was founded upon melody, spectacular guitar playing and Mogg's vocal style. Thankfully, all three are still to the fore. At the end of the day, the album represents a triumph – the spirit of UFO has been recaptured."

Speaking about the release in 2002, Mogg admitted to *Revelationz*: "... I played it the other day and it's very good. I was surprised myself ..."[218]

High Stakes & Dangerous Men has sadly faded into relative obscurity since its initial release, which is a crying shame as it remains one the band's best non-Schenker era albums. It's been reissued over the years via different labels, but that has not helped raise the album's appeal. UFO fans, however, continue to rate it rather highly. It has emphatically stood the test of time.

An excellent version of the album, which is a worthy addition to any fans collection, is the two-disc set, *One of Those Nights – The Collection*, which was released in 2006 by Sanctuary Records. Not only does it contain the twelve track *High Stakes & Dangerous Men* album with the bonus track "Long Gone", but also seven live tracks on disc two which were recorded at Midland, Texas on 21 March 1979 and eight live tracks recorded at Club Citta, Tokyo on 20 June 1992. The studio version itself is certainly long overdue a reissue with sleeve notes detailing this era of the band's career.

Woolven: "I don't know if I was or wasn't [pleased with it]. I think I probably wasn't. I was probably frustrated by it because it did take so long. I like to get into an album, really work it and leave on a high, and when it's so long you squeeze the blood out of the stone. You don't enjoy it and so therefore I don't think you're putting your best effort in. I listened to it today; I'm quite surprised – I thought it was really quite good. I do have the sort of nature whereby no matter how bad it's going, you wake up fresh the next morning and go 'Right, today's a new day. Be positive. Today we're gonna to do it.' I started out that way but three hours later, fuck me ..."[219]

He continues: "I spent a lot of my time in Los Angeles. I think I came back from LA to do the album and after I finished it I went back to LA to do some stuff out there. Listening to the album this morning, it's amazing – you can hear the bloody Los Angeles influence. Fucking hell, that's transparent."[220]

1992 also saw the release of *The Essential UFO*, a collection of songs from 1974 to 1979 covering the famed Schenker years. The Chrysalis-released compilation derives tracks from *Phenomenon*, *Force It*, *No Heavy Petting*, *Lights Out*, *Obsession* and the legendary *Strangers In The Night*.

Keyboardist Jem Davis, known for his stints in Stranger and Tobruk, not to mention Doogie White's band Midnight Blue and Praying Mantis, continued to join them on the road throughout the year. The band ventured to mainland Europe for some gigs to promote the new studio release. Ray Zell of *Kerrang!* reviewed the band's show at Stuttgart's The Longhorn on March 12. He wrote: "Most excellent. I bopped my bits that were boppable and smiled 'til my teeth hurt."

They played a second round of UK dates, which began at Rock City in Nottingham on April 21. The band then committed themselves to a series of sold out gigs in Japan, where they performed some classic UFO material. "Japan was great," says Archer. "I had a solo album out in Japan in the eighties. The band I had, Stampede, had a big following in Japan, also. The gigs were really good. I really enjoyed it. It was great."[221]

The band's gig at Club Citta in Tokyo on June 20, 1992 was recorded and released as *Lights Out In Tokyo*. Speaking about the *Lights Out In Tokyo* live album in 2012, Clive Edwards says: "We were a very, very energetic band. We played a lot quicker. When I listen to the new band I think they're playing a ballad. 'Lights Out' has got so slow and 'Rock Bottom' – how slow can you play that before the song's unrecognisable? Myself and Laurence with the X-UFO lot, we are very much faster players and we like that three piece kind of vibe.

'People talk about how overdubbed *Strangers In The Night* was, that live album from Tokyo is a genuine live album. There are no overdubs. It was only done once – there was nothing done at soundcheck. It was done on the equipment the PA hire firm had and we had an engineer come out to record it. It was done with separate mics, so we had separate feeds for some of the stuff. Some of it was going straight out into the PA, but that is a genuine – more so than 99.9% of live albums like [Thin Lizzy's] *Live And Dangerous* – one night live and seven days in the studio. There's a lot of stuff done in soundcheck. We had no money. If it had gone wrong there would have been no album. That's the way everything was done, on such a shoestring. We had no money. A lot was done on a wing and a prayer. It was amazing that we managed to get anything done."[222]

A set list for 1992 ran as follows: "Running Up The Highway", "Borderline", "Too Hot To Handle", "She's The One", "Cherry", "Backdoor Man", "Love To Love", "Only You Can Rock Me" and "Lights Out", with an encore of "Doctor Doctor", "Rock Bottom", "Mystery Train" and "Shoot Shoot".

Given the positive reviews that greeted the album upon its release, and the rave write-ups the band were getting on tour, it was evident that they were well on their way to capturing the glory days of old. UFO were empathically back in action.

Longstanding UFO fan Mark Blake reviewed 1992's gig at Birmingham's Institute for *Metal Forces*, writing: "The *High Stakes* ... material just sounds better and better as the band clock up those road miles ... They may be from a bygone age, but they're still capable of laying to waste so many of today's young upstarts. Where will it end? Hopefully not in tears. I'm still backing them every inch of the way!"

In 1993, UFO played two UK tours with Red Dogs and Wraith as support. The band also toured mainland Europe in 1993. The 1993 set list was certainly robust: "Natural Thing", "Mother Mary", "Let It Roll", "Out In The Street", "This Kid's", "Only You Can Rock Me", "Positive Forward", "Open And Willing", "Hot 'N' Ready", "Too Hot To Handle", "Love To Love", "Lights Out", "Doctor Doctor", "Rock Bottom" and "Shoot Shoot". It was inevitable that it would be the old songs which fans greeted enthusiastically. Sets usually ran for around 90 minutes and the overall playing was very skilful especially from guitarist Laurence Archer.

"The touring was great. It was great being with Pete," Archer reflects. "Pete's a prankster and it was always a good laugh on tour. Clive's always been a mate, a close friend of mine. It was good fun. I enjoyed the recording part of it. There wasn't anything I didn't really enjoy. It was just the end, really."[223]

However, the tour ended in literal pain after a drunken Mogg fell offstage and broke his leg on the last night during a performance at the White Nights Festival in St Petersburg, Russia, where the band mimed to a backing tape. This incident essentially brought about the end of this particular line-up.

Archer: "We were in St Petersburg in Russia. Phil had fell off the stage drunk and it had been a couple of years building the reputation back up with the promoters showing them that we could do it again and that we were pretty good. Phil fell off the wagon and in one fell swoop decided to launch himself off the stage and that was that for a period of time. When I came back to London, on reflection, it just didn't seem that it was going to happen. It seemed a little fragile. It must have been two years because we had toured Spain, Japan and various other countries. In Spain, Phil, without telling anybody, had got on a flight and flown home. Me, Clive and Pete turned up at the gig in the minibus from the hotel unknown that Phil had actually scarpered with the manager on a plane. Things added up. It was wild, varied and interesting. It was a very good laugh."[224]

Speaking about his experience of working with Mogg, on and off the wagon, Edwards says: "Phil would reach that point when he was really not nice to be around. He'd go into a very dark mood and be rude to people. He never was violent, but there was always the threat of violence. Like they say with whiskey drinkers, the eyes go and all of a sudden there's this demon there. Phil when he is sober is one of the nicest men in the world. He really is gentle and kind, an absolute sweetheart to be with and to work with. After the album, he sobered up and we went out on tour. He stayed sober until towards the end, then he got completely pissed and fell off the stage."[225]

Despite the various line-up changes, UFO have always been a people's band. There have been times when they have lost touch with their fans, but they've learned over the years not to take their fans for granted. The music business is a fickle world. Mogg has never been in a limo, nor does he have a cocky rock star attitude typical of so many lower grade musicians. He is, essentially, a regular London geezer.

High Stakes & Dangerous Men came as something of a Godsend for many seasoned rock fans; especially those that had no appetite for grunge. Grunge was a style of alternative rock that had largely spawned in the Seattle area. Bands such as Nirvana, Pearl Jam, Soundgarden, Alice In Chains and lesser known names like Melvins and Mad Season were just as influenced by Black Sabbath as they were The Clash and Misfits. Grunge, at its most basic, was a combination of metal and alternative rock and punk. They had no love whatsoever for the glam scene that dominated LA in the 1980s; in fact, grunge was the polar opposite.

However, many seasoned rock and metal fans did not care for grunge at all as it effectively put a spike in the head of the hard rock scene, thus recalling the days when punk killed prog and, what is now termed, classic rock. UFO was an inspiration to many of those bands; especially Pearl Jam. Pearl Jam's guitarist Mike McCready would even form a UFO tribute band with his fellow UFO fanboy friends called Flight To Mars. UFO's legacy continued to influence a wealth of musicians even if the band, in some fans' eyes, had become a former shadow of itself in the post Michael Schenker years. However, the band's latest release was something of a return to form.

The arrival of *High Stakes & Dangerous Men* may have only made a minor dent in the rock world, but it garnered enough enthusiasm from hardened UFO fans to warrant a reunion of the classic late 1970s line-up of Phil Mogg, Pete Way, Michael Schenker, Paul Raymond and Andy Parker. It was obvious to both Archer and Edwards that Mogg and Way wanted the Schenker era line-up to go ahead, so they quit UFO and joined Medicine Head.

The amount of money that Mogg and Way would make with Schenker far eclipsed anything they'd make in another incarnation of UFO. It was hard for Mogg to find any common ground with Schenker, but money talks and a reunion with Schenker could prove a financial pleasure. "As far as UFO goes it's unlikely there'll be another album unless it's with that line-up" Mogg admitted in 1993 to *RAW's* Dave Ling regarding a Schenker reunion. "The thing with Michael's been on and off for ten years. It's being discussed as we speak, so Pete and I have been writing songs and they're going very well, in the vein of *The Wild, The Willing And The Innocent*; good, heavy and with dynamic choruses."[226]

Fans were enthralled by the idea of a Schenker UFO reunion. Schenker had just come off the back of his debut solo album *Thank You* in 1993, but it's his work in MSG and UFO that he remains best known for. The new line-up was announced in 1993 – Schenker was back, baby. However, it did leave a somewhat bitter taste in the mouth for the rest of the *High Stakes* era line-up, namely, Clive Edwards and Laurence Archer. There was a strong feeling that the *High Stakes* album and line-up was merely a springboard to reunite the *Strangers In The Night* line-up.

Edwards: "It got to the point with the record company that there's still life in the old dog yet in terms of the band and the people. And of course the moment you do that, everyone starts talking, 'Well, I'll come up with this much money for Michael to be in the band ...' and you've got the original *Strangers In The Night* band and people know that it's only to last for one album and one tour. Phil and Michael are like the opposite ends of a piece of string. One's black and one's white. They can't be alone for longer than five minutes but it's money. Nobody had much money at that time, so there's a lot of pressure from the US."[227]

He continues: "We'd done a lot of the donkey work. When we got together, Phil and Pete couldn't get arrested off their previous incarnations. Phil had just fucked off home and left the band, and people knew about their demons. People wanted to see them as being serious and that they could still function. Myself and Laurence did a huge amount of work to get it off the ground and we got kicked in the nuts and pushed to one side and told, 'Fuck you, we're gonna go and earn some money now.' It's frustrating because if there had been another album it would probably have been better than *High Stakes* and I still rate that as an album – a lot better than the UFO albums that have vanished without a trace, especially the more recent ones. There's not a lot of tracks on them you'd listen to twice."[228]

Archer: "Well, basically there was a lull anyway, because when we came back from Russia I made my feelings known to the management and to the guys, and Phil had broken his leg, so he wasn't really doing anything for a couple of months. Nothing really happened for a while. I just called it a day, really, and went on to do some bits and pieces with a band called Medicine Head. I had put quite a bit of work in to getting that album done and wanted it to be right. It was a bit of a blow when things like that happen. I'm not blaming anybody. I'd say the management were at fault at the time. I understood what Phil was like. I knew how precious and fragile the whole thing could be and was. I understood that when I got the thing together. It was moving forward at that point, depending how much damage had been done to the promoters in Europe, and without having Michael involved."[229]

One idea that was thrown around was that, besides the *Strangers In The Night* line-up, they would have both Archer and Schenker in the band but, in all honesty, that was never going to work. Edwards and Archer felt like they had both been kicked in the balls, because they had done all the donkey work in getting the band rejuvenated. However, it's all water under the bridge, and Archer and Edwards do see Mogg and Way from time to time; they tend to laugh about the old days and recall all the funny incidents that happened throughout that period.

Not only was Schenker back in the team, but original drummer Andy Parker was returning too. Mogg's comments from an interview with *Kerrang!*'s Dave Dickson back in 1984 would be somewhat ironic in hindsight. He said: "I never liked, since I was a kid, a group whose members chop and change. I like to see a group and remember them as a group. We'd been through so many changes and that was one of the things that got me down ... chopping and changing people."[230]

However, many would agree that the true line-up of UFO has always been: Mogg, Way, Schenker, Raymond and Parker. The classic late 1970s line-up of UFO played a low-profile week-long tour of Germany and such was the rushed nature of the reunion that promoters were not even aware that the prodigal Schenker had returned to the band. The gigs were a big success for UFO, which saw them supported by the LA glam metal band Quiet Riot.

In the old days on the German tours, members of the band always enjoyed drinking and when they weren't rehearsing or doing a soundcheck they'd be having fun. On the Germany tours they'd sometimes place bets with the promoters for a game of five-a-side football in the afternoon. They'd play football, start partying, do the gig and then finish the party well into the early hours of the morning before going to bed.

Everyone from the band to their fans were rather shocked by the reunion. Some fans in attendance at the first German show thought it was going to be Paul Chapman playing lead guitar; they could not believe their eyes when Schenker walked onstage. There was almost a sense of, how the hell did it happen? Mogg and Way had spoken to Schenker at some acoustic gigs Scorpions had played; talks progressed from there into the real thing. The timing was right for all concerned and there's no doubt that the money was a big incentive to kiss and make up.

As soon as they started rehearsing, it just felt right. Certainly, they had a turbulent friendship but they always worked well musically and the band had known Schenker since he was a teenager, so there was significant personal history. Way had since moved to Copenhagen, where he'd bought a new apartment with his wife, and had to travel back to England for rehearsals. Nevertheless, big things were expected of UFO now that arguably Germany's greatest hard rock guitarist export had returned.

Misdemeanor producer Nick Tauber shared his thoughts about the band's line-up changes: "The problem with Phil is he keeps changing his mind … It's not good. There are great bands like the Stones that don't change the line-up and it's worked. The trouble with UFO is they keep going back to the original line-up. It's such a moving carpet that the fans don't know where they are. The only consistency is Phil's voice. Everything else keeps bloody changing. He doesn't realise that it's not helpful. I know he doesn't mean it … It's not good. If you have a great line-up you should just stick with it. If anyone comes back and says: 'I'd like to rejoin.' Just say, 'Look we've got a line-up now. That was the past and we just wanna keep going.'"[231]

Indeed, it was felt by some quarters of the band's fanbase that not enough time and effort had been given to the *High Stakes* line-up. After all, they had released an excellent album and played brilliantly together onstage, but not everyone felt the same way. Mogg spoke to *Kerrang!*'s

Dave Reynolds in 1994 about that line-up: "It had nowhere left to go. That was more or less the point where me 'n' Pete decided to have another chat with Michael, and get Andy and Paul involved."[232]

UFO played not only material from the legendary *Strangers In The Night* live album, but also material off Schenker's *Thank You*. Europe was obviously not a problem for the rejuvenated UFO, but what about the notoriously fickle American market? In April 1994, they played at a festival in San Antonio which also included Motörhead, Blue Öyster Cult and Yngwie Malmsteen. "I think that when they went out to America with Michael, Pete was a little bit alone," says Laurence Archer. "He never spent that much time with Phil really. I think he became a bit of a loner."[233]

In June, they flew to Japan where they performed "Natural Thing", "Mother Mary", "Let It Roll", "Out In The Street", "This Kid's", "Only You Can Rock Me", "Love To Love", "Hot 'N' Ready", "Too Hot To Handle", "Lights Out", "Doctor Doctor", "Rock Bottom", "Shoot Shoot" and "C'mon Everybody". What was initially arranged as a taster tour of Germany ended up being far longer than planned, with other countries involved simply because word of mouth had spread about how brilliantly UFO were playing with Schenker back in the band.

The band's initial aim was to concentrate on playing live. They did not approach a label straight away. The one label that approached the band questioned whether the five members could stay in the same rehearsal room for more than a week without the whole thing falling apart. The band decided that they needed to reconnect with the industry machine by getting organised with a record deal, management and so on. Later in the year the band signed to the label Zero Corporation for a high advance, with the label owning Asian rights while the band owned Rest of World rights.

UFO set about recording a new album. The new material had a great deal to live up to. They could not make anything half-baked. It simply had to be of the same quality as past releases.

Gearing up for the new album, a compilation called *TNT* was released in 1994 via Essential Records. It consists of *Lights Out In Tokyo* as well as some previously unreleased live material notably songs culled from *Parker's Birthday* bootleg recorded in Texas back in 1979.

Way offered his views on life in a rock band to *RAW*'s Kirk Blows in 1991: "Being in a rock band is like running a business in some ways and somebody should've said: 'Look, take two months off, and why don't you have a few days of not drinking? What do you need to do those drugs for? Why don't you have a rest, go and play football.' We touched the Twilight Zone, it was extremely excessive."[234]

Even with Schenker's return, could UFO top the previous studio album they recorded together: 1978's *Obsession*? The jury was out.

CHAPTER
EIGHT

Swimming With Sharks –
The Many Returns Of Michael Schenker
(1995 –2002)

*"I don't think we ever thought of ourselves as rock stars.
We were just a bunch of blokes playing in a band and getting
to a reasonably successful level."*

Phil Mogg[235]

With Schenker back on board, the band hit the studio in 1995 to record *Walk On Water*. Schenker: "I'd always known that this classic line-up never quite fulfilled its true potential. It's always been my hope that one day we would get back together and realise what we could still be achieved [*sic*]. For whatever reason it took this long for it to happen, but we're all glad that it did."[236]

For Schenker, the notion was for everyone to forget about anything that had happened in UFO from 1979 to 1995, meaning that *Walk On Water* was intended as a continuation of *Phenomenon*, *Force It*, *No Heavy Pettin'*, *Lights Out*, *Obsession* and *Strangers In The Night*. Throughout those years, the band had a special chemistry which made them one of the most recognised and influential hard rock bands of their era. So in a sense they were now completing unfinished business.

Walk On Water was recorded at Rumbo Recordings in Canoga Park, California with producer Ron Nevison back at the helm and the line-up of Mogg, Way, Schenker, Raymond and Parker. Of course, Nevison had worked with the band in LA before, with the *Obsession* album back in 1978. Had the band changed their working methods after so much time had elapsed?

Nevison: "It was fun to get back together with everybody. Everybody was reasonably sober. Everything was smoothed out between them at that point. With the other two studio albums I had done, Phil Mogg always waited till the last minute to write the lyrics. I'd only have working titles and I wouldn't even know what the songs are about, which is not real popular with me. Nothing changed!"[237]

Could the band recreate the magic of the late 1970s? Mark Philips added backing vocals as did Denny Godber, the band's hairdresser from the 1970s. It was obvious that the reunion was all about nostalgia, especially with Nevison onboard who'd last worked with the band on *Strangers In The Night*, and the fact that they re-recorded the vintage classics "Doctor Doctor" and "Lights Out" was simply a dose of nostalgia. The fundamental reason why they chose to revisit those songs was a way of linking the past with the present.

"We talked about it," explains Nevison about re-recording "Doctor Doctor". "I thought it was one of their best songs. I had recorded it on *Strangers In The Night*, the live album. It was not something I had recorded, originally. It was a staple of their live show. I said let's update it and they were up for it and it was nice to have a familiar song on the new album, so it was almost like a cover of themselves. I don't remember whose idea it was exactly, but everybody agreed that it would be a good idea. We tried it and if it didn't work out we would have tried something else."[238]

For Parker, it was like stepping into a time warp. He'd been out of UFO for over a decade. "I was surprised that Andy made it over," says Nevison. "There was talk that he wouldn't be able to come. He had pretty much gotten out of the rock 'n' roll business and was working with his family in the construction business. It was great. Everybody was fine. It went really fast as far as I remember. No problems with anybody."[239]

Inevitably, it was a strange experience for all concerned because of the amount of time they'd had apart, but they made it work. Once they settled into the recording routine, it was like they'd never been apart. The way each of them worked musically hadn't changed and they each still maintained a love of making songs.

Nevison did not have any problems with Schenker, having not only worked with Schenker on *Lights Out*, *Obsession* and *Strangers In The Night* but also 1981's *MSG*, the second album from the Michael Schenker Group. Nevison had problems with Schenker during that album, but *Walk On Water* was a breeze. Nevison: "There's no question he's one of the most brilliant, musical and talented guitar players that has ever been born, especially in that genre. There's no question about that."[240]

Walk On Water opens with the hard-hitting and edgy "A Self-Made Man", while "Venus" has Paul Raymond's stamp all over it and Schenker gives as good as he gets with a terrific riff in full motion. "Pushed To The Limit" is a speedy rocker with a suitably powerful lead lick, while "Stopped By A Bullet (Of Love)" sees a charismatic vocal performance from Phil Mogg. "Darker Days" is a heavy number with a wailing frontal riff. "Running On Empty" proves that, even in the 1990s, UFO were still accomplished musicians. "Knock, Knock" is a cheerful rocker with some pounding drums. "Dreaming Of Summer" is an effective mid-paced song with some memorable lines. "Doctor Doctor" (new version) achieves the impossible by sounding both modern and classic, and "Lights Out" (new version) still has the ability to get the listener to perform air guitar. The three bonus tracks are more like advertisements for the solo projects of various band members. "Fortune Town" by Mogg and Way is curiously heavy and almost aggressive in its rock stomp, while "I Will Be There" by MSG is somewhat more controlled. "Public Enemy #1" by Paul Raymond Project, the final song on the album, sees Raymond venturing back to his blues roots.

Walk On Water is an excellent album and remains one of the band's finest achievements. The title itself implies a belief that this band is the business and can do anything including, walking on water. It's both modern and fresh, yet unmistakeably UFO. A return to form, indeed. Released in April 1995 by Eagle Records, it failed to chart in the USA and UK. Would UFO ever return to the charts?

Critics gave *Walk On Water* very positive reviews. A majority of rock scribes were of the collective opinion that it was undoubtedly a worthy follow-up to the magnificent *Strangers In The Night*.

One reviewer declared on *House Of Shred*: "Michael Schenker soars through this record with the speed of light. Yes the mighty UFO are back! With the killer riff of the opener 'Self Made Man', this album catches your attention immediately."

Fondly referred to by UFO fans, *Walk On Water* has not attained the sort of longevity that previous Schenker era UFO albums have, although it is an excellent release and one of the band's finest albums. If anything, *Walk On Water* should be in a poll of rock's most undervalued releases.

Asked which is his favourite of the three studios albums, Nevison responds: "They're all totally different but I guess I'm proudest of *Lights Out*. It has 'Love To Love' which is one of my favourite songs ever."[241]

The reunion may not have been as highly publicised as those of KISS or Black Sabbath, but it was still a red letter day for fans. During an age of Britpop and American college-rock-bands-done-well such as REM, UFO were staying true to the hard rock sound of the 1970s, which in the mid-1990s seemed like such a bygone era of music. Rock had seemingly disappeared from view and, while it remained popular with loyal fans of the genre, it had dropped out of the mainstream consciousness. But that is the capricious nature of the industry; when fundamentally brilliant bands like UFO and Thunder fight against music industry ignorance and snobbery, it is obvious why many bands from that period struggled to survive. Regardless of what the mainstream media assumes, there will always be a fanbase for rockers such as UFO. Artists don't survive for over 30 years without having talent and drive, but above all else it is about music.

Pete Way was asked by the Dutch rock magazine *Aardschok* for his thoughts on the album. He replied: "With pride. The recording was very natural and very disciplined. There have been times that it was different. It is a good album that shows that a band like UFO has a right to exist in 1996. I am already looking forward to the new album that hopefully will be released this year. Whether we will be working with Ron Nevison again? I do not know. It would be a challenge to work with Mike Clink, a former assistant to Ron."[242]

In 1995, the band hit the road with former AC/DC drummer Simon Wright on the drum-stool after Parker decided to leave the band to help run his family business rather than tour.

Wright explains: "A friend of mine put me in touch with Michael's then manager, Bella Piper. Michael was looking for musicians for his MSG project and, as far as she told me, that was what I was going to audition for. As the weeks passed, with many phone calls back and forth with her, she finally confided that it was UFO I was gonna play for and there was no audition, I had the job if I wanted it. So, my wife and I drove to Phoenix with my drums, I met them and we seemed to get along great and things just progressed from there."[243]

There were still noticeable tensions between Mogg and Schenker, so things hadn't really progressed for Parker since he was last in UFO. Parker praised the album and enjoyed the experience of being back in the band to an extent, but felt it was best to quit again in order to do his own thing. Unfortunately, Parker felt that there would be problems with Schenker when it came to touring. Would he be proven right?

Born in Lancashire, Wright first sat behind a drum kit aged 13 and joined a number of bands in his youth including Tora Tora and the New Wave Of British Heavy Metal band, A II Z. He joined AC/DC in 1983 after Phil Rudd was fired. Leaving AC/DC in 1989 (his replacement was Chris Slade) after three albums with the band, he joined Dio for the 1990 *Lock Up The Wolves* album.

The American tour in June 1995, which included a headlining performance at the Milwaukee Festival, saw UFO supported by Triangle and Lode. Americans really took to the Schenker reunion and ticket sales were healthy. The band played two sold out nights in Hollywood, three in Palo Alto and four in Chicago at the Vic Theatre. Touring continued throughout the year and surprised critics and record labels, because most venues were sold out despite the band not having an American record deal or any financial backing.

"Interesting to say the least, never a dull moment!," enthuses Wright when asked what it was like to tour with UFO. "They like a good laugh! Playing wise, I thought the band sounded great, we got really tight ... Michael sounded awesome; I've admired his playing for years. We seemed to get along O.K. too which was nice, I had heard he can be a little strange at times, but as I said his playing was incredible and to actually play alongside him was a great honour."[244]

However, Schenker left the outfit part way through the road jaunt, which caused the band to cancel several high-profile concerts. The seemingly friendly atmosphere in the band was disrupted on October 20 before they were due to go onstage at the Hollywood Palace. Schenker approached a T-shirt bootlegger outside the venue, but the bootlegger attacked the guitarist, hitting him twice in the face before running off. At the band's next gig, the following night in Redondo Beach, they sailed through the set, but on October 22 at the Modesto California Ballroom, Schenker failed to turn up. Some reports at the time suggested that Bella Piper informed the band that Schenker thought the group had the night off.

The band's scheduled performance at the Sacramento Boardwalk on October 24 was cancelled, as were the next fifteen shows in the USA and Canada going right through to the end of November. The German gigs planned for the same month were also axed. There was no other way around the situation except to cancel the gigs because contractual obligations stated that Schenker had to appear onstage, thus ruling out the possibility of a replacement.

"I think he's [Schenker] a brilliant guitar player," says producer Leo Lyons. "I always hear him as an example of somebody who doesn't do verbal diarrhoea on a guitar. He actually thinks about what he's going to do and works it out. It's perfectionism and that's what Schenker was. You put a perfectionist with a load of party guys and there's bound to be a little bit of friction."[245]

Rumours circulated that there had been fights between Mogg and Schenker, and that Mogg had slipped back into alcohol abuse. It was a sad end to what had started out so promisingly.

Pete Way responded to those rumours when he spoke to the Dutch rock magazine *Aardschok* in March 1996. "Absolutely not true! On the contrary, Phil was the man who kept us all going. I think it is a pity that the press has printed this story, it does him great injustice. I am the last one to deny that there was not any drinking and pill taking, but it was not Phil. Such things happen during a tour, you start off as a priest and end up as the devil. Certain habits have a way of coming back during a tour. But I can say that if you compare it to the old days, we were all clean on stage."[246]

Although some reports alleged that Schenker's contract stated the band could not work as UFO at all without his involvement, Mogg, Way, Raymond and Wright hooked up with guitarist John Norum of the Swedish band Europe for some rehearsals in mainland Europe. Wright had contributed to Norum's *World's Away* but the UFO collaboration did not work out and failed to go beyond the rehearsal stages, which also included some sessions with guitarists George Bellas and possibly keyboardist Matt

Guillory, known for his band Dali's Dilemma and his work with James LaBrie. UFO once again became seemingly dormant.

Further compilations followed with the release of *The Best Of UFO* (Gold series) in 1996, focusing mostly on Schenker material from the 1970s, but also taking songs from *No Place To Run, The Wild, The Willing And The Innocent, Mechanix* and *Misdemeanor*.

For a proposed, unnamed project the original UFO duo had signed to Motörhead's manager Todd Singerman and hooked up with Dio drummer Vinnie Appice and guitarist Tracy G, but nothing materialised as the duo spent time trying to get a reunion with Schenker and Chapman off the ground. The *Parker's Birthday* bootleg resurfaced again but in an official capacity, which was released in the hope of enticing Schenker and Chapman to consider a reunion.

Phil Mogg and Pete Way had put UFO on the backburner to concentrate on the Mogg/Way side project with the debut album, *Edge Of The World* in 1997. They teamed up with the American guitarist George Bellas and drummer Aynsley Dunbar for the first album, which included backing vocals from Mr Big's Eric Martin. The Liverpool born drummer had long been established as one of Britain's greatest. He famously auditioned for The Jimi Hendrix Experience, but despite facing a tough decision, Hendrix chose Mitch Mitchell. Dunbar went on to drum for John Mayall And The Bluesbreakers, Frank Zappa, David Bowie, Lou Reed, Ian Hunter, Journey, Sammy Hagar, Whitesnake, Jefferson Airplane and Ronnie Montrose.

A surprise came in 1997 when UFO – Mogg, Way, Schenker, Raymond and Wright – played two sold out gigs at Hollywood Palace in August. The second show on August 4 was attended by some of rock's most well known musicians, including Joe Elliott and Vivian Campbell of Def Leppard, Mike Inez of Alice In Chains, Europe's John Norum, Motörhead's Phil Campbell and Mikkey Dee and Slash, who joined the band for a version of "C'mon Everybody". UFO then arranged a tour of the States through October.

Wright: "Michael would keep to himself most of the time, travelled separately from the rest of us, I think because of disagreements in the past, so really that seemed the only way they could tour. Michael was happy and the band did our own thing, it seemed to work! He was always very polite to me and everyone else before we went on stage, but I think he needed his own space."[247]

From November 13 through to early 1998, UFO toured Europe with Danger Danger as support on the continent, while the lengthy UK tour had Dirty Deeds as opening act. The tour included a performance at the legendary London Astoria, where they played "Natural Thing", "Mother Mary", "Self-Made Man", "Electric Phase", "This Kid's", "Out In The Street", "One More For The Rodeo", "Venus", "Pushed To The Limit", "Love To Love", "Too Hot To Handle", "Only You Can Rock Me", "Lights Out", "Doctor Doctor", "Rock Bottom" and "Shoot Shoot". There was evidently a balanced mix of vintage UFO songs with some obscure tracks and a few sprinklings of more recent material.

However, Schenker left the band during a Japanese tour in early 1998. Paul Raymond reflected on this period in 2005 when discussing the highs and lows of his history with UFO: "The low point has to be at the Nakano Sun Plaza, Tokyo in 1998, when Michael slammed his guitar down and stormed off stage in the middle of the show. It was the worst place he could have chosen to do such a thing as the Japanese are such honourable people and it disgraced the whole band, and damaged our reputation over there irreparably."[248]

While Paul Raymond was working on a solo album, which included vocals from Mogg, Way, Raymond and Wright, Mogg started to work on some new UFO material for a proposed studio album but nothing materialised, even though they had rehearsed in London in 1998. Raymond subsequently left UFO and the group was seemingly laid to rest. Or was it?

The future of UFO remained uncertain especially as the case surrounding Schenker's possible ownership of the name UFO, and that he'd made the rest of the band sign contracts stating that they could not perform as UFO without his involvement, were still ongoing.

1999 would see the band's 30th anniversary, so fans were eager for the band to push aside whatever arguments they had and simply get back to making music and playing live. But rock 'n' roll does not work like that, not in the post-grunge years, anyway. One idea to call themselves Lights Out without Michael Schenker was discussed, but it would that mean they had become their own tribute band. Would such a project sit well with fans? Raymond: "I don't know why we signed it, the idea was that a group contract would cement us together, but it was wickedly done ... It's a problem because Michael only wants to be in UFO when it suits him ..."[249]

Even though Schenker (who had dyed his hair jet black), had left UFO, he nevertheless chose to tour on the 1998 all-star G3 guitarists' road jaunt with Uli Jon Roth and Joe Satriani, and released the MSG album *The Unforgiven* the following year. Interestingly, it was around this time that former UFO guitarist Tommy McClendon reappeared with a new band called Soulmotor, that also featured Tesla bassist Brian Wheat. McClendon also played guest guitars on Tommy Tutone's album *Rich Text Files* in 1998.

While Mogg and Way were still trying to negotiate a UFO reunion with Schenker, the duo released the second Mogg/Way album, *Chocolate Box,* in 1999. It features former Edwin Dare And The Truth guitarist Jeff Kollman and contributions from Raymond and Wright. With UFO seemingly out of action for the time being, Way resurrected his side-project Waysted, whilst Raymond released his third solo album *Man On A Mission* with guest vocals from Mogg and a re-vamped version of "Lights Out". Wright, meanwhile, had left UFO altogether to rejoin Dio. The semi-official live album *Werewolves Of London* with Schenker on guitars was released towards the end of 1999.

In 2000, Schenker rejoined UFO yet again and the band began work on their first album of new material since 1995's *Walk On Water*. That same year, Michael Schenker released his fourth instrumental album, the Mike Varney produced *Adventures Of The Imagination*, with Aynsley Dunbar on drums. Schenker stated that the individual projects helped strengthen the chemistry between the band members and this aided them with creating better music for the upcoming album.

Way: "Spirit within UFO has never been better. It doesn't sound like a tired record. Its basis is hard rock, but the choruses are very catchy, some are almost Beatle-ish. We weren't trying to re-tread old ground, but as soon as you hear it you know it's us."[250]

Covenant, featuring Aynsley Dunbar, Pete Way, Phil Mogg and Michael Schenker, was recorded at the Prairie Sun Recording Studios in Cotati, California and LCM Studios in Novato, California. The band co-produced the album with Mike Varney and associate producer Ralph Patlan, with additional musicians Jesse Bradman (backing vocals) and Kevin Carlson (keyboards).

With personal grudges seemingly a thing of the past, the band appeared to work much better this time around recalling the old days back in London in the mid-1970s. They were able to work on a new set of material and even harboured thoughts of touring the USA for the first time in a few years. There was more spontaneity in the studio this time round and positive vibes helped fuel the band's muse. There was a strong feeling within the camp that they were on the right path. But the question that has always plagued UFO is: would it last?

Covenant opens with "Love Is Forever" before the pounce of "Unraveled" takes the album into harder territory. "Miss The Lights" is a more melodic song though Mogg's vocals sound a tad too forced. "Midnight Train" is a furiously charged rocker with some stunning guitar-bass-drums interplay. "Fool's Gold" slows down the pace considerably; it is a somewhat average ballad. "In The Middle Of Madness" is a nifty song aided by Schenker's finely-tuned guitars and controlled performance. "The Smell Of Money" is a hard-hitting number with plenty of grit and gusto in Mogg's voice. "Rise Again" is an interestingly arranged track with slight shifts in tempo, while "Serenade" sees a sustained performance from drummer Dunbar – though it is hardly a standout track. "Cowboy Joe" is one step closer to the blues and "The World And His Dog" closes the album in a raucous fashion.

The album features a second disc of live classics with a tracklisting that was incorrectly printed on the artwork. The live songs, titled *Live USA*, feature Simon Wright on drums and Paul Raymond on guitar and keyboards. UFO have always been a great live band regardless of the changes in personnel. The tracklisting runs as follows: "Mother Mary", "This Kid's", "Let It Roll", "Out In The Street", "Venus", "Pushed To The Limit" and "Love To Love".

Covenant has some standout rock songs, yet it is a flawed album. It does not have the immediate intimacy of *Walk On Water*, though it deserves more attention than it has been given since its release in July 2000. The new millennium saw the band failing to chart in both the USA and UK.

Covenant received distinctly average reviews with the generally consensus being that it failed to better *Walk On Water*.

Dave Ling wrote in *Classic Rock*: "... after the benefit of five or six spins *Covenant* (the initial copies of which come with an official seven-track live bootleg) proves well worthy of investigation. Not a classic but a fine return to form." Also, Chris Yancik wrote in *House Of Shred*: "Obviously, Messrs Schenker and Mogg are intelligent enough to know which side their bread is buttered on, and they have proven once again that the product is indeed greater than the sum of the parts. With any luck, they'll keep it together long enough to hit these shores (US) as tentatively slated for early next year. 'Til then, crank it up and keep your fingers crossed!"

Covenant has slipped into the misty corners of rock history and it's doubtful it will ever resurface, given the generally lukewarm reception it received on its original 2000 release. Better things were expected of the band at the time.

Fans were pleased that UFO – given the nature of their history – had even managed to come out with a new album at all, even if there was a general feelings that it was slightly below par. "My analysis of it is, that a band goes through a growing process," Pete Way said to Steph Perry of *Rocknotes Webzine* in 2000, "for example if I was in the Eagles and after we came out with *Hotel California*, we came out with *The Long Run*, people might say that one is better than the other, but both were hugely popular."[251]

The band hit the road for some more live shows to promote *Covenant*. They toured the UK with support from German guitar wizard Uli Jon Roth, while the European shows saw the band supported by "The Voice Of Rock" Glenn Hughes and Moon' Doc. The tour featured yet another new line-up of UFO, with Luis Maldonado from Mogg/Way on rhythm guitar and keyboards and drummer Jeff Martin, best remembered for his tenures in Badlands, Black Symphony and Racer X. Their set list was a suitable mix of the old and the new: "Love Is Forever", "Unraveled", "Miss The Lights", "Mother Mary", "Self-Made Man", "Out In The Street", "This Kid's", "Venus", "Pushed To The Limit", "Love To Love", "Too Hot To Handle", "Midnight Train", "Only You Can Rock Me", "Rock Bottom" and "Doctor Doctor", before an encore of "Cherry", "Shoot Shoot" and "Lights Out".

However, trouble hit the band when they played a now infamous gig at the Manchester Apollo on 24 November 2000. They just had a few dates to finish off in the UK when all hell broke loose. Mogg's voice was not in the best of shape and there was a reported incident between Schenker and the band at a dressing room in Newcastle, which they had played 24 hours previously. The German guitarist walked onstage in front of the Northern English rock crowd with a black eye and the word "Spike" penned on his forehead, which was reportedly in reference to Spike of The Quireboys who'd given him the black eye the day before in Newcastle. Apparently, inebriated by alcohol, the now slightly overweight guitarist refused to play guitar solos and bashed into Mogg on purpose. Schenker even offered his guitar to Mogg at one point for the singer to play. The audience, rightfully angry and slightly confused, booed the guitarist who shouted back "This audience sucks and so do I!" The band left the stage, but Schenker ran back to encourage the audience. The rest of the tour was cancelled.

Schenker spoke to *Classic Rock*'s Dave Ling about the night: "It had been very painful for me to watch Pete Way lose it concert after concert. His behaviour was obnoxious; he would constantly bump into me and distract me from doing a good job. I wanted to show Pete what it would be like if I did what he does."[252]

Ever restless, Way also released a solo album called *Amphetamine* in 2000 that was recorded at the legendary Rockfield Studios in Wales, which was followed by *Pete Way (Alive In Cleveland)* in 2002 and *Acoustic Animal* in 2007.

Following the Manchester debacle, UFO again went dormant. However, a high-profile tribute album called *Only UFO Can Rock Me* was released in early 2001. It features contributions from Rainbow's Doogie White, Motörhead guitarist Phil Campbell, Fastway singer Lea Hart, guitarist Bernie Tormé, Wishbone Ash's Bob Skeat and former Grim Reaper singer Steve Grimmett. Former UFO keyboardist Jem Davis also guest starred on the album.

Mogg, Way and Schenker joined Uli Jon Roth onstage at the Rock & Blues Festival at Donington, England in 2001 and Cream's bassist/singer Jack Bruce also joined them. The performance was released as *Live At Castle Donington* in Japan by Nippon Crown and through the German label SPV in Europe. The makeshift band played not only Uli Jon Roth material but also UFO's "Let It Roll", "Rock Bottom" and "Doctor Doctor".

Having released the MSG album *Be Aware Of Scorpions* in 2001, Schenker teamed up with Way and drummer Jeff Martin for some studio sessions in July and August 2001 under the moniker The Plot. The results of those sessions were finally released in 2003 as *The Plot*. It was announced that the band would also tour as support to Schenker's own group on an American tour in late 2001, beginning with three nights at the Chicago House Of Blues from November 26.

However, it turned out that The Plot would only perform four songs during the middle section of MSG's gigs. The guitarist continued to display some odd behaviour despite beginning the road jaunt with solid performances. On December 6 at the Icon Supperclub in Palo Alto, Schenker struggled to finish the opening song "Into The Arena" causing the show to be cancelled. The audience were informed that the guitarist was suffering from an illness and they would be able to get a refund. Subsequent gigs were re-arranged before full cancellation. The tour was a disaster and 2001 to 2002 was a truly dreadful period for Schenker.

Phil Mogg also found time to create the side project $ign Of 4 (originally called Stonetowne); releasing just one album *Dancing With St Peter* in 2002. Danny Peyronel re-emerged with his debut solo album *Make The Monkey Dance*, which included a new version of "Highway Lady" from *No Heavy Petting*.

In 2002, UFO went back in the studio to record *Sharks*. It would be their final album with Michael Schenker, the last to feature Aynsley Dunbar, who'd worked with the band in the studio since 2000, and UFO's sixteenth album in total.

"He's a funny guy," Mogg said about Dunbar. "Aynsley fits right in, he comes from Liverpool and he still retains his Liverpool sense of humour, very clever and very amusing. I knew him since we did a Mogg/Way album six years ago, though we did a gig with him when he was in Journey – I don't remember the gig but we must have met about then."[253]

UFO now consisted of Mogg, Way, Schenker and Dunbar, while in the studio they were joined by Mike Varney (playing guitar fills and outro guitar solo on "Fighting Man"), keyboardist Kevin Carlson and backing vocalists Jesse Bradman and Luis Maldonado.

The album was produced by Varney with Steve Fontano – who also engineered and mixed it – at Prairie Sun Recording Studios in Cotati, California in 2002. They had a tight schedule which didn't work especially well for the band as they preferred to work at their own leisurely pace, as we've seen! Varney had some ideas of his own, as did Mogg and Way, and together the trio would come up with enough strong material for an album. Mogg and Way flew to California about twelve days in advance of the first day of recording to rehearse, jam and run through the new material. It's a pity that Dunbar never went on the road with UFO because of schedule clashes, as in the studio he worked brilliantly with them.

As a side note, the band photography by Pat Johnson shows Schenker sporting a thick scruffy beard, beanie hat and glasses. The good looking blonde haired Aryan guitar god of the 1970s was emphatically in the past. Schenker looked worn down and pale during this era.

Sharks opens with plenty of grit and dirt on the track "Outlaw Man", though "Quicksilver Rider" fails to make a long-lasting impression. "Serenity" is an average ballad lacking a memorable chorus, but "Deadman Walking" is a surprisingly cheerful little number with a sturdy lead lick. "Shadow Dancer" has an aggressive riff which some of the other songs need, while "Someone's Gonna Have To Pay" sees Way offering a steady bass line on a track that is very bluesy and almost funky with its melody. "Sea Of Faith" is nothing special; the melody is fairly insubstantial though Mogg's voice sounds impassioned. "Fighting Man" brings a rock sound back to proceedings; the drums and guitars are excellent. "Perfect View" opens with a strong lead riff while "Crossing Over" offers a strong melodic texture. "Hawaii", an instrumental, closes the album and leaves little impression.

The Japanese version typically included some bonus tracks: live versions of "Only You Can Rock Me", "Too Hot To Handle" and "Rock Bottom" that had been recorded in Buffalo during the band's USA tour in 1995, when they were promoting *Walk On Water*.

Sharks has its flaws, but it is an album which is worth revisiting from time to time. It is not perfect by any means and there are some rough edges, but in time it grows on the listener.

Sharks was released through Shrapnel Records in September 2002 and guess what? Yeah, it didn't chart on either side of the Atlantic.

Speaking about the album to *Revelationz*, Mogg enthused: "I think it's more rocky. More kind of how we used to go in and ... you know, we picked songs that really worked rather than working for ages on material that comes out maybe not sounding that great. We have gone for the ones that kinda grab you."[254]

Some fans felt that both *Covenant* and *Sharks* failed to follow in the footsteps of the acclaimed *Walk On Water*. There was a sense that Schenker's playing was by numbers. Critics gave *Sharks* the tentative thumbs up although it did not go without its detractors.

Andrew McNeice wrote on *Melodicrock.com*: "Flat. Generally, the album sounds loose and raw. It will be personal choice whether this album rates higher or lower than *Covenant*. Musically there are some blues rock moments and some '70s classic rock attitude, not to mention some of the feel of the last two albums." Also, Shelly Harris stated on *Rough Edge*: "While this particular album may not be the best vehicle to illustrate to the new generation of retro rockers precisely just why UFO were (and still are) so beloved as hard rock royalty (it might take one of their legendary – but all too rare – live performances to really convince most of the next wave of up and coming guitar-rock connoisseurs of the heaven-on-earth charm, substance, and historical impact of UFO on the genre), *Sharks* is definitely a tasty and satisfying morsel for the already converted."

Sharks has since garnered little attention. It appears that with the possible exception of *Walk On Water*, the second Michael Schenker era was somewhat underwhelming. Also there was too much to live up to, considering how highly revered the first era remains. It seemed that *Covenant* and *Sharks* represented the winding down of this particular phase of the band's career. It had essentially peaked too soon with *Walk On Water*.

However, UFO did not tour to support *Sharks*, much to the frustration of fans. Instead, Way took his solo band (guitarist Walt James and drummer Scott Phillips), from his first album, on the road with him for some low key gigs in Ohio. Mogg also planned his first ever solo gig at the London Marquee Club on November 19. If anything, UFO had become something of a sporadic and uncertain band. Fans simply did not know what was going to happen next.

In a seemingly never ending series of UFO compilations, the ten track *The Best Of UFO* was released in 2002, focusing on material from 1976 to 1980. It was part of EMI's 'Ten Best' series, while Smallstone Records released *Sucking In The 70s*, a collection of cover versions of famous 1970s rock songs, where Fireball Ministry recorded a version of "Doctor Doctor". 2002 also saw the release of the Riot album *Through The Storm*, which includes a version of "Only You Can Rock Me". "Lights Out" was also issued as a one track single, limited to just a 1,000 copies, by Zoom Club label in October to promote their *Re-Active Live* archive collection.

If this is all starting to sound a bit depressing, just remember that you can't keep old rockers down. UFO were about to embark on one of their most creative and successful periods in many years.

CHAPTER
NINE

The Wild Ones –
The Rebirth Of UFO
(2003 –2008)

"We take the music seriously, obviously.
But we're out to have fun and for everyone else to have fun."

Andy Parker[255]

UFO released *Live On Earth* in September 2003, featuring most of the classic late 1970s line-up: Mogg, Way, Schenker and Raymond, with Wright on drums. It was recorded on 29 January 1998 in Vienna. The reissue of the album also includes two bonus tracks from concerts recorded in 1977 and 1995. The original version features classic UFO material with a few new songs from *Walk On Water* plus the tracks "Electric Phase" and "One More For The Rodeo". As with most veteran rock bands, there is a thirst amongst UFO collectors for live material.

UFO has always been a hardworking live band. Pete Way: "Sure you get paid, but it's not about the money. It's about the enjoyment. One thing that's special about UFO, is to be on stage with UFO, and see people that have been with you for 20 years getting a sheer delight out of the band. We owe them another album."[256]

After the release of 2002's *Sharks*, Michael Schenker left the band again, which was announced in January 2003. This time it was final. Schenker struggled with some personal problems after he left his wife and their two children, and he reportedly underwent some financial difficulties after his manager supposedly ran off with his money. He was at a very low ebb, even selling three of his famous Gibson Flying Vs – his Number 1 Flying V sold for a reported $18,000; a pittance for such an iconic guitar. Later auctions also included various personal items such as clothing and several more guitars. He also sold a tour bus. Schenker then released the eighth MSG album, *Arachnophobiac,* in 2003, having signed to the independent label Mascot Records and, with two years of touring, he was able to help get his business and finances back on solid ground.

Pete Way announced plans to rejuvenate Waysted with Paul Chapman and original singer Fin, while UFO released a statement saying that Europe guitarist John Norum was hired as Schenker's replacement for the second time. Months later, Norum issued a press statement saying he had declined the offer.

Phil Mogg expressed his opinions on UFO to *Get Ready To Rock*'s Jason Ritchie: "I did say in other interviews that maybe we would do some festivals in the summer. But the way things look now, unless something dramatic happens in terms of health and fitness, I can't see UFO playing live."[257]

In July 2003, rumours began to circulate that former Vicious Rumors guitarist Vinnie Moore had been hired. He was eventually announced as Schenker's replacement, joining officially in 2004.

Vinnie Moore is one of the most iconic guitar shredders in rock, standing alongside Yngwie Malmsteen, Eddie Van Halen and Tony MacAlpine. Born Vincent Moore in New Castle, Delaware, USA on 14 April 1964, he had a quick hand on the guitar and by age 12 was already playing professionally. He caught the attention of Mike Varney of Shrapnel Records, appeared in a Pepsi commercial in 1985 and released his debut solo album *Mind's Eye* in 1986, which also features MacAlpine on keyboards, Andy West on bass and Tommy Aldridge on drums.

The album, released via Shrapnel, was a hit and sold over 100,000 copies. Moore went on to play guitar on the debut album by the metal band Vicious Rumors. *Soldiers Of The Night* features a solo song by Moore called "Invader" which is akin to Van Halen's "Eruption" in terms of its axe shredding dexterity. He joined Alice Cooper's band for the 1991 *Hey Stoopid* album and tour. Moore continued to release solo albums, as well as some instructional videos on how to play the guitar, before he joined UFO.

Moore received a phone call one day from a friend, who'd also been a tour manager for UFO. He told Moore that UFO were on the lookout for a new guitarist to replace Schenker. Moore sent a CD of his work to UFO's manager Peter Knorn (of United Talents Management in Hannover) who'd also managed Michael Schenker. Moore had previously opened for Schenker on a USA tour, so he had met Knorn before.

About two weeks later, after thinking he wouldn't hear anything back, Knorn called Vinnie and told him that Mogg thought highly of his guitar playing, so he got the gig after he auditioned in person. Moore grew up idolising Schenker, Eddie Van Halen, Robin Trevor and Larry Carlton, so he knew in a way that he would immediately feel at home in UFO.

However, once it was announced that Moore was the new UFO guitarist, some fans chatted online that he was not going to be the right fit for the band, so he had to prove to them he was more than capable of replacing Schenker.

It did not seem so long ago that Moore was just the usual rock loving American kid, listening to UFO albums and mimicking Michael Schenker. Moore fitted into UFO with ease right from the get-go, although it took him some time to learn that a sense of humour is a priority in the band. Life in UFO is so unpredictable, so crazy, that to take it seriously would probably lead one to a nervous breakdown.

There are *Spinal Tap* moments and many pranks that are typical of English rock bands from UFO's era. Many bands, in the wake of the cult rock comedy *This Is Spinal Tap* from 1984, have laid claim to having influenced the film's more outlandish and memorable scenes, but UFO could justifiably say they have inspired many of the film's standout comedic moments. Moore simply learned to go with the flow. He had a great deal of talent and an abundance of ideas to contribute to the band, and a style of his own, which would in time manifest itself in UFO's music.

However, the addition of Vinnie Moore did not sit well with everyone, including former guitarist Laurence Archer. "I've always loved Phil. I've always loved Phil's vocals and I love UFO songs. To me now it sounds like a session band. Don't get me wrong Vinny's [*sic*] a great player. It lacks the edge for me, which is something that UFO always had. The project [X-UFO] I'm doing now with Clive [Edwards] and Danny [Peyronel], we're still playing like teenagers. We still have loads and loads of energy. I know we haven't been knocking the same songs around for fifteen years or whatever. When I joined the band, Phil and Pete had been in America looking for guitar players for quite some time and they said to me at that point that they never wanna see another guitar player because they interviewed like five hundred of them or something in America. Pete called me up from the States, initially, and said: 'Are you gonna be around?

We want a British guitar player.' I was surprised really that they went down the Vinnie route. He's a great player but to me that's not UFO."[258]

UFO in 2004 featured Phil Mogg, Pete Way and Vinnie Moore, with Paul Raymond back in his rightful place. Jason Bonham, meanwhile, landed on the drum stool covering for Andy Parker. Bonham's father, of course, was the late great Led Zeppelin drummer John Bonham, but Jason has stepped out of his father's shadow and forged a career himself as a drummer of great talent and style. He had drummed for Jimmy Page, Paul Rodgers, Airrace and The Quireboys prior to joining UFO, and had even appeared in the 2001 movie *Rock Star*.

It was the connection to The Quireboys that landed Bonham the UFO job. Phil Mogg got chatting to The Quireboys' front man Spike when he was doing a solo tour. Mogg told Spike that they'd only used Aynsley Dunbar in the studio and that they didn't really have a permanent drummer. Spike invited Mogg to his gig at the London Underworld and Mogg caught up with Spike's band, which included Bonham on drums. They started talking and Mogg asked Bonham if he fancied joining UFO.

The fresh line-up of UFO set to work on the band's seventeenth studio album, *You Are Here*. Now under the management guidance of Peter Knorn of United Talents Management, UFO were about to enter a new creative high.

You Are Here was recorded at Area 51 Studios in Celle, Germany with producer Tommy Newton. The touring had helped the band gel and develop a sound that was modern yet unmistakably UFO. Bonham, for example, wasn't aiming for a Led Zeppelin sound in the studio, but there are some Led Zep moments, especially during "The Spark That Is Us". Bonham had some ideas of his own, which he brought to the band.

Jason Bonham: "Phil [Mogg] was very nervous about anything that I came up that had a little bit of Zep in it, and he was like, 'No, no, no, let's not do that.' The press could have gone straight away, 'Jason's in the band, listen to this.' They would have been on it – they would have ripped us apart and say, 'Oh look, just because Jason's in the band now, they're gonna try to do a Zep sound.' Phil was very good. Without talking the fun out of me, he was being the Zep police [laughs]."[259]

Bonham worked especially well with Vinnie Moore, whose 1980s guitar style was held in high esteem by the drummer. Naturally everyone's ambition was to make a strong-sounding, solid UFO album. "It's been great," Moore told *Metal-Rules* scribe Marko Syrjala at the time. "I mean [the] whole band seems more energetic than before. Jason adds a lot of energy with his drumming you know? There is no laid back from him, just real energetic which makes it heavier you know. Doing a record was really a lot of fun."[260]

Moore made a large contribution to the album. He wrote much of the music, while Mogg wrote the lyrics. The songs started with an idea like "The Spark That Is Us" from Bonham or "Sympathy" from Raymond and they progressed with it from there.

You Are Here opens with the gutsy "When Daylight Goes To Town", before "Black Cold Coffee", a feisty blues rock number, kicks into play. "The Wild One" sees Vinnie Moore offer a terrific lead riff. "Give It Up" is a cheerful rocker with a squealing riff. "Call Me" is more of a rock pounce than its predecessors, while "Slipping Away" is a musically effective ballad with a passionate vocal performance. "The Spark That Is Us" proves once again that UFO are just as accomplished at making ballads as they are rock songs; this one is a wonderful ballad. "Sympathy" begins softly before the pace picks up with plenty of guitar work, then "Mr Freeze" continues the band's run of mid-paced songs. "Jello Man" is somewhat more rugged than previous songs, whereas "Baby Blue" is a ballad straight out of the late 1970s. There is plenty of activity during "Swallow", giving the album a plausible closing. The Japanese version of the album features the bonus track, "Messing Up The Bed".

You Are Here is a fine return to form; it's filled with all the ingredients that have made previous UFO albums so great. It remains a wonderful release and one of the band's more worthwhile efforts from the 1980s onwards. However, it's most obvious flaw is that it is too safe, too mid-paced.

You Are Here was released in March 2004, via the German label SPV, and did not chart in the USA and UK, as was becoming the custom.

Critics greeted *You Are Here* with glowing reviews. The band no longer needed Schenker now that they had Vinnie Moore. Rock critics applauded the new release and so commenced a new era in the band's history.

Geoff Barton raved about the album in *Classic Rock*. He enthused: "... 53 minutes and 12 tracks later, and after a severe jolt to the system, I began to wonder whether this might be the finest studio album of UFO's entire 35 year career."

It is an album that belongs up there with the best of the band's releases.

A European tour was scheduled for February and March with shows in Greece, France, Spain, Italy, Austria, Germany and The Netherlands, with Uli Jon Roth as support. UFO returned to Europe in June for some festival dates. The band's set list usually looked like this: "Midnight Train", "Mother Mary", "When Daylight Goes To Town", "Let It Roll", "I'm A Loser", "This Kid's", "The Wild One", "Fighting Man", "Call Me", "Too Hot To Handle", "Jello Man", "Only You Can Rock Me", "Lights Out" and "Love To Love", with encores of "Rock Bottom", "Doctor Doctor" and "Shoot Shoot".

The band hit the UK from June 14 to June 24. Rumours had been circulating for some time about a possible Led Zeppelin reunion featuring Jason Bonham on drums. Naturally, he was an obvious choice. "Robert [Plant] came to see UFO during the English tour," Bonham said to *Glam Metal*. "I mentioned to him that I hear all these rumours, and I said: 'What do you think, Robert? Tell me what's going on, I hear all this stuff.' He said: 'Don't believe any of them, nothing's happening.'"[261]

I attended the band's gig at the Manchester Apollo on June 16 and penned a review for *BBC Online* (Manchester): "Other than a tight-knit sound and some heavy duty riffs, two other things are memorable from this night: one is how tired Mogg looked after playing just the first few songs, and the other is having to watch bassist Pete Way (looking like a Las Vegas drag queen) run all over the stage with his belly flopping out."

A tour of the USA was planned for early 2004; however, it was hampered by immigration problems as Pete Way was unable to get his passport authorised in time for the start of the tour. Richie Scarlet, known for his work with Ace Frehley, Sebastian Bach and Mountain, was announced as Way's temporary replacement for the first batch of shows, which began at the Jaxx venue in Springfield, West Virginia on April 22. If that wasn't a big enough problem, the whole tour had to be called off after the American embassy in London refused to give Phil Mogg a work permit.

Mogg's fingerprints had been taken in Buffalo, NY, 24 years previously, which prompted the FBI to conduct some security checks. The officials at the US embassy quizzed Mogg by asking him questions about his experiences with the law in America. Had he been arrested over there?

Mogg had forgotten that he had been arrested back in 1982 when he mooned in Lubbock, Texas.

The tour was rearranged for September. Jason Bonham spent the summer period touring with the Anglo-American melodic rock band Foreigner.

However, the rescheduled USA tour dates were hit by further immigration trouble after Pete Way was denied a visa, reportedly on the grounds that he'd outstayed the amount of days he was allowed to work there on his last visit. Consequently, the band hit the road for their rescheduled USA tour in mid-2004 with bassist Barry Sparks filling in for Pete Way.

Sparks was the perfect bassist to cover for Way, as he was heavily inspired by him. Sparks was in MSG from 1995 to 2000, playing on their 1996 album *Written In The Sand*, as well as two live albums (*The Michael Schenker Story Live* and *The Unforgiven World Tour*) and a DVD. He returned briefly to MSG in 2007, only to be replaced by Frank Rummler. In the 1990s, he'd also played bass for Yngwie Malmsteen on *I Can't Wait* (1994) and *Magnum Opus* (1995) and was a member of Dokken in the early 2000s, replacing Jeff Pilson. He also appears on Vinnie Moore's 2000 album *Live*. Mogg later told *Classic Rock*'s Geoff Barton. "He plays bass like John Entwistle a little bit. He's real cool."[262]

2004 also saw the return of Michael Schenker with a new project called Schenker-Pattison, featuring singer Davey Pattison (who is best known for his work with Gamma and Robin Trower). The album includes covers of 1970s hard rock songs, with bassist Gunter Nezhoda and former UFO drummer Aynsley Dunbar. Guitarist Leslie West of Mountain also guest stars. *Schenker-Pattison Summit – The Endless Jam* sank without a trace.

Waysted re-emerged from hibernation once again in 2004, with Paul Chapman and singer Fin Muir. Despite the myriad of line-up changes, Way had never fully lost interest in Waysted. The band had been put on the backburner while he toured with UFO throughout the 1990s, and he had resurrected the outfit in 2000 with *Wilderness Of Mirrors,* after a long period of dormancy: 1986's *Save Your Prayers*, which also features Paul Chapman, being the last Waysted album. Further albums continued throughout the 2000s.

2004's Waysted album, the aptly titled *Back From The Dead*, the band's first since 2000's live release *You Won't Get Out Of Here Alive*, was recorded in the UK and USA and mixed by Robin George. The Japanese version of the album saw UFO covers "No Place To Run" and "The Wild,

The Willing And The Innocent" added as bonus tracks. The band released two further albums with *The Harsh Reality* in 2007, followed a year later by a three disc compilation, the wonderfully titled *Totally Waysted*

With the frustration of 2004 firmly in the past, UFO toured Europe in May 2005, with The Lizards as support. The band's performance at the Pumpwerk in Wilhelmshaven in Germany, on May 13, was released as the double DVD *Showtime* in 2005 via SPV, which was also issued on CD with a selection of re-recorded studio songs. The DVD did not win over everyone in the band, as Vinnie Moore explained in 2009: "I personally don't think that it was our strongest show. We had done better shows than that, but we had problems with electricity that night. I don't know, I feel [a] little bit critical about it ... the way it was shot ... I felt like there was a detachment from it. It might have had something to do with the way they mixed it or something. I think it was cool to get a DVD out there, but I do think that up to that point we had done better shows on that tour."[263]

Reviewing the 2008 HD DVD release of *Showtime* for *Fireworks: The Melodic Rock Magazine*, I enthused: "The band – Messrs Phil Mogg, Pete Way, Paul Raymond with guitarist Vinnie Moore and drummer Jason Bonham – are in fine shape displaying bouts of energy and enthusiasm. Personal highlights include powerful renditions of classics 'Rock Bottom', 'Let It Roll' and 'Lights Out'."

Interestingly, a UFO family tree collection, called *Alien Relations*, was released by Majestic Rock Records. It contains songs by the various UFO related projects, such as Waysted, The Plot, Paul Raymond Project and Snowblind.

UFO headed across the Atlantic, once again, for the band's USA tour. However, Pete Way's visa problems persisted, which caused the band to hire Jeff Kollman known for his work with Mogg/Way and $ign Of 4. The set list was revamped for their American fans: "Only You Can Rock Me", "Let It Roll", "When Daylight Does To Town", "I'm A Loser", "This Kid's", "The Wild One", "Fighting Man", "Mother Mary", "Baby Blue", "Cherry", "Love To Love", "Too Hot To Handle", "Rock Bottom", "Shoot Shoot" and "Doctor Doctor".

The band headed back to Europe for some more live dates later in the year. On November 12, 2005 Andy Parker briefly rejoined the band to play at the Piorno Rock Festival at the Salle Polyvalente in Granada, Spain. Parker had not hit a drumkit in anger for many years, because he was too busy with his day job. He had played drums with a local covers band in a pub, but that was about it. He did not feel as though he could carry a full UFO set at the time. However, things would change. His return would soon be permanent and, though Bonham was a great addition to the band, Parker is the rightful heir to the UFO drum stool.

There was a lot of substance abuse in UFO and Bonham found it uncomfortable, so he separated himself from the band much of the time. Maybe he was mindful of his father's premature death due to alcohol in 1980. He was more suited to Foreigner, the band he joined after leaving UFO. Bonham also went on to fill his father's shoes by playing drums at the famous Led Zeppelin reunion at the O2 Arena in London on 12 December 2010. He has also worked with the Glenn Hughes fronted supergroup Black Country Communion and Jason Bonham's Led Zeppelin Experience.

Pete Way admitted to *Metal-Rules'* Marko Syrjala: "To be honest with you, Jason got on my nerves, he didn't like my lifestyle or attitude, he'd given up drink and drugs. Jason was already doing things with Foreigner, but would have liked to have done some more things with UFO I'm sure ..."[264]

The planets appeared to be aligned, because Parker had decided to leave his family business, which manufactured plastics and metals, and move back to the USA. He'd been in the corporate world for a while but wanted to make a return to music, though not necessarily back to UFO. While Parker was working with his family in their very successful Perspex business, working 60 hours a week, even working Saturdays, his wife was also in a very stressful job working for the huge pharmaceuticals company, GFK.

They decided to change their lifestyles after his daughter, from his previous marriage, graduated from college in England. They were also fed up of England and the cost of living. Parker's wife has family in Dallas, but he was not too keen on moving there, because it is another big city. They had a number of options to discuss.

When Parker first moved to the States with the band in the mid-1970s, he stayed in LA and got his Green Card through his first marriage to an American. He left the band in the early 1980s, went through a divorce and was trying to obtain custody of his daughter. He'd chosen to give up music and work in construction because there was no travel involved and he could earn a living from a steady job with a regular paycheck. However, as well as moving to California, to run the family business in the 1980s, he also owned a recording studio with Axe/Blackfoot guitarist/vocalist Bobby Barth, and was the drummer in an aborted line-up of Axe that did some recordings in 1989; two of which recently appeared on the Axe compilation *Axeology*.

Parker remarried and stayed in LA until an earthquake struck in 1994. As they were not happy there anyway, they decided to move. Parker got an offer to work with his family back in England, so they upped sticks and left. But then came the *Walk On Water* album, so he had to spend time working back in Southern California. However, he stayed in England for about twelve years before deciding to move back across the Atlantic.

Parker had been out of the country for so long, his Green Card had expired and, post 9/11, America's immigration policy had become much tougher. They went through the immigration routine and, when Parker finally got his Green Card, they arranged the arduous move. One of Parker's wife's friends, who was a property developer, recommended a small town about an hour and a half's drive outside of Dallas and 45 minutes from Fort Worth, called Granbury. Parker and his wife bought two houses in Granbury over the Internet. They rented those houses out while they stayed in England.

"... when we decided to move back we fixed this one house we had in the historic district," he told Lisa Torem of *Penny Black Music* in 2011. "We said: 'We'll buy houses and fix them.' At the time I was out of the band. I was a licensed contractor. My whole family were in the building business when I was a kid. So, I was just planning on coming back to this house and living in the historic district and we wanted to buy houses, maybe rent them, maybe flip them, whatever. And that was the plan."[265]

It was a sunny Bank Holiday in England when Raymond rang Parker in August 2005. Raymond told Parker that Bonham was leaving the band and would he be interested in joining UFO for a show that was planned for Spain in November? Parker mentioned that he was planning to move back to the States, but he gave it some thought and said he'd commit to the Spanish gig on November 12. Parker played the show and enjoyed it.

There was a different vibe in the band, which Parker noticed right away. There was no longer any tension and there was a great deal more fun in the band's camp, just like the old days. It felt right for Parker to be back. They asked Parker if he was interested in staying in UFO on a permanent basis. Parker jumped at the chance and said yes without a second's thought.

Having older members back in the band was like a trip back to the past for Phil Mogg. The singer's friendship with Parker and Way – though stormy at times – goes right back to the late 1960s. "We've been together for so long, it feels comfortable knowing what dramas going to come next," Mogg told *Relix*'s Phil Freeman.[266]

2005 saw Schenker celebrate the 25th anniversary of MSG and the release of Michael Schenker's covers album *Heavy Hitters*, which includes a version of "Doctor Doctor" with AOR singer Jeff Scott Soto, bassist Marco Mendoza and drummer Brett Chassen. However, the guitarist suffered from bad publicity in 2007 due to his return to heavy drinking. Shows were cancelled and performances were lacklustre.

UFO fans were intrigued when news broke in 2005 that Pete Way had founded the band Damage Control, with guitarist Robyn George, singer Spike from The Quireboys and drummer Chris Slade (who had previously been AC/DC's drummer for around five years from 1989). They later released their lacklustre self-titled debut album in 2007. The band's second album, 2008's *Raw*, was released minus Spike, with vocals shared by George and Way. Slade actually went on to join MSG and its newest recruits Gary Barden, Chris Glen and Wayne Findley, in 2008 for a tour.

UFO – Mogg, Way, Moore, Raymond and Parker – set to work on their eighteenth studio effort, *The Monkey Puzzle*. With Vinnie Moore in the band, it was a different experience for Parker. Prior to the release of the band's latest album, they played some sporadic live dates in early 2006. They performed at the Princess Pavilion in Falmouth on July 26; the Cheese & Grain public house in Frome on July 27 and the Rock & Blues Festival in Derby on July 28, before heading to Germany to perform at the Rock Of Ages event on July 29, and the Roots Rock Festival in Nidrum, Belgium on July 30. The band then played shows in Seoul and Busan in South Korea in early August.

They tailored their set lists for the country they were in, but one set of songs included "Mother Mary", "When Daylight Goes To Town", "Let It Roll", "I'm A Loser", "This Kid's", "Hard Being Me", "Drink Too Much", "Fighting Man", "Only You Can Rock Me", "Baby Blue", "Heavenly Body", "Love To Love", "Too Hot To Handle", "Lights Out", and "Rock Bottom" with Doctor Doctor" and "Shoot Shoot" closing the set.

The Monkey Puzzle was recorded at Area 51 Studios in Celle, Germany with producer Tommy Newton in early 2006. Since working on *You Are Here* and the DVD *Showtime*, Newton had become a friend of the band's so there was really no other option but to hire him when it came to working on *The Monkey Puzzle*. It was important for the band not only to have a producer onboard who understood them, and the classic sound of UFO, but who also had a good knowledge of contemporary rock.

In the studio, Vinnie Moore pulled out his slide guitar for "Hard Being Me" and the band returned to that undeniable UFO sound by adding piano and organ sounds to "Rolling Man". Melodic, yet hard and heavy, the harmonica was added to "Some Other Guy". It was obvious the band's old muse was back and what they had started with *You Are Here*, they were continuing with *The Monkey Puzzle*. Moore was just the right ingredient for the band – his youth, relentless energy and talents unleashed a new potential in the camp.

Parker was also pleased to be back in the band as they had returned to their hard blues rock roots, which he was more than content with. Although Moore is not an especially bluesy guitarist, the band's melodies had drifted back to that 1960s and 1970s blues rock sound. Parker was happy with the direction the band were going.

Andy Parker: "This band, is an interesting thing – when I started playing with them, which was back in 1969, it was kind of the end of the blues boom, especially in the UK with bands like Chicken Shack and Savoy Brown; we were part of that as we were influenced by the blues, and when I came back in 2005, lo and behold, it's just gone full circle back to the blues. I just think it was a natural progression ..."[267]

As a fan of the blues and guitarist Albert King, Vinnie Moore was pleasantly surprised to discover just how much a fan of the blues Phil Mogg is. Moore got to check out Mogg's personal record collection, which contains a dense set of blues records. Even on tour, Mogg would listen to the likes of Muddy Waters in his hotel room. The pair would chat about all the old Delta blues players. They had a great rapport through their shared love of the blues.

Vinnie Moore may have begun his career as a guitar shredder, but he had developed his own style and a strong sense of melody, which was now a major part of his contribution to UFO. Moore had also become a prolific and talented songwriter in his own right. He was never brought into UFO as a mere hired hand, but rather as a full-time permanent member and his contributions have been valid, without question. Moore spends time crafting new songs throughout most of the year and, once he has a collection of material, he creates demos at his home studio before sending the music files to Mogg. The band usually have a lot of material to work on in the studio, for which Mogg will then pen the lyrics. Mogg then picks the best songs for the finished album.

It is not always easy writing for a singer from a guitarist's point of view, so the guitarist has to create a song that fits the singer's frame of mind. Mogg opts for the songs that best suit his voice, and he has the final say on which numbers make it to the finished album.

UFO have always followed their instincts. They've never been a contrived and calculated band. They continue to produce music that feels natural to them, and a return to the blues was a gut feeling. They've never sat down and said: "Right, this is how the album is going to sound." They simply create music that feels right.

The band had no interest in revisiting past squabbles and the only baggage they brought into the studio were their instrument cases. They were in a rather agreeable and enjoyable place and, with Tommy Newton, they were enthusiastic about creating some new music. "Fortunately for this band, when you mix in everybody's musical differences, it blends into one identity," Mogg confessed. "We should eventually end up in one spot together. Bits of everyone's influences are scattered throughout."[268]

The Monkey Puzzle opens with the thrilling "Hard Being Me", which is just the sort of blues rock that UFO have always excelled at. "Heavenly Body" is a sturdy rocker with gritty vocals and metal guitars. "Some Other Guy" is undoubtedly Mogg's tribute to some of his blues heroes, whereas "Who's Fooling Who?" is an effective and passionately sung ballad, which starts slowly, until the drums and bass kick into action. "Black And Blue" is a fantastic rock song that would not sound out of place on a recent AC/DC album. "Drink Too Much" is a laid back track, while "World Cruise" is a mid-album punch in the guts. "Down By The River" is a solid mid-paced rock song, perfect for where the band are at during this stage in their career. "Good Bye You" is perhaps too middle of the road but it does have a strong melody. "Rolling Man" is a joyous hands-in-the-air sort of anthem that's perfect for the live stage. The band sounds great on this particular track. "Kingston Town" is perhaps too laidback to close the album, but it is obvious that Mogg is no longer interested in making the type of fast rock songs that the fans were used to in the previous decade.

The Monkey Puzzle is a further step forward for the band after the triumphant *You Are Here*. It's the band's ode to the classic rock sound of the 1970s, and there's plenty of blues and enough energy to show that they haven't ran out of steam; far from it. *The Monkey Puzzle* is as far away from *Misdemeanor* as the band could possibly get. It was released in September 2006 through SPV and, again, failed to chart in the USA and UK. Would the band ever get an even break?

Certainly the reviews were generally positive, although some felt it was not quite as strong as *You Are Here*.

Andrew McNeice wrote on *Melodicrock.com*: "The overall feel of the album is fairly laid back, but the band is clearly at ease with themselves and I'm finding more guitar riffs and melodies in this album than I have heard in quite some time. The production is perfect for what the band needs – solid sound, evenly mixed, but without the life being squeezed out of the performance." Jeb Wright enthused on *Classic Rock Revisited*: "UFO continues to release great old school hard rock. The band's second release featuring guitarist Vinnie Moore is a power pack of lightning guitar riffs and rock anthems. UFO have discovered a second life and is taking advantage of the new energy that Moore brings." I wrote in *Big Cheese*: "Phil Mogg's voice is in great shape; his bluesy-rock vocals show no signs of waning with songs like 'Some Other Guy' being particularly effective. Equally, the musicianship of Pete Way on bass, guitarists Vinnie Moore and Paul Raymond, and drummer Andy Parker is superlative."

Its significance within the band's back catalogue remains to be seen as it is still relatively new, but it is part of an era of the band's career that is highly lauded.

To promote the release of the new album, the band played shows in Germany and Switzerland in late October through to November with support from Mob Rules, while gigs in Czech Republic, Italy, France, Spain and The Netherlands saw Kriesor and Vengeance opening on selected dates.

UFO then toured the UK from 20-30 November with Spike of The Quireboys as support. I went to the Liverpool Academy gig on November 2 and noted at the time: "Mogg started off well enough, ripping through the old hits but by the end of the hour-and-forty-five-minute set, he was well and truly knackered and his voice showed it. He still managed to belt out the encore songs, 'Doctor Doctor', and 'Shoot Shoot'. It was a chilly night in Liverpool, but having warmed up the few hundred (if that) capacity audience with the likes of 'Too Hot To Handle' and 'Rock Bottom', Mogg was justifiably beat. He is very much like Paul Rodgers, an aging singer with young meaty blues-vocals."

UFO closed 2006's live performances with gigs in Greece on 2 and 3 December. They began 2007 with a tour of Europe in March, with support from Mob Rules before sporadic live dates and festival performances in the UK and Ireland, Germany and Belgium from May to September.

It was business as usual and, for the next couple of years, the band went on the road for a steady stream of touring, although Texas-based Andy Parker had to undergo leg surgery after breaking his ankle in a fall in February 2007, causing UFO to redraft Simon Wright for a small stint during the first half of the year. Wright was on shore leave from Dio, as mainman Ronnie James Dio was on tour with Heaven And Hell. Wright was a more than competent drummer and was perfectly suited to UFO. It would have been interesting to find out what UFO would sound like had he recorded material with the band.

"Phil, Pete and Paul Raymond were great to get along with too," enthuses Wright. "I think me being an Englishman and us, most times, sharing the same sense of humour, helped a lot. Phil and Pete were very tight as friends; you could tell they go way back together. I still remain good friends with all of them; I really enjoyed my time in UFO."[269]

Despite Mogg's past assertions that he was not interested in playing older UFO material, it is evident that in order to please the band's fanbase he had to give in and include much of the band's classic 1970s material. How could they not? The band blitzed through "Mother Mary", "Lettin' Go", "Black And Blue", "When Daylight Goes To Town", "Let It Roll", "This Kid's", "I'm A Loser", "Hard Being Me", "Baby Blue", "Only You Can Rock Me", "Fighting Man", "Love To Love", "Too Hot To Handle", "Lights Out" and "Rock Bottom" before closing with an encore of "Doctor Doctor" and "Shoot Shoot".

They worked in a similar fashion to any other band in that they rehearsed the songs ready for the gig, though the soundchecks were never long, which suited Wright. When asked who was the dominant member of the band, Wright responds: "Well my impression was Phil. It's funny but they are really a quiet bunch of people until they go off at each other, which happened on a couple of occasions."[270]

During the 2007 tour, Vinnie Moore – who'd begun work on a new solo album in October 2006 with drummer Van Romaine at Spin Studios in Queens, New York – performed some Engl guitar clinics.

Asked about his fondest memories of his two stints in UFO, Wright replies: "Just the camaraderie; well the great catalogue of music as well. We played some great shows together, but we also seemed to get along really well. There were fights and disagreements between Michael and the other lads but all in all very fond memories of my time in UFO. We always socialised, I was never really a part of the business side of things, that was dealt with by the original members of the band, and rightly so I think!"[271]

With Parker comfortably back on the drum stool, UFO played some festival dates and isolated shows around Europe and the UK throughout the summer months. They then began the Red October 2007 Tour on October 23 in Cologne, Germany and finished the tour with a performance at the UK's Hard Rock Hell Festival on November 10. The band also played a batch of live dates in Russia as part of the tour, hence its moniker. There was seemingly no end to UFO's touring schedule and their commitment to fans to deliver some outstanding live performances, and the band would continue to stay on the road into the following year.

Schenker meantime had by now shifted from a Gibson Flying V to a Dean V, with Dean Guitars producing a signature Schenker Dean V as well as two acoustic signature models with Schenker's iconic black and white V design. Dean Guitars issued a hundred limited edition models signed and numbered personally by Schenker. There's no doubting, however, that Schenker is most famous for his Gibson Flying V. He typified the guitar rock god in the late 1970s and in the early years of MSG. Incidentally, Tyson Schenker, Michael's son, has his own band Raiders Of Rock n' Roll, proving that rock runs deep in the Schenker DNA.

Schenker also had visa issues with the American immigration department, which caused dates in March 2009 to be cancelled. It wasn't the first time Schenker had been troubled by red tape.

A year earlier, Pete Way was unable to get a visa yet again, so he was substituted in UFO by Rob De Luca from Sebastian Bach's band. De Luca, who joined Bach's band in 2005, is an accomplished bassist who formed the LA glam metal band Spread Eagle in 1989. De Luca has also toured/ played bass with Joan Jett And The Blackhearts, George Lynch of Dokken and Lynch Mob, Mike Chlasciak of Halford and New York rockers, Helmet.

It was De Luca's manager Peter Kalish who heard about the possible vacant slot on the tour, after searching the Internet. De Luca had also been tipped the wink by his buddy Ron "Bumblefoot" Thal, so the bassist emailed Vinnie Moore and it progressed from there. Obviously it was a great opportunity for De Luca who saw the band live onstage as a kid growing up in Philadelphia. "Well, as a musician you try to make something that lasts, something that's classic. UFO have done that and I'm honoured to be involved and helping out. So that's what I'm looking forward to," he said to *Get Ready To Roll* before the tour commenced in 2008.[272]

The tour ran from April 9 with a show in Baltimore, Maryland to May 9 in Coeur D'Alene, Idaho. During the tour Vinnie Moore performed several guitar clinics.

It was not only the addition of Vinnie Moore that had brought about a new lease of life for the old dogs, but also the return of Andy Parker. It took several months for Parker to get back to match fitness, because it had been so long since he'd played the drums professionally, prior to rejoining the band. Parker worked brilliantly with Way onstage during those shows though. There was a positive feeling in the band and they were playing excellent sets to growing audiences. The material from the new album was going down well with fans.

However, American fans in particular wanted to hear some Paul Chapman era material, so the band rehearsed "Long Gone" from *The Wild, The Willing And The Innocent*. They also wanted to include "Lettin' Go" from *No Place To Run*, but never got around to it. Of course, they simply had to play the classic Schenker era material such as "Love To Love" if they wanted to get out of venues in one piece.

UFO's USA set list, filled mostly with classic songs, ran as follows: "Long Gone", "Mother Mary", "Hard Being Me", "Pushed To The Limit," "This Kid's", "Only You Can Rock Me", "Ain't No Baby", "Heavenly Body", "Baby Blue", "Too Hot To Handle", "Lights Out", "Love To Love", "Rock Bottom", "Doctor Doctor" and "Shoot Shoot".

Aside from a show at the Würth Open Air Festival in Künzelsau, Germany, UFO spent much of the first half of the year in the USA, with further dates played during July and August; all of them being festival appearances, including Rocklahoma. In August, Vinnie Moore appeared onstage at a Blue Öyster Cult gig. On August 23, Pete Way returned to the band for a performance at the Leyendas Del Rock in Puerto de Mazarron, Murcia. In September, the band played shows in Korea and then performed a six date tour of Germany.

2008 also saw the release of MSG's tenth studio album, *In The Midst Of Beauty*. In 2008, the excellent compilation *The Best Of UFO (1974-1983)* was also released and, while the band had made some terrific material after 1983, it is evident that fan interest largely concentrates on the band's first Schenker phase and the years immediately thereafter. The album includes all the band's classics, digitally remastered.

With *You Are Here* and *The Monkey Puzzle*, UFO had showed that they could still cut the mustard and, while there's no doubting that the band's output from 1974 to 1979 continues to have an enormous impact on the rock and metal world, it's certainly time for the band and their fans to look ahead. The nostalgic compilations are a great way to entice new fans, but the abundance of UFO collections is simply overkill. There are only so many versions of "Doctor Doctor" that fans want to own. Mind you, the same is true with Motörhead and Status Quo and other veteran bands that have had record deals with different companies who all want to milk the cash cow until it's dry.

UFO were on a roll, but would it come to an end?

CHAPTER
TEN

Seven Deadly –
More Than 40 Years Of UFO
(2009 –2013)

*"It's exciting to get discovered by a younger generation.
I really do think this band has a lot to offer, with not just the past
material, but the present and future as well."*

Andy Parker[273]

The 2009 line-up of UFO of Pete Way, Phil Mogg, Andy Parker, Paul Raymond and Vinnie Moore began work on the band's nineteenth album, *The Visitor*. Given the strengths of *You Are Here* and *The Monkey Puzzle*, their forthcoming album was eagerly awaited by fans. This particular line-up had established itself as UFO's most consistent and creative incarnation since the revered Michael Schenker 1970s era.

As soon as the band had come off the road they felt it was time to make a new album, Andy Parker's second since his return. Although the band's regime may sound hectic, it is not as gruelling as it used to be. Long gone are the days when they'd tour for nine or ten months before going straight into the studio without a break. These days they take some time off to recuperate. Being on the road for months at a time continues to be hard work, but they had their training in the 1970s when it was far tougher. After the first few shows they'd find the energy to carry on for the rest of the tour. Once the break was over and done with, they'd be craving to go back into the studio.

Each member had their own ideas and after about two weeks they pooled their ideas together via email. They flew over to Germany where their manager is based, with about 30 fresh ideas for the forthcoming album. They spent about five days going over the ideas in Germany before going into the studio, although Vinnie Moore works from his own studio in Delaware.

Phil Mogg was as unpredictable as ever. He rarely has any trouble coming up with ideas, it's just that his cohorts never know when he's going to bring those ideas to the table. It's usually at the end!

Andy Parker: "... what seems to work for him, is he likes to hear the song structure and he has different ideas and then he figures out which idea works well with what song. He'll come in and sing a couple of lines and then go off to a corner again with his pen and paper and scratch things down. So it's kind of interesting for us because you'll get a flavour of what's coming but not the whole song."[274]

The Visitor was mostly recorded at the familiar haunt, Area 51 Recording Studio in Celle, Germany in early 2006 with Tommy Newton and studio assistant Andre Bargmann. The band initially wanted Martin Birch – famed for his work with Iron Maiden, Deep Purple, Black Sabbath, Rainbow and Whitesnake – but they worked efficiently with Newton. Birch has now retired and has faded from public view, despite his legendary status in the world of rock and metal.

"... it was the same process as we followed in the past," Moore said to *About.com*'s Chad Bowar when speaking about the recording process. "It all starts off with the music and then vocals and lyrics are added. We get together and rehearse and then go into the studio to record drums and bass. Guitars are done at my studio."[275]

Moore's guitars were recorded at The Core in the USA. The bass tracks were recorded by Peter Pichl (from German outfit Nektar) because Pete Way was absent from the recording of the album due to his persistent liver condition, which caused concern amongst hardened fans. Pichl joined Mogg, Raymond, Moore and Parker with producer Tommy Newton for the recording of the album during February and March 2009. It was an undeniably tough decision for the band to make, knowing that Pete Way is irreplaceable.

"The initial plan when we were rehearsing was to have a local guy just so we could have bass there," Vinnie Moore explained to Ruben Mosqueda of *Sleaze Roxx* in 2009. "Everyone liked the feel of his [Pichl's] playing and he's a good guy, it just progressed from there and we wound up asking him to play on the record."[276]

Also, Raymond's keyboards and additional guitars (on the tracks "Forsaken", "On The Waterfront" and "Villains & Thieves") were recorded at the RMS Studio in Selhurst, South London with engineer Andy Le Vien. Backing vocals were provided by Martina Frank, Melanie Newton and Olaf Senkbeil. Recording became fragmented, because after the initial ten day rehearsal in Hannover, the band members worked on their own pieces either at home or in Germany and then emailed files back and forth. However, it is much cheaper than having everyone work in a studio for weeks at a time.

There was an extensive amount of material to pick from, so they had a lot of leftover songs that didn't make the final cut. There were songs that Mogg and Way had worked on; there were songs that Mogg wrote with Nick Crutchley; Raymond submitted twelve songs; Parker submitted eight, while Moore also submitted more than half a dozen, if not more.

"Villains & Thieves" was an original track, which Raymond devised and Mogg penned some lyrics for. "On The Waterfront" was inspired by Eric Clapton and Traffic; Raymond is a fan of Steve Winwood. "Forsaken" was very much in The Rolling Stones vein, from their country phase. The working title for the track in the studio was "Keef", because it reminded Raymond of classic 1970s Rolling Stones. When Raymond wrote it, before Mogg added his own lyrics and title, it was called "More Than My Fair Share". Raymond was not sure if it was suited to UFO, but Mogg made it work.

Both Raymond and Mogg allowed their blues influences to manifest themselves in the music. There would later be some comparisons with Deep Purple, but Raymond has admitted he has never been a major fan of the Deep Purple organist, the late Jon Lord. Raymond did not like how Lord ran his Hammond organ through a Marshall rather than a Leslie cabinet. Raymond was always more in favour of Keith Emerson of ELP.

Given Raymond's contributions to UFO over the years, it was pleasing that he was finally getting fully credited for his songwriting talents. He admitted: "Yes, I laid that demon to rest a long time ago. Most of the fans know now that Pete Way had to pay back all the money owed to me over the years for songwriting. Considering it was over twenty years, it was quite a lot. So, we're all straight on that."[277]

The band had basically followed the same blueprint that was laid down with *You Are Here*, in that they wanted to create a set of hard blues rock songs that could be played live. Not all songs worked as well in the studio as they did onstage and vice versa. "Saving Me" was another song that was soaked in blues music, right from Vinnie Moore's slide guitar; no doubt influenced by B.B. King and Albert King.

Mogg's voice has matured over the years and, while the higher notes of the 1970s songs may be beyond him, his voice is still very distinctive and strong. With age, it has become perfect for the sort of blues rock that Mogg and the rest of the band evidently aspire to create. One of Mogg's all-time heroes is the blues singer Howlin' Wolf and, for the past couple of albums, Mogg has almost mimicked Wolf's distinctive vocal style. It's as if Mogg has gone full circle, going back to the blues.

The Visitor was as much of a representation of the band's blues rock identity as it was a homage to their musical heroes. The blues had not been so apparent in UFO's music since the 1970s and there's no doubt that Vinnie Moore had helped Mogg rediscover it. *The Visitor* is a raw, earthy and rootsy album which was made specifically for Mogg's bluesy voice. Mogg may not have lived the healthiest lifestyle (how many rock stars do?), but his voice is in fine form as displayed on the band's current recordings.

Mick Glossop, producer of *Making Contact* and *Headstone*, says of Mogg's voice: "Everyone is different. Everyone has their style. Certainly as a rock singer he's one of the most well-known and respected singers in the English rock genre. He certainly was at the time, in the '70s. He's quite a soulful singer when he puts his mind to it. Unlike Ian Gillan, who is a very ballsy singer – that's his whole style – Phil's not that sort of singer. His voice is not what you'd call a strong voice, but that's not the point. He can deliver songs without having a physical, strong presence."[278]

UFO have never been trendsetters and neither have they followed trends. They're very much a band which has created its own agenda. UFO was formed at the tail-end of the British blues boom, of which Mogg was an ardent follower, and the Vinnie Moore era of the band has seen them delve deeper into their collective well of musical inspirations.

The Visitor opens with the blues rock vibes of "Saving Me". "On The Waterfront" has a gentle and joyous feel to it, and Moore throws in some nifty guitar work. "Hell Driver" offers some much-needed grit, while Mogg sounds like he is in his element. "Stop Breaking Down" is a fantastic song; there is an atmospheric feel to it thanks to Raymond's keyboards, while Vinnie Moore gives a very controlled performance. "Rock Ready" is another one of Mogg's obvious tributes to his American blues heroes, with its references to Mississippi. "Living Proof" is a funky R&B style number with some strident vocals. "Can't Buy A Thrill" is a nod to UFO's melodic rock sound of the 1980s and offers a welcome change from some of the more blues orientated songs. "Forsaken" is a laidback affair, in contrast to "Villains & Thieves" which sees Moore employ a dirty hard rock riff. "Stranger In Town" is the perfect song to close such a gutsy sounding album.

The Visitor continues the band's run of bluesy classic rock style albums. The songwriting is strong, Mogg sounds fantastic, while Vinnie Moore offers plenty of meat and grit to a band that were looking as though were on the ropes in the late 1990s. Both Parker and Raymond are playing brilliantly, too. Perhaps some rock fans would argue that UFO have slowed down too much and that all their songs are now stuck in mid-paced territory, but, for others, the band have not sounded this strong in a long time. Mogg is certainly sounding enthusiastic.

The digipak version of the album includes the bonus track "Dancing With St Peter", which is a remake of a song Phil Mogg recorded in his past project $ign Of Four. The album's cover sleeve has a band shot showing Andy Parker, Paul Raymond, Vinnie Moore and Phil Mogg, which left some fans wondering if UFO was really the same without Pete Way, though Pichl does a good job.

The Visitor was released in June 2009 via SPV. Did it chart? Yes! Scraping in at number 99 in the UK Top 100. Their first appearance in nearly fifteen years. It didn't grace the US charts, but it was a step in the right direction.

The Visitor was released to ecstatic reviews from rock journos. The band was going from strength to strength since Vinnie Moore signed up.

Writing in *Classic Rock*, Geoff Barton said: "Throughout, American guitarist Vinnie Moore eschews his shreddy past to deliver a mature, commanding performance, contributing a wealth of sublime solos."

The Visitor is an album which, like *You Are Here* and, to an extent, *The Monkey Puzzle*, represents the best of UFO in the 2000s. Many critics voted it one of the best rock albums of 2009.

The band hit the road yet again, but this time bassist Barry Sparks replaced Peter Pichl for the live shows. They played a short tour of Britain to promote *The Visitor*, though the band were hesitant to call it their 40th anniversary tour. Mogg spoke to *Classic Rock*'s Geoff Barton: "We are not in our 40th anniversary. Status Quo does that. We don't. No. Do you know what? I don't look too deep. This is, like, rock. If you start looking too deep then you get carried away with your own stuff. You disappear up your own arse, basically."[279]

I was at the Manchester Academy 2 on June 20 and noted at the time: "Temporary bassist Barry Sparks did a great job. Admittedly, they leaned too heavily on new material, but what was played from their newbie *The Visitor* and the one before last *You Are Here* were engaging. As usual with a band of their ilk it was the classics like 'Only You Can Rock Me', 'Cherry' and 'Too Hot To Handle' which got the biggest applause and lifted the ceiling. Some of the riffs ('Rock Bottom') were over-extended, which was unnecessary, but Phil Mogg's voice held up throughout the evening."

2009 not only saw the release of the revised *Headstone* compilation courtesy of EMI, but also the *Official Bootleg Box Set 1975-1982*. UFO fans have always been eager to record and archive UFO's live performances, and the official released EMI box set is a terrific contribution to the band's back catalogue. It consists of six discs featuring gigs recorded at the Record Plant in NYC on 1 September 1975; London's Roundhouse on 25 April 1976; London's Roundhouse on 2 April 2 1977; an unknown venue in Cleveland, Ohio on 16 October 16; Hammersmith Odeon on 20 February 1981 and Hammersmith Odeon 'BBC In Concert' on 28 January 1982.

The band continued touring, but, in 2010, Pete Way – who was still suffering from his liver problem – was *hors de combat*. The band felt Way wasn't cutting it anymore. With Pete Way it is a case of – to quote the cliché – what you see is what you get. He continues to live the rock 'n' roll lifestyle that he embraced back in the hedonistic 1970s. However, discipline has never been one of the bassist's strong points and he does not necessarily have the stamina that it takes to get better. Although the band felt Way would be better off trying to sort himself out than staying on the road, they did miss him and his presence. He always was a laugh.

Andy Parker: "Unfortunately, because he won't curb his lifestyle, they won't give him the treatment in England. We've got social medicine, which is great, but they're not going to give the treatment to someone who is drinking and taking drugs. The guy is smoking 60 cigarettes a day. It just doesn't work like that. So, a) he isn't getting treated, and b) he's just continuing his old self and, I'm sorry, but the time has come in UFO's career that it's really affecting his performance, and, as much as we love him, I think people deserve to see something a little bit better. Until he sorts himself out, I'm afraid he's sitting on the bench.[280]

Since his last stint in UFO, Sparks had played with Scorpions and Ted Nugent as well as continuing as Dokken's bassist. However, Sparks was forced to fly back to the States in early May due to illness in his family and was briefly replaced by Peter Pichl.

They'd kicked off the tour in support of their new album with a performance at the Rock Hard Festival in Gelsenkirchen, Germany on 31 May, before further shows on the continent. Their UK tour commenced on 9 June in Brighton and finished in London on the24th.

Yet another batch of shows were arranged for June through to August, on the continent, with the band returning to England to play at the Bulldog Bash at Avon Park Raceway in Stratford-Upon-Avon on 7 August.

The band bulldozed through "Saving Me", "When Daylight Goes To Town", "Mother Mary", "I'm A Loser", "This Kid's", "Cherry", "Baby Blue", "Only You Can Rock Me", "Ain't No Baby", "Love To Love", "Lights Out", "Too Hot To Handle", "Rock Bottom", "Doctor Doctor" and "Shoot Shoot".

UFO then kicked off their USA tour on 2 October at the Jaxx venue in West Virginia and wound up the extensive road jaunt in San Francisco on 1 November. The band flew back across the Atlantic to start a tour of Europe from November 16 (Germany) to December 8 (Switzerland).

Meanwhile in London, Alice Cooper presented Michael Schenker with the Marshall '11' award for his dedication to rock 'n' roll. Jimmy Page, Slash, Ron Wood, Tony Iommi and John Paul Jones were in attendance. Schenker released his ninth solo album *Temple Of Rock* in 2008, which features Pete Way on bass. Vinnie Moore finally issued his new solo album *To The Core* in 2009; his first since 2001's *Defying Gravity*.

Moving *The Visitor* tour into 2010, and with Rob De Luca back on bass, UFO began a tour of Europe, including UK dates, on 14 April in Hannover and finishing in Dresden on 8 May.

They flew to Brazil for some shows at the end of the month, before performing at the High Voltage Festival in London on 25 July, which followed three gigs in Germany and one show in The Netherlands, from 20-23 July. The band had a short break before another European tour commenced in Bremen on 11 October, finishing in Copenhagen on 1 November. The band finished 2010 with a tour of their native UK from 2-7 December.

2010 also saw the release of the collection *The Best Of A Decade*, which celebrates the band's SPV albums of the 2000s. Some fans would have liked to see songs from *Covenant* and *Sharks* but, as the collection was released by SPV, one can only assume that the CD was released purely to capitalise on the band's remerging success post *You Are Here*. It includes songs from said *You Are Here* as well as *The Monkey Puzzle*, *The Visitor* and live recordings of classic songs such as "Too Hot To Handle" culled from *Showtime*.

The world does not need another UFO compilation, although this particular release does have an interesting angle. Pete Pardo wrote a review of the collection on the *Sea Of Tranquility* website: "If you are looking for a snapshot of the Vinnie Moore era of UFO, this is not the best place to start. Seeing as there are only three studio releases so far, your best bet is to go out and either buy the individual CDs or download them, so you can really get an idea of where the band is at today. There's no doubt that the current line-up lacks the magic of the first Schenker era (and possibly even the Paul Chapman years for that matter), but UFO still rock out and can deliver better than plenty of bands half their age. *The Best Of A Decade* is only the tip of the iceberg to what this current line-up is all about."

UFO began work on their next studio album, *Seven Deadly*, in December. Way was out of action again, so Lars Lehmann joined Mogg, Parker, Moore and Raymond in the studio.

However, the band were not entirely sure if they would be able to release another album after SPV filed for bankruptcy in May 2009. On 25 May, Manfred Schutz submitted an application to commence insolvency proceedings, which is similar to Chapter 11 bankruptcy protection in the USA. Inevitably, lots of background work went on while the label continued as normal. They chose to keep UFO on their books, which was excellent news for the band. SPV and their A&R representative have supported UFO since the band first signed to the label.

Seven Deadly was recorded at Area 51 in Germany with Tommy Newton, but it was not the Area 51 the band were used to, it was a new studio in a brand new building, but Newton decided to keep the studio moniker. The band – especially AC/DC fan Paul Raymond – were aiming for some killer 1970s hard blues rock riffs. "Paul and Vinnie pretty much wrote this album between them with Phil. The stuff that Phil wrote was actually centred more around guitar," Parker said to *Teeth Of The Divine*'s Scott Alisoglu. " ... It's still got that blues thing going on, but it's more edgy this one I think, a little heavier to please some of the fans."[281]

Additional recording was completed at RMS Studio in Selhurst, England by Andy Le Vien and by Steve Ward at SW Sounds. Vinnie Moore, who recorded his guitars at The Core at home in Delaware in the USA, has a strong sense of melody and songwriting which was influenced by some of his heroes, mostly the late great blues guitarist Stevie Ray Vaughan and Jimi Hendrix. By the time of *Seven Deadly*, it felt like Moore had been in UFO for more than a generation, such was his chemistry with the rest of the band. Never short of ideas and always one for a challenge, Moore had many melodies developed for the new album.

Moore had never felt left out of the band, nor was he pushed aside despite being the newest and youngest member. Distance is not a problem when it comes to working on an album (Parker also lives in the USA) and, in an age of instant digital technology, music files can be emailed back and forth within seconds.

As ever, Phil Mogg kept his lyrics under wraps until the last minute. As soon as Andy Parker had laid down his drum tracks in Germany, he'd fly back home to Texas without knowing what Mogg was going to do with the final arrangements, so the rest of the band would hear the tracks without vocals. Listening to those songs with vocals was akin to listening to them for the first time. This kind of procedure would not work for every band, but Phil has been doing it for 40 years and you can't teach an old Mogg new tricks!

The new building, where the band recorded, had an empty swimming pool, which Parker used as a makeshift drum room. He thought the sound was very powerful. They laid out a makeshift floor on the bottom of the empty pool and Parker set up his drums there and banged away. Parker thought it was the best drum sound he'd heard in years, much heavier and more solid than he was previously used to. It was important for the band to take their influences and their sound forward in order to progress. They emphatically had a strong set of recordings for the new album.

Seven Deadly opens with "Fight Night", a suitably strong and steady rock song with a fantastic vocal performance. "Wonderland" is a surprisingly fast number with plenty of adrenaline and energy. "Mojo Town" is charged by a terrific melody and is also notable for some powerful backing vocals. "Angel Station" is a sturdy track, almost soulful with its backing vocals and Mogg's passionate performance. "Year Of The Gun" is a strong, hand-clapping little tune, whereas "The Last Stone Rider" is an anthemic number, perfect for the live stage. "Steal Yourself" is another mid-paced composition, but Mogg sounds at home here. "Burn Your House Down" is woken from a slow start by Moore's controlled guitars. "The Fear" is a groovy Southern American sounding track. Mogg's voice is evidently very appropriate for such a song. "Waving Good Bye" is a curiously alluring number and "Other Men's Wives" (bonus track) has plenty of grit and stomp. "Bag O' Blues" (bonus track) closes the album, leaving the impression that Mogg is now only interested in revisiting the blues singers and songwriters that inspired him in the first place. He has the perfect voice to imitate his heroes yet, at the same time, has an identity all his own.

Some fans had complained that UFO were sounding too middle of the road, too mid-paced, but *Seven Deadly* counter-attacks such criticisms with some aggressive sounding guitars and faster songs. The band sounds modern, energetic and Mogg shows no signs of fatigue or lack of enthusiasm. UFO fans mostly greeted the album with open arms and continued to praise this particular incarnation of the band. Mogg has now set a pattern for the future sound of UFO; there's no doubt that there will be more albums to come and they will sound similar (though not too close) to all albums post *You Are Here*. It is also a sound which UFO fans are mostly thrilled by, especially after the lacklustre sound of *Sharks*.

The careers of many musicians often come full circle; they begin with one particular sound, which was influenced by their heroes, and then try their hand at different styles, before re-discovering the music which they loved right at the beginning and which prompted them to commence a career in music in the first place. Mogg has done just that; he has gone full circle. The resurgence of rock music has probably had a role to play in helping Mogg rekindle his muse. Mogg sounds right at home, while the rest of the band bring along enough energy and drive to ensure that UFO will continue to make more albums of worth in years to come.

The title for the album was originally *Last Of The Bone Riders,* but Mogg didn't get the feedback from the band or the label that he wanted. Some even mocked it by saying it sounded like a gay porno movie! The name Bone Riders actually came from a motorcycle T-shirt Mogg had spotted somebody wearing in the States, when they were on tour. However, it got negative feedback from fans on the band's website, so it was switched to *Seven Deadly*.

Although it was initially slated for June 2011 release, *Seven Deadly* was actually released in February 2012. Their twentieth album peaked even higher than *The Visitor* in the UK, hitting Number 63, although it failed to chart in the USA. Charting higher in Germany and Sweden than *The Visitor, Seven Deadly* received high praise from rock writers. It was hailed as the band's finest album since *You Are Here*, the first to feature Vinnie Moore, while others praised it as one of UFO's strongest ever records.

William Clark wrote on *Ultimate Guitar*: "... the album shows that UFO only continues to progress and improve after 42 years of excellent rock music! Lead singer Phil Mogg can no longer hit the higher notes that dominated 70s hits 'Doctor Doctor' and 'Rock Bottom', but that does not stop him from rocking! In fact, this album shows the band moving into several different genres of music, which sound better with Phil's deeper singing voice."

Metal Underground stated: "Though only 10 tracks long, the album could've probably used some judicious trimming here and there. 'Angel Station' and 'Waving Good Bye' both overstay their welcome a little. Still, only one track – 'Steal Yourself' – feels like it doesn't add anything to the mix (other than another killer solo on an album full of them). Yes, UFO's *Seven Deadly* is more hip-shaker than headbanger, but when the vocals have this much soul and the guitars have this much swing, even the most dedicated mosh pit veteran won't mind mellowing out for a while."

Rebecca Miller enthused on *Metal-Temple*: "To say that Phil Mogg has got an outstanding voice would be an understatement, especially considering that he's been UFO's front man for 43 years. His voice is consistently good on *Seven Deadly* and he shows an awesome range. The guitar work from Vinnie Moore is brilliant, with the guitar solos allowing him to show off his skill. Raymond and Parker provide the rhythm of the album, with excellent style, bringing it all together. The band sound as good as ever, and haven't lost anything, even after all this time."

Seven Deadly has become one of UFO's most popular albums and will no doubt remain a firm fan favourite. It featured in a number of polls of the best rock albums of 2012, including *Classic Rock* and *Get Ready To Rock*.

With a succession of excellent, critically acclaimed and commercially successful albums under their belts, since the somewhat underwhelming reunion with Schenker, UFO quashed any notions that they were nothing but an average rock band without Michael Schenker on guitar. The band have been on fire since 2004's *You Are Here* and have gone from strength to strength ever since.

Rob De Luca continued as their touring bassist. Some long-term fans even commented that UFO were much tighter onstage without Way. The band kicked off the year's touring commitments with a road jaunt around the USA from 5-22 May, before a tour of Germany from 10-16 June. Their USA set list consisted of "The Wild, The Willing And The Innocent", "Mother Mary", "Saving Me", "Let It Roll", "I'm A Loser", "Hell Driver", "Venus", "This Kid's", "Ain't No Baby", "Only You Can Rock Me", "Try Me", "Too Hot To Handle", "Love To Love", "Doctor Doctor", "Lights Out" and "Rock Bottom".

When it comes to the set list, it tends to be down to Phil Mogg – although it is open to discussion. Mogg is not going to sing something he is not comfortable with, yet he will often let the audience decide. If a song does not go down too well with the crowd, he'll change it to something more popular. "The Wild, The Willing And The Innocent" replaced "Long Gone", which was also from the Paul Chapman era. The latter song had not gone down too well with the crowd, even though the band had been getting hits on their website from fans wanting to hear material from the Chapman albums. UFO fans were also pleased that the band opted to include "Venus" from the excellent *Walk On Water* album.

UFO made an appearance at France's Hellfest on 18 June, followed by a gig in Poland at the Dolina Charlotty Resort & Spa in Slupsk on 12 August. UFO could not seem to get enough of the USA, so much so that they ventured back across the Atlantic for a second leg running from 15 September to 8 October.

In 2011, former members Danny Peyronel, Laurence Archer and Clive Edwards, with bassist Rocky Newton of McAuley Schenker Group, formed a UFO covers band called X-UFO. Michael Schenker, on the other hand, had rebuilt his life yet again and was playing better onstage than he had in years. He also took over the financial responsibilities for his children after their mother died unexpectedly.

Both UFO and Michael Schenker are doing well in their own right. "If you live life consciously and you believe that you're developing then you just become a part of life," Schenker told *Classic Rock Revisited*'s Jeb Wright. "You don't just go up. You go down as you go up, some people more, some people less. As I develop and go through my life there are certain things that I have to deal with. I was very shy when I was young and I grew out of it. Other things, as you develop, you overcome difficulties. I think that is all there is to it."[282]

With twenty albums under their belt and a 40 year plus history, it appears that the band have come full circle. In September 2011, EMI released the exhaustive box set *The Chrysalis Years – 1973-1979*, to celebrate the classic Michael Schenker era of the band. Remastered by Peter Mew, it includes the first batch of Schenker albums (*Phenomenon, Force It, No Heavy Petting, Lights Out, Obsession* and the live album *Strangers In The Night*) as well as a live recording of a UFO gig from 5 November 1974 (recorded at the Electric Ballroom in Atlanta). The collection also includes other live recordings and bonus tracks. *The Chrysalis Years 1980-1986* was released in 2012 and celebrates the first phase of the post Schenker years.

Parker spoke to *Hard Rock Heaven*'s Steve Patrick about Pete Way, whom he had not seen in over a year, just after Christmas: "Poor old Peter. He started off with a good attitude, but he kind of fell by the wayside, so I don't see him returning anytime soon. I mean, obviously we're all hoping that he will be back and that he will sort himself out, but the last time I saw him he was still pretty much in the same state that he had been for a while."[283]

At the time of writing, it seems unlikely that Pete Way will rejoin UFO any time soon. The band are still very fond of him despite some of the comments Parker may have made in the press, but the drummer has nothing but respect and love for Way. The bassist has to get his life and health back on track before any negotiations to rejoin UFO can take place.

Laurence Archer says about Pete Way: "When you look at classic UFO, Pete is a massive part of that; his tracks are onstage and his whole presence because nobody else moves around in that band. Pete was drinking but Pete was harmless. He never changes. He's just a smiley drunk. If he got drunk he'd be happy and then he'd fall asleep. Phil was different. He had some darker places."[284]

However, Way did resurface to make a return to the stage when he joined X-UFO for a rousing version of 'Lights Out' at Grimsby Yardbirds in February 2012.

Edwards: "The guy has given his life to rock 'n' roll and being a rock 'n' roller. He's got hepatitis and liver damage. It's not great. He's on a lot of pills. He still falls off the wagon. Pete is Pete. I can't see him changing enough. People said: 'Oh, you shouldn't have got Pete up with X-UFO.' Pete wanted to do it. We wanted Pete to do it. The worst thing you can say to Pete is: 'Pete you're never gonna play live again.' He is a rock 'n' roller. He's got demons but his demons aren't onstage. His demons are when he's off stage. He came up and he played. People got the wrong idea why we do it. We do it because we love Pete. We played the stuff that he wrote and we're mates. We all want to see him back out there. We all want to see him sort himself out, but I don't think he's got the motivation to do it. He's kind of sealed his fate on that and we can just hope he can go for as long as he can keep going. I don't think Pete will suddenly change into a health freak, and if he did I don't think he'll be the same kind of person."[285]

Kit Woolven elaborates: "I suppose they were a bit like an old married couple [or] were, I mean they're divorced. The last time I spoke to Phil he was quite pleased about it. It's so much easier going onstage knowing the bass player is going to play the right song."[286]

Still, it is undeniable that some fans yearn to see Pete Way back in the band. "I heard an interview with Andy Parker recently and I really didn't like the way he spoke about Pete," says Laurence Archer in early 2012. "Pete's in a really bad way at the moment. He's really ill. He was still in Birmingham. I spoke to Spike [of The Quireboys] at the weekend because we both played the Rock & Bike Festival [July 2012] and The Quireboys were on the bill with us. He said he's living above a shop, an off licence in Birmingham. I hope that Pete can hang on and get himself together."[287]

However, you can't keep a good rocker down. I spoke to Pete Way's manager who says he is living in Bournemouth these days and working on a solo album being produced by the wonderful Mike Clink of Guns N' Roses *Appetite For Destruction* fame. This could be the hard rock album Way fans are desperate for. Watch this space. 2013 also saw the Hear No Evil (an imprint of Cherry Red Records) reissues of the Waysted albums, *Vice* and *Save Your Prayers*.

I reviewed the two reissues for *Fireworks* magazine and enthused: "Two different studio releases from a vastly underrated and all-but-forgotten band from one of Britain's greatest rock 'n' roll heroes, Pete Way."

To begin the New Year, UFO performed at Revolution Live in Florida on February 24, before they took part in the Monsters Of Rock Cruise which set sail from Fort Lauderdale, Florida to Key West and Nassau, Bahamas from 25-28 February 2012. The classic rock bill also included Cinderella, Tesla, Kix, Stryper, Y & T and Night Ranger.

A European tour in support of *Seven Deadly* began at the Rock Café in Czech Republic on April 26, with shows going right to May 19 in Holland. On May 11, UFO supported Judas Priest in Mantova, Italy for the first time since 1979's *Hell Bent For Leather* Tour. Priest were on their Epitaph Tour, purportedly their farewell road jaunt.

UFO's eagerly awaited UK tour commenced in Cambridge at The Junction on March 15, going right through to April 4 with a gig at the London Forum, with Rob De Luca on bass. Support on selected dates came from Heavy Metal Kids.

UFO won praise for these live performances, proving that they are still a thrilling live band and that the new material blends in with the classics perfectly. Ian Murtagh was enthusiastic enough about UFO's performance at the Newcastle O2 Academy on March 17, yet he pointed out on *Rush On Rock*: "Maybe, Moggy and the boys could tamper with the running order which during the closing stages of the gig is a little too predictable. There is nothing wrong with keeping the best till last and few bands can produce such a classy finale as 'Too Hot To Handle', 'Lights Out', 'Rock Bottom' followed by encores 'Doctor Doctor' and 'Shoot Shoot'. But if memory serves me right, 'Shoot Shoot' has been the final song they've played at every UFO concert I've attended since the late-70s – and that's quite a few. So next time lads, don't change too much but keep us guessing just that little bit more."

Sue Ashcroft, writing in *Fireworks: The Melodic Rock Magazine*, wrote about the band's gig at the HMV Ritz in Manchester on March 30: "It seems Mr Mogg is in fine form despite reading lyrics from an autocue, his bizarre between song raps are as confusing as they are funny but it all adds to the fun atmosphere of the gig."

The band played "Let It Roll", "Fight Night", "Wonderland", "I'm A Loser", "This Kid's", "Saving Me", "Burn Your House Down", "Only You Can Rock Me", "Love To Love", "Venus", "Too Hot To Handle", "Lights Out" and "Rock Bottom" with an encore of "Doctor Doctor" and "Shoot Shoot". With over 40 years of material to choose from, it can be a headache trying to please the fans with a set list. "It does get difficult. I'm not absolutely sure at this stage what we're going to use from the new album," Andy Parker confessed to Scott Alisoglu of *Teeth Of The Divine*. "I'd imagine it'll be two, maybe three songs at the most. I mean you've got to cut something. Otherwise, we'd have to go about four hours. Normally we get about two hours; that's been our limit."[288]

Mogg, on the other hand, does not find touring as much fun as it used to be. In a post 9/11 world when travelling and airport procedures are more rigorous than ever, it's frustrating for artists to go through all the bureaucratic malarkey. In the old days, Mogg was psyched to be hitting the road and playing to audiences anywhere and everywhere but things have changed, as he told *The Guardian*'s Michael Hann at the start of the *Seven Deadly* tour: "Whereas now it's: are we getting paid? How much are we getting paid? Because in the mid-80s I ended up completely skint."[289]

After spending much of the first half of the year in Europe, the band journeyed around the USA from November onwards. During this time, Repertoire Records released *The Decca Years –1970-1973*. The first disc includes eighteen songs with tracks from the first two albums and various single A-sides and edits. There's UFO's famous cover of "C'mon Everybody", which made the band huge in Japan. There's also a cover of "Loving Cup", a song originally by the American white blues guitar player Paul Butterfield. The second disc contains extended versions of just four songs, although the shortest is a lengthy nine and a half minutes. The extended versions of "Who Do You Love" and "Boogie For George" are both live.

In my review of the collection for *Fireworks: The Melodic Rock Magazine*, I said: "Historically speaking this is a good, interesting collection of songs but don't expect anything near the quality of 'Rock Bottom', 'Lights Out' and 'Only You Can Rock Me' *et al*. UFO is a British rock institution and it's interesting to explore their roots. *The Decca Years* is also a nicely produced package."

The likelihood of Schenker rejoining UFO is slim. His history with the band is a tumultuous one, and knowing how Parker felt during the time of the *Walk On Water* album, it's doubtful anyone in the band would engineer his return. It is equally doubtful Schenker would want to rejoin the camp. UFO is now an incredibly steady band. The instability of the Schenker and, even Way years, has gone.

Dez and Mick Bailey – best known as the Bailey Brothers – were *Metal Hammer* journalists and broadcasters throughout the 1980s. They came in contact with Schenker on a number of occasions. "We go back with UFO from the prime time of Schenker," they told me "[We] followed them to Newark, Birmingham and Blackpool in three days [and] met the band backstage every time. By the time we got to Blackpool, Pete Way told the tour manager to give us passes for the rest of the tour. We ended up in the police cells two nights out of three but that's another story. Pete Way taught me how to play 'Doctor Doctor' in his hotel room, and later when I started playing I had a custom made Flying V. I had Schenker's name put on the headstock. Later when he was with MSG we were at the infamous Sheffield gig when Graham Bonnet walked offstage and Schenker played the rest of the set with no vocalist. We met before backstage and had pics [taken] … things seemed fine. For me *Strangers In The Night* is one of the all time great albums and that original line-up was never beaten."[290]

There have been so many different line-ups of the band, yet it's still the *Strangers In The Night* era which everyone holds in the highest regard. Certainly the Paul Chapman era has its advocates and the *High Stakes* era of the early 1990s deserves more praise.

Clive Edwards: "One thing that's disappointing is that when we went out we used to play virtually the whole of the *High Stakes* album with a bit of the old stuff and immediately it's back to *Strangers In The Night* live and one track off the new album, and they're still doing that now. When we were working, Phil had this thing that he wanted to go somewhere new. He wanted it to be different and he wanted to promote that rather than just playing all the old stuff. It's what they do now."[291]

Mogg did not settle with each subsequent line-up after the classic *Strangers In The Night* incarnation, although there was stability with the Chapman era. It takes a long time for a band to become tight and well-crafted around the edges; years of graft and fine-tuning. It must have been difficult for Mogg to deal with the fact that in between the first and second Schenker periods, he was basically back to square one with the band.

Nick Tauber: "Since the first line-up they've never settled much. I think Phil gets bad press. He gets a lot of bad press. He's one of those people that shouts at people when people don't understand what he's trying to say. 'Let me make it a bit clearer,' and he shouts at them. He's not a bad guy. It's hard to dissect that. I found him a really nice guy. He's been given a lot of bad press. We've all got our faults. Listen to some of his vocals – they're brilliant. Incredible vocalist. When he puts his mind to it he's a fucking good songwriter as well. He's done some incredible vocals like 'Doctor Doctor' and he's done some incredible lyrics."[292]

UFO have never been a band that focuses on creating music for the charts, nor do they gain much mainstream airplay. The band has lasted 40 years because it consists of a group of individuals that love music. It just comes naturally to them and they still have the talent, drive and stamina to create music. UFO's music is not formulaic and, while they may have an identifiable trademark sound, there have been periods of their career when they have wandered off into other musical territories, whether it be blues or space rock, hard rock or melodic rock. Indeed, they have their own style; a musical framework, but they are not formulaic nor are they lazy.

They have never had any notion of creating a hit single (although the money would be handy), because it has always been the music that is important to them and not the opportunity to chase chart success. They treat everything with a sense of humour and fun, except for the music itself about which they are absolutely serious. The humorous side of the band was something that Schenker could not relate to, which is why he isolated himself from everyone else.

They are not a worldwide band such as The Who or Led Zeppelin – who are regularly played on mainstream radio – and neither is there a generation of young rock fans that wear T-shirts bearing their name as they do with AC/DC or Iron Maiden. UFO exists very much in their own self-contained world, below mainstream radar, but they have a fanbase that is vehemently loyal. And kudos to Phil Mogg, whose lyrics have touched on a vast array of subjects; not just the rock clichés about women, booze and drugs but historical subjects too. The music industry needs bands like UFO, even if it has little or no respect for such experienced rock outfits.

Seasoned rock bands such as UFO – now all lumped together under the classic rock umbrella – have seen a return to favour. Whilst UFO may not be filling the large stadia as AC/DC do, they are just as influential, with younger bands declaring their love of (nearly) all things UFO. They say everything goes around in circles and, while the 1990s was a fairly terrible time for hard rock music, the 2000s saw a gradual rise in popularity, thanks in no small part to nostalgia and package tours featuring more than two bands on the same bill, festivals such as Sweden Rock and of course the British magazine, *Classic Rock*.

2013 began for UFO with a UK tour. Continuing to promote the highly acclaimed *Seven Deadly* album, their road jaunt began at Komedia in Bath on February 21. Before climaxing at the Forum in London, they travelled to Bournemouth, Portsmouth, Oxford, Cardiff, Holmfirth, Glasgow, Preston and Birmingham. UFO have always travelled to places that are not only rock strongholds, such as working class towns and cities in the Midlands and the north of England, but also locales that are not typically frequented by rock bands.

Following on from the UK tour, the band headed to mainland Europe for shows in France, Spain and Germany beginning on March 6. It was also announced that the band would perform at the Sweden Rock Festival in June, which would also feature sets from Rush, KISS and Status Quo, amongst dozens of other bands. UFO also performed at the UK's Download Festival in June alongside Iron Maiden, Rammstein and Slipknot, which hopefully introduced them to some new fans.

EMI also pleased fans with more live releases: *On Air: At The BBC 1974-1985* and *Hot 'N' Live – The Chrysalis Years 1974-1983* in 2013.

The final words are best left to Andy Parker, who said to Kelley Simms of *Hails And Horns* in 2011: "The one thing I love about this band is we've never been trend followers. UFO has always been about what comes from the heart. We just play what comes from within. That's always kind of our M.O., and I don't think I could do it any other way."[293]

AFTERWORD

BY PETER MAKOWSKI

To paraphrase an old '60s maxim: if you can remember the times you spent with UFO then you obviously weren't having fun. I know that I saw the band in America in the early '80s, because I have the feature I wrote for *Sounds* to prove it. I am also told that I saw them quite a few times in the US and UK by their former manager, good friend and general fount of wisdom, Mr Wilf Wright.

That bloke who wrote 'The road of excess leads to the palace of wisdom' obviously hadn't spent time on the road with UFO. 'Excess All Areas' would be an appropriate title for a biography of the band, but rather than dwell on the past indiscretions and missed opportunities (another good title) I am going to focus on the music.

My only clear recollections of encountering the band were the first and last time I saw them. The first was when I interviewed them in the mid '70s when *Phenomenon* came out. It was in a cramped office at Chrysalis Records, where I was confronted with the scrawny, worse for wear dynamic duo – Phil Mogg and Pete Way – wearing tight women's tops and leopard skin pants resembling a pair of corvine tranny hookers you'd normally expect to see cruising down the reeperbahns of Hamburg. It was of course a look most rock bands would embrace in the '80s, most with much less panache. It was an uncomfortable interview; I wasn't a fan of their music, which lacked the balls to walls ferocity of Purple, Sabbath and Grand Funk Railroad that informed my record collection, and was less impressed with Leo Lyons production. In fact, the only thing we bonded on was – surprise, surprise – drugs, and Mogg/Way recalled their late nights at the legendary Roundhouse all-nighters fuelled by a mix of Methedrine amps mixed with orange juice.

A few years later, like many thousands of other people, I converted to the UFO cause after hearing *Strangers In The Night* which, along with

199

Made In Japan, easily stands out as one of the most exciting heavy rock albums of all time and was the primer for hundreds of aspiring musicians all over the world.

My most memorable encounter with UFO was as chaotic as anything the band could come up with. Due to a courtesy lounge at Heathrow Airport, 'The Very Legendary' Ross Halfin and me managed to miss our plane and somehow managed to book two seats on Concorde, charging it to Chrysalis. An alcohol-fuelled binge ensued at Supersonic speed and we eventually arrived in LA, with one set of clothes (our luggage was on another plane), jet lagged with our hangovers baking in the merciless Hollywood sunshine. It was 1981 and, by this time, UFO were at their peak as a live band (a fact underlined by their stunning performance at Oakland's Day On The Green where they played to an ecstatic crowd of almost 100,000 people). Confident and armed with an artillery of anthemic crowd pleasers, this, coupled with the fact that it was my first experience of an event of this magnitude, immediately put the band into my all time Top 5 list. A few days later I saw them create the same magic at the Long Beach Arena (with a then unknown Iron Maiden as support), where I bumped into über UFO fan and Cockney Reject Mickey Geggus who flew over to see his heroes in action.

For me, the main strengths of the band are the songs. Classic songs are what give any group or artist an enduring appeal. Next comes Phil Mogg's voice, which easily ranks him as one of the UK's top vocalists alongside Gillan, Rodgers and Plant. Listen to his other band $ign Of Four and you'll realise what an underrated talent he is. Visually the double act of Mogg and Way were unbeatable. And then there was the backline – Parker, Raymond and Paul "Tonka" Chapman, completing what for me was the classic line-up.

The last time I saw UFO was about three years ago at The Brook in Southampton (true music lover's venue, small in size, huge in heart). I was apprehensive about the gig as it was my first sighting of the band since their glory days and a lot of blood, cocaine, Jack Daniel's and managers had gone under the bridge. I needn't have worried, UFO were on fire that night, playing a set that featured highlights from the *Strangers In The Night* album. Mogg's voice was still in magnificent shape ('It's hard rock with the voice of a crooner!' enthused an American pal). Although older, less flexible and bearing the scars of chemical warfare, Pete Way still embodied the spirit of the band. With the same humour and humility that captured the hearts of the blue collar workers and punks alike, the band's enthusiasm and rapport with the audience left me with the same feelings of euphoria I had that afternoon in Oakland almost 30 years ago.

UFO are, and always will be, classic rock at its best.

Peter Makowski
Classic Rock/Mojo

UFO SELECTED DISCOGRAPHY (UK)

UFO's discography is a long and convoluted one. The following list is restricted to official UK releases only and to the original versions unless otherwise stated.

ALBUMS

UFO 1
Beacon, 1969
Unidentified Flying Object/Boogie/C'mon Everybody/Shake It About/ (Come Away) Melinda/Timothy/Follow You Home/Treacle People/Who Do You Love?/Evil

UFO 2: FLYING
Beacon, 1971
Silver Bird/Star Storm/Prince Kajuku/The Coming Of Prince Kajuku/ Flying

PHENOMENON
Chrysalis, 1974
Oh My/Crystal Light/Doctor Doctor/Space Child/Rock Bottom/Too Young To Know/Time On My Hands/Built For Comfort/Lipstick Traces/ Queen Of The Deep

FORCE IT
Chrysalis, 1975
Let It Roll/Shoot Shoot/High Flyer/Love Lost Love/Out In The Street/ Mother Mary/Too Much Of Nothing/Dance Your Life Away/This Kid's (Including Between The Walls)

NO HEAVY PETTING
Chrysalis, 1976
Natural Thing/I'm A Loser/Can You Roll Her/Belladonna/Reasons Love/
Highway Lady/On With The Action/A Fool In Love/Martian Landscape

LIGHTS OUT
Chrysalis, 1977
Too Hot To Handle/Just Another Suicide/Try Me/Lights Out/Gettin'
Ready/Alone Again Or/Electric Phase/Love To Love

OBSESSION
Chrysalis, 1978
Only You Can Rock Me/Pack It Up (And Go)/Arbory Hill/Ain't No Baby/
Lookin' Out For No.1/Hot 'N' Ready/Cherry/You Don't Fool Me/Lookin'
Out For No. 1(Reprise)/One More For The Rodeo/Born To Lose

NO PLACE TO RUN
Chrysalis, 1980
Alpha Centauri/Lettin' Go/Mystery Train/This Fire Burns Tonight/Gone
In The Night/Young Blood/No Place To Run/Take It Or Leave It/Money,
Money/Anyday

THE WILD, THE WILLING AND THE INNOCENT
Chrysalis, 1981
Chains Chains/Long Gone/The Wild, The Willing And The Innocent/It's
Killing Me/Makin' Moves/Lonely Heart/Couldn't Get It Right/Profession
Of Violence

MECHANIX
Chrysalis, 1982
The Writer/Somethin' Else/Back Into My Life/You'll Get Love/Doing It
All For You/We Belong To The Night/Let It Rain/Terri/Feel It/Dreaming

MAKING CONTACT
Chrysalis, 1983
Blinded By A Lie/Diesel In The Dust/A Fool For Love/You And Me/When

It's Time To Rock/The Way The Wild Wind Blows/Call My Name/All Over You/No Getaway/Push, It's Love

MISDEMEANOR
Chrysalis, 1985
This Time/One Heart/Night Run/The Only Ones/Meanstreets/Name Of Love/Blue/Dream The Dream/Heaven's Gate/Wreckless

AIN'T MISBEHAVIN'
FM/Revolver, 1988
Between A Rock And A Hard Place/Another Saturday Night/At War With The World/Hunger In The Night/Easy Money/Rock Boyz, Rock/Lonely Cities (Of The Heart)

HIGH STAKES & DANGEROUS MEN
Razor/Griffin, 1992
Borderline/Primed For Time/She's The One/Ain't Life Sweet/Don't Want To Lose You/Burnin' Fire/Running Up The Highway/Back Door Man/One Of Those Nights/Revolution/Love Deadly Love/Let The Good Times Roll

WALK ON WATER
Eagle, 1995
A Self-Made Man/Venus/Pushed To The Limit/Stopped By A Bullet (Of Love)/Darker Days/Running On Empty/Knock, Knock/Dreaming Of Summer/Doctor Doctor/Lights Out/Fortune Town/I Will Be There/Public Enemy #1

COVENANT
Shrapnel, 2000
(Disc 1) Love Is Forever/Unraveled/Miss The Lights/Midnight Train/Fool's Gold/In The Middle Of Madness/The Smell Of Money/Rise Again/Serenade/Cowboy Joe/The World And His Dog
(Disc 2 – UFO Live In The USA) Mother Mary/This Kid's/Let It Roll/Out In The Street/Venus/Pushed To The Limit/Love To Love

SHARKS
Shrapnel, 2002
Outlaw Man/Quicksilver Rider/Serenity/Deadman Walking/Shadow Dancer/Someone's Gonna Have To Pay/Sea Of Faith/Fighting Man/ Perfect View/Crossing Over/Hawaii

YOU ARE HERE
SPV, 2004
When Daylight Goes To Town/Black Cold Coffee/The Wild One/Give It Up/Call Me/Slipping Away/The Spark That Is Us/Sympathy/Mr Freeze/ Jello Man/Baby Blue/Swallow

THE MONKEY PUZZLE
SPV, 2006
Hard Being Me/Heavenly Body/Some Other Guy/Who's Fooling Who/ Black And Blue/Drink Too Much/World Cruise/Down By The River/ Good Bye You/Rolling Man/Kingston Town

THE VISITOR
SPV, 2009
Saving Me/On The Waterfront/Hell Driver/Stop Breaking Down/Rock Ready/Living Proof/Can't Buy A Thrill/Forsaken/Villains & Thieves/ Stranger In Town/Saving Me

SEVEN DEADLY
SPV, 2012
Fight Night/Wonderland/Mojo Town/Angel Station/Year Of The Gun/ The Last Stone Rider/Burn Your House Down/The Fear/Waving Good Bye/Other Men's Wives *(Bonus Track)*/Bag O' Blues *(Bonus Track)*

LIVE ALBUMS

UFO LIVE
Toshiba Musical Industries/Stateside, 1971 (Japan), 1972 (World)
C'mon Everybody/Who Do You Love/Loving Cup/Prince Kajuku/The Coming Of Prince Kajuku/Boogie For George/Follow You Home

STRANGERS IN THE NIGHT
Chrysalis, 1979
Natural Thing/Out In The Street/Only You Can Rock Me/Doctor Doctor/
Mother Mary/This Kid's/Love To Love/Lights Out/Rock Bottom/Too Hot
To Handle/I'm A Loser/Let It Roll/Shoot Shoot

LIVE ON EARTH
Zoom Club, 2003
(Disc 1) Natural Thing/Mother Mary/A Self Made Man/Electric Phase/
This Kid's/Out In The Street/One More For The Rodeo/Venus/Pushed To
The Limit
(Disc 2) Love To Love/Too Hot To Handle/Only You Can Rock Me/Lights
Out/Doctor Doctor/Rock Bottom/Shoot Shoot
(Disc 3) Lights Out/Getting' Ready/Love To Love/On With The Action/
Doctor Doctor/Out In The Streets/This Kid's/Shoot Shoot/Rock Bottom/
Too Hot To Handle
(Disc 4) Natural Thing/Mother Mary/Let It Roll/This Kid's/Out In The
Streets/Venus/Pushed To The Limits/Love To Love/Only You Can Rock
Me/Too Hot To Handle/Lights Out/Doctor Doctor/Rock Bottom/Shoot
Shoot/C'mon Everybody
NOTE: This was released as a two CD and four CD set.

HEADSTONE – LIVE AT HAMMERSMITH 1983
EMI, 2003
We Belong To The Night/Let It Rain/Couldn't Get It Right/Electric Phase/
Doing It All For You/Long Gone/Chains Chains/Lonely Heart/Blinded By
A Lie/No Place To Run/Mystery Train

NOTE ON LIVE RELEASES: *There are many more official, unofficial and
non UK released UFO live releases. Here is a list of the most well-known and
widely circulated ones.*

Misdemeanor Tour LIVE (1986)
Lights Out In Tokyo Live (1992)
T.N.T (1993)
BBC 1 – Live In Concert (1995)
Heaven's Gate (1995)

On With The Action (1998)
BBC – In Session And Live (1999)
Werewolves Of London (With Schenker, Mogg, Way, Raymond, Dunbar) (1998)
Live In Texas (2000)
Regenerator – Live 1982 (2001)
Big Apple Encounters – Live At The Record Plant NYC 1975 (2004)
Showtime (2005)
Live Throughout The Years (2007)
Classic Studio Recordings And Essential Live Hits (2007)
Impact Live (2009)
Live On Air (2010)
Live In Texas 1979 (2011)
On Air: At The BBC 1974–1985 (2013)
Hot 'N' Live – The Chrysalis Years 1974–1983 (2013)

COMPILATIONS

SPACE METAL
Nova, 1976
Loving Cup/Shake It About/Silver Bird/(Come Away) Melinda/Evil/
Flying/A Boogie For George/Star Storm/Timothy/C'mon Everybody/
Follow You Home/Prince Kajuku

ANTHOLOGY
Castle, 1986
Rock Bottom/Built For Comfort/Highway Lady/Can You Roll Her/A Fool
For Love/Shoot Shoot/Too Hot For Handle/Getting' Ready/Only You Can
Rock Me/Looking For No.1/Something Else/Doing It All For You/When
It's Time To Rock/Diesel In The Dust

THE BEST OF THE REST
Chrysalis, 1988
The Writer/Mystery Train/Makin' Moves/Night Run/You And Me/Alpha
Centauri/Lettin' Go/Something Else/Blinded By A Lie/Diesel In The
Dust/Chains Chains/This Time/Back Into My Life/The Way The Wind
Blows/Money, Money/Let It Rain/A Fool For Love

THE ESSENTIAL UFO
Chrysalis, 1992
Doctor Doctor/Rock Bottom/Out In The Street/Mother Mary/Natural Thing/I'm A Loser/Only You Can Rock Me/Lookin' Out For No.1/Cherry/Born To Lose/Too Hot To Handle/Lights Out/Love To Love/This Kid's/Let It Roll/Shoot Shoot

THE BEST OF UFO: GOLD COLLECTION
EMI, 1996
Doctor Doctor/Only You Can Rock Me/Let It Roll/Shoot Shoot/Let It Rain/When It's Time To Rock/Rock Bottom/Love To Love/High Flyer/Can You Roll Her/Pack It Up (And Go)/Hot & Ready/This Time/Long Gone/Young Blood/Lonely Heart

THE BEST OF UFO
EMI, 2002
Lights Out *(Live)*/Only You Can Rock Me *(Live)*/Too Hot To Handle/Love To Love/Doctor Doctor/Rock Bottom/Lettin' Go/Cherry/Out In The Street/Mystery Train

THE BEST OF UFO (1974-1983)
EMI, 2008
Rock Bottom/Oh My/Let It Roll/Shoot Shoot/Can You Roll Her/I'm A Loser/Natural Thing/Lights Out/Love To Love/Too Hot To Handle/Only You Can Rock Me/Doctor Doctor *(Live)*/Lettin' Go/Young Blood/Lonely Heart/Chains Chains/Let It Rain/We Belong To The Night/When It's Time To Rock

NOTE ON COMPILATIONS: *There are many more official, unofficial and non UK released UFO compilation releases. Here is a list of the most well-known and widely circulated ones.*

UFO C'mon Everybody (1981)
UFO Headstone – The Best Of UFO 1983 (1983)
The Collection (1985)
X-Factor: Out There & Back (1987)
Essential (1992)

UFO – Rock Champions (2001)
The Decca Years (2002)
Then & Now (2003)
Flying: The Early Years 1970–1973 (2004)
An Introduction To UFO (2007)
All The Hits & More – The Early Days (2001)
Alien Relations (2005)
One Of Those Nights – The Collection (2006)
The Best Of '74–'83 (2008)
Broadcast Rarities (2008)
Orange Collection (2008)
The Best Of A Decade (2010)
Hard Rock Legends (2010)
The Best Of A Decade (2010)
Time To Rock – Best Of Singles (2011)
Too Hot To Handle – The Very Best Of UFO (2012)
The Best Of The Decca Years (1970–1973) (2012)
All The Hits & More – The Early Years (2012)

BOX SETS

THE OFFICIAL BOOTLEG BOX SET (1975–1982)
EMI, 2009

(Disc 1) *(Live At Record Plant; New York, 1/9/75)* Intro/Let It Roll/Doctor Doctor/Oh My/Built For Comfort/Out In The Street/Space Child/Mother Mary/All Or Nothing/This Kid's/Shoot Shoot/Rock Bottom

(Disc 2) *(Live At The Roundhouse; London 25/4/76)* Can You Roll Her/ Doctor Doctor/Oh My/Out In The Street/Highway Lady/I'm A Loser/Let It Roll/This Kid's/Shoot Shoot/Rock Bottom/C'mon Everybody/Boogie For George

(Disc 3) *(Live At The Roundhouse; London 2/4/77)* Lights Out/Getting' Ready/Love To Love/On With The Action/Doctor Doctor/Try Me/Too Hot To Handle/Out In The Street/This Kid's/Shoot Shoot/Rock Bottom/ Let It Roll/C'mon Everybody

(Disc 4) *(Live In Cleveland; Ohio, 16/10/78)* Hot 'N' Ready/Pack It Up/ Cherry/Let It Roll/Love To Love/Natural Thing/Out In The Street/Only

You Can Rock Me/On With The Action/Doctor Doctor/I'm A Loser/Lights Out/Rock Bottom

(Disc 5) *(Live In Hammersmith; London, 20/2/81)* Chains Chains/Long Gone/Cherry/Only You Can Rock Me/No Place To Run/Love To Love/ Makin' Moves/Mystery Train/Lights Out

(Disc 6) *(Live In Hammersmith – 'BBC In Concert'; 28/1/82)* We Belong To The Night/Let It Rain/Long Gone/The Wild, The Willing And The Innocent/Only You Can Rock Me/No Place To Run/Love To Love/Doing It All For You/Makin' Moves/Too Hot To Handle/Mystery Train

THE CHRYSALIS YEARS – VOLUME I (1973–1979)
EMI, 2011

(Disc 1) *(Single, 1973)* Give Her The Gun/Sweet Little Thing *(Phenomenon, 1974)* Oh My/Crystal Light/Doctor Doctor/Space Child/Rock Bottom/ Too Young To Know/Time On My Hands/Built For Comfort/Lipstick Traces/Queen Of The Deep/Doctor Doctor *(Bonus Track) (Bob Harris Record Session, October 28, 1974)* Rock Bottom/Time On My Hands/Give Her The Gun

(Disc 2) *(Live At The Electric Ballroom; Atlanta, GA, November 5, 1974)* Oh My/Doctor Doctor/Built For Comfort/Give Her The Gun/Cold Turkey/ Space Child/Rock Bottom/Prince Kujuku *(Force It, 1975)* Let It Roll/ Shoot Shoot/High Flyer/Love Lost Love/Out In The Street

(Disc 3) *(Force It, 1975)* Mother Mary/Too Much Of Nothing/Dance Your Life Away/This Kid's *(No Heavy Petting, 1976)* Natural Thing/I'm A Loser/ Can You Roll Her/Belladonna/Reasons Love/Highway Lady/On With The Action/A Fool In Love/Martian Landscape *(Lights Out, 1977)* Too Hot To Handle/Just Another Suicide/Try Me/Lights Out

(Disc 4) *(Lights Out, 1977)* Getting' Ready/Alone Again Or/Electric Phase/Love To Love/Try Me *(Bonus Track) (John Peel Recording Session, June 27, 1977)* Too Hot To Handle/Lights Out/Try Me *(Obsession, 1978)* Only You Can Rock Me/Pack It Up (And Go)/Arbory Hill/Ain't No Baby/ Lookin' Out For No.1/Hot 'N' Ready/Cherry/You Don't Fool Me/Lookin' Out For No. 1(Reprise)/One More For The Rodeo/Born To Lose/Only You Can Rock Me *(Bonus Track)*

(Disc 5) *(Strangers In The Night)* Natural Thing/Out In The Street/Only You Can Rock Me/Doctor Doctor/Mother Mary/This Kid's/Love To Love/ Lights Out/Rock Bottom/Too Hot To Handle/I'm A Loser/Let It Roll/

Shoot Shoot/Doctor Doctor *(Bonus Track)*/On With The Action *(Bonus Track)*

THE CHRYSALIS YEARS – VOLUME II (1980–1986)
EMI, 2012

(Disc 1) Alpha Centauri/Lettin' Go/Mystery Train/This Fire Burns Tonight/Gone In The Night/Young Blood/No Place To Run/Take It Or Leave It/Money Money/Anyday/Young Blood *(7" Edit)*/Hot 'N' Ready *(Live In Cleveland, Ohio)*/Lettin' Go *(BBC In Concert)*/Young Blood *(BBC In Concert)*/No Place To Run *(BBC In Concert)*/Out In The Street *(BBC In Concert)*/Cherry *(BBC In Concert)*/Only You Can Rock Me *(BBC In Concert)*/Love To Love *(BBC In Concert)*

(Disc 2) Mystery Train *(BBC In Concert)*/Doctor Doctor *(BBC In Concert)*/Too Hot To Handle *(BBC In Concert)*/Lights Out *(BBC In Concert)*/Rock Bottom *(BBC In Concert)*/Chains Chains/Long Gone/The Wild, The Willing And The Innocent/It's Killing Me/Makin' Moves/Lonely Heart/Couldn't Get It Right/Profession Of Violence/Lonely Heart *(7" Edit)*

(Disc 3) The Writer/Somethin' Else/Back Into My Life/You'll Get Love/Doing It All For You/We Belong To The Night/Let It Rain/Terri/Feel It/Dreaming/Heel Of A Stranger

(Disc 4) Blinded By A Lie/Diesel In The Dust/A Fool For Love/You And Me/When It's Time To Rock/The Way The Wild Wind Blows/Call My Name/All Over You/No Getaway/Push, It's Love/Everybody Knows/When It's Time To Rock *(7" Edit)*/We Belong To The Night *(Live At Hammersmith)*/Let It Rain *(Live At Hammersmith)*/Couldn't Get It Right *(Live At Hammersmith)*/Electric Phase *(Live At Hammersmith)*/Doing It All For You *(Live At Hammersmith)*

(Disc 5) This Time/One Heart/Night Run/The Only Ones/Mean Streets/Name Of Love/Blue/Dream The Dream/Heavens Gate/Wreckless/The Chase/Night Run *(US Remix)*/Heavens Gate *(US Remix)*/One Heart *(US Remix)*

SINGLES

'Shake It About'/'Evil' *(1970)*
'(Come Away) Melinda'/'Unidentified Flying Object' *(1970)*
'Boogie For George'/'Treacle People' *(1970)*

'C'mon Everybody'/'Timothy' *(1970)*
'Boogie For George'/'Follow You Home' *(1971)*
'Prince Kajuku'/'The Coming Of Prince Kajuku' *(1971)*
'Give Her The Gun'/'Sweet Little Thing' *(1974) (Germany only)*
'Doctor Doctor'/'Lipstick Traces' *(1974)*
'Rock Bottom' *(1974)*
'Rock Bottom'/'Doctor Doctor' *(1975)*
'High Flyer' *(1975)*
'Shoot Shoot'/'Love Lost Love' *(1975)*
'High Flyer'/'Let It Roll' *(1975)*
'Can You Roll Her'/'Belladonna' *(1976) (Japan only)*
'Highway Lady'/'Fool In Love' *(1976) (Japan only)*
'Too Hot To Handle'/'Electric Phase' *(1977)*
'Getting' Ready'/'Too Hot To Handle' *(1977)*
'Alone Again Or'/'Electric Phase' *(1977)*
'Try Me'/'Getting' Ready' *(1978)*
'Only You Can Rock Me' *(EP) (1978)*
'Doctor Doctor' *(Live EP) (1979)*
'Couldn't Get It Right'/'Hot 'N' Ready' *(1980)*
'Lonely Heart'/'Long Gone' *(1980)*
'Shoot Shoot' *(1980)*
'Young Blood' *(1980)*
'Lonely Heart' *(1981)*
'The Writer' *(1982)*
'Let It Rain' *(1982)*
'When It's Time To Rock' *(1983)*
'Night Run' *(1986)*
'This Time' *(1986)*

VIDEO/DVD

UFO – The Misdemeanor Tour Live (VHS, 1985)
Too Hot To Handle (VHS, 1994)
Showtime – Live In Germany (DVD, 2005)

BIBLIOGRAPHY & SOURCES

The following publications and websites were integral in making this book possible ...

Special thanks to Classic Rock, Kerrang!, Melody Maker (RIP) and *Sounds* (RIP).

REFERENCE TEXTS

Betts, Graham. *Complete UK Hit Singles 1952-2005.* London: Collins, 2005.

Betts, Graham. *Complete UK Hit Albums: 1956-2005.* London: Collins, 2005.

Larkin, Colin. *The Virgin Encyclopaedia Of Rock.* London: Virgin Books, 1999.

Roberts, David (Ed). *British Hit Singles & Albums. (19th Edition).* London: Guinness World Records Ltd, 2006.

Strong, Martin C. *The Great Rock Discography. (6th Edition).* London: Canongate, 2002.

GENERAL BOOKS ON ROCK

Christe, Ian. *Sound Of The Beast: The Complete Headbanging History Of Heavy Metal.* London: Allison & Busby Limited, 2004.

Konow, David. *Bang Your Head: The Rise And Fall Of Heavy Metal.* London: Plexus, 2004.

Popoff, Martin. *The Collector's Guide To Heavy Metal – Volume 1: The Seventies.* Collector's Guide Publishing: Toronto, 2003.

Popoff, Martin. *The Collector's Guide To Heavy Metal – Volume 2: The Eighties.* Collector's Guide Publishing: Toronto, 2005.

Popoff, Martin. *The Collector's Guide To Heavy Metal – Volume 3: The Nineties*. Collector's Guide Publishing: Toronto, 2007.

BOOKS ON UFO

Popoff, Martin. *UFO: Shoot Out The Lights* (Metal Blade Records: California, 2005).

MAGAZINES

Aardschok
Beat Instrumental Magazine
Big Cheese
Billboard
Bravo Magazine
Circus
Classic Rock
Fireworks
Goldmine
Guitar World
Hard Roxx
Kerrang!
Melody Maker
Metal Edge
Metal Forces
Metal Fury
Metal Hammer

NME
Pop
Powerplay
Prime Crime
Record Mirror
Revolver
Riff Raff
Rock Power
Rock Scene
Rolling Stone
Scene
Sounds
Sounds: Guitar Heroes
Trouser Press
Way Ahead
Waxpaper

SELECTED ARTICLES

Alisoglu, Scott, 'UFO – The Spark That Is Us'. *Teeth Of The Divine.com*, 2012.
Bowar, Chad, 'A Conversation With Vinnie Moore'. *About.com*, 2009.
Epstein, Dmitry. 'Interview With Phil Mogg'. *Let It Rock/dmme.net*, 2002.

Hann, Michael, '54 Minutes With ... Phil Mogg'. *The Guardian*, 2012.

Hash, Tommy, 'Andy Parker: Seven And Seven Is'. *Ytsejam.com*, 2012.

Patrick, Steve, 'Andy Parker Of UFO Is No Bone Rider'. *Hard Rock Heaven. com*, 2012.

Perry, Steph, 'Pete Way Interview'. *Rocknotes Webzine*, 2000.

Reese, Joel, 'Michael Schenker Interview'. *Chicago Herald*, 2001.

Rettman, Tony, 'The King Of Oblivion Slings Mud – Larry Wallis Interview'. *Furious.com*, 2002.

Ritchie, Jason. 'Interview: Phil Mogg'. *Get Ready To Rock.com*, 2002.

Ritchie, Jason, '10 Questions With Paul Raymond'. *Get Ready To Rock.com*, 2005.

Seaver, Morley, 'Morley Views – UFO'. *Antimusic.com*, 2009.

Simms, Kelley, 'UFO: Interview With Andy Parker'. *Hails And Horns.com*, 2011.

Smith, Todd K. 'An Interview With Phil Mogg'. *Cutting Edge Rocks.com*, 2004.

Syrjala, Marko, 'UFO's Vinnie Moore and Pete Way'. *Metal-Rules.com*, 2004.

Torem, Lisa, 'UFO Interview'. *Pennyblackmuisc.com*, 2011.

WEBSITES

http://dmme.net
http://heavymetal.about.com
http://rocknoteswebzine.com
http://rushonrock.com
www.allmusic.com
www.antimusic.com
www.bbc.co.uk/news/england/manchester
www.beatsworking.tv
www.classicrockmagazine.com
www.classicrockrevisited.com
www.cuttingedgerocks.com
www.fullinbloommusic.com
www.furious.com
www.getreadytorock.com
www.getreadytoroll.com

www.glam-metal.com
www.guardian.co.uk
www.hailsandhorns.com
www.hardrockheaven.com
www.houseofshred.com
www.live4metal.com
www.melodicrock.com
www.metal-temple.com
www.metalexpressradio.com
www.metalunderground.com
www.pennyblackmusic.com
www.relix.com
www.revelationz.net
www.roughedge.com
www.seaoftranquility.org
www.sleazeroxx.com
www.teethofthedivine.com
www.ultimate-guitar.com
www.ytsejam.com

ACKNOWLEDGEMENTS

Thanks to the following rockers and metalheads for making this book possible and for their ongoing support: Phil and Sue Ashcroft, Andy Brailsford, Steve Calzaretta, Kevin Elson, Doug Flett, James Gaden, Richard Galbraith, Phil and Sue Godsell, Nigel Hart, Peter Makowski, Derek Oliver, Ian Parry, Martin Popoff, Brian Tatler, Eddie Trunk, John Tucker and Richard Ward.

Thank you again to the following people for allowing me to interview them for the purposes of this book and/or for their contributions: Laurence Archer, Dez and Mick Bailey, Neil Carter, Clive Edwards, Kevin Elson, Mick Glossop, Myke Gray, Paul Gray, Colin Hart, Leo Lyons, Peter Makowski, Tony Mills, Ron Nevison, Danny Peyronel, Brian Slagel, John Sloman, Nick Tauber, Brian Tatler, Eddie Trunk, Kit Woolven and Simon Wright.

Thank you to the follow journalists and writers whose articles, interviews and reviews helped the author during research for this book and whose work is fully credited and referenced in the main text: Scott Alisoglu, Michael Ameen, Jason Anderson, Sue Ashcroft, Geoff Barton, Philip Bell, Mark Blake, Kirk Blows, Chad Bowar, Mick Burgess, Garry Bushell, Steffan Chirazi, Robert Christgau, William Clark, Peter Crescenti, Mike Daley, Mark Day, Dave Dickson, Harry Doherty, Peter Douglas, Barbara Drillsma, Jill Eckersley, Bob Edmands, Dmitry M. Epstein. Jerry Ewing, Gordon Fletcher, Doug Flett, Richard Foss, Phil Freeman, David Fricke, Steve Gett, Andy Gill, Ronnie Gurr, Lyn Guy, Mike Guy, Michael Hann, Brian Harrigan, Shelly Harris, Karen Harvey, Tommy Hash, Paul Henderson, Matthew Honey, Andy Hughes, Del James, Howard Johnson, Bill Landers, Merryl Lentz, Dave Ling, Pete Makowski, Andrew McNeice, Cliff Michalski, Rebecca Miller, Ruben Mosqueda, Ian Murtagh, Pete Pardo, Steve Patrick, Steph Perry, Roger St Pierre, Mark Putterford (RIP), Joel Reese, Tony Rettman, Dave Reynolds, Jason Ritchie, Joe Robinson, Al Rudis, Simon Rushworth, Morley Seaver, Garry Sharpe-Young (RIP), Kelley Simms, Robert L. Smith, Robin Smith, Todd K. Smith, Tony Stewart, Marko Syrjala, Lisa Torem, Mick Wall, Chris Watts, Chris Welch, Jeb Wright, Chris Yancik and Ray Zell.

Apologies if I have missed any names ... it was not intentional. Honest!

Visit *neildanielsbooks.tumblr.com* and *neildanielsbooks.wordpress.com* for details on my other books.

ENDNOTES

Interview material used throughout this book is taken from the author's own original interviews and conversations, unless noted in the text or below.

INTRODUCTION

1 *"It is so important however as a band to keep moving forward ..."*: Paul Raymond quote; Mick Burgess interview, *Metal Express Radio*, 2007.

CHAPTER ONE
Unidentified Flying Object – The Early Space Rock Years (1969-1972)

2 *"We try to do more than just play music – we entertain ..."*: Phil Mogg; Roger St. Pierre interview, *NME*, January, 1972.

3 *"I discovered the blues from the English blues and ..."*: Phil Mogg quote; Todd K. Smith interview, *Cutting Edge Rocks*, 2004.

4 *"My mum always warned me about loud music ..."*: Pete Way quote; Bob Edmands interview, *NME*, 1978.

5 *"My mother always had to sing ..."*: Andy Parker quote; Lisa Torem interview, *Penny Black Music*, 2011.

6 *"It's just my style that I developed over the years ..."*: Andy Parker quote; Tommy Hash interview, *Ytsejam*, 2012.

7 *"At this distance from events I don't have ..."*: Doug Flett quote; author correspondence, 2012.

8 *"We were torn between doing something that was bluesy ..."*: Phil Mogg quote; Todd K. Smith interview, *Cutting Edge Rocks*, 2004.

9 *"We want to develop melody, lyric ..."*: Phil Mogg quote; interviewer unknown, *Beat Instrumental Magazine*, September, 1971.

10 *"Japanese audiences are great. They will accept anything ..."*: Mick Bolton quote; Roger St. Pierre interview, *NME*, January, 1972.

11 *"We have noticed that people seem more into ..."*: Pete Way quote; Mike Guy interview, *Melody Maker*, October, 1971.

12 *"Oh ... I suppose you could say we were sexual and possibly slightly bizarre ..."*: Phil Mogg quote; Chris Welch interview, *Melody Maker*, 1972.

13 *"I don't know. Perhaps it's because the public has become a little ..."*: Phil Mogg; Roger St. Pierre interview, *NME*, January, 1972.

14 *"He signed us a publishing deal for £8,000 ..."*: Larry Wallis quote; Tony Rettman interview, *Furious*, 2002.

CHAPTER TWO
UFO's Rise To Prominence – The Michael Schenker Years Part 1 (1973–1976)

15 *"This a rock band. The thing is that you are what you do ..."*: Pete Way quote; Marko Syrjala interview, *Metal-Rules*, 2004.

16 *"So there we were, no guitarist and no gear ..."*: Phil Mogg quite; Cliff Michalski interview, *Scene*, June, 1976.

17 *"We've already been through the super star treatment ..."*: Phil Mogg quote; Chris Welch interview, *Melody Maker*, 1972.

18 *"Oh, Bernie's just an easy-going, nice guy to get on with ..."*: Pete Way quote; Marko Syrjala interview, *Metal-Rules*, 2007.

19 *"... Bernie was great, Bernie was very funny ..."*: Phil Mogg quote; Dmitry M. Epstein interview, *Let It Rock/dmme.net*, 2002.

20 *"I would call it original – as original as it gets ..."*: Michael Schenker quote; Joel Reese interview, *Chicago Daily Herald*, 2001.

21 *"We could not have fulfilled our visions as accurately as we ..."*: Michael Schenker quote; Jeb Wright interview, *Classic Rock Revisited*, 2001.

22 *"... I was on stage with the Scorpions and about to play ..."*: Michael Schenker quote; Matthew Honey interview, *Hard Roxx*, 1997.

23 *"He will bring us luck ..."*: Phil Mogg quote; interviewer unknown, *Bravo* magazine, 1973.

24 *"Because basically they'd sold a few records in Germany ..."*: Leo Lyons quote; author interview, 2012.

25 *"I don't think there was too much translating ..."*: Leo Lyons quote; author interview, 2012.

26 *"Pete was always the guy that had a million excuses ..."*: Leo Lyons quote; author interview, 2012.

27 *"They liked it. They put it out in America and Jerry Moss s ..."*: Leo Lyons quote; author interview, 2012.

28 *"We were a team of people that were going to show ..."*: Leo Lyons quote; author interview, 2012.

29 *"That's why we're a looser organisation than many ..."*: Phil Mogg quote; Michael Ameen interview, *Trouser Press*, 1979.

30 *"Working in a studio is very stressful ..."*: Leo Lyons quote; author interview, 2012.

31 *"Sometime during that period the band came to me without ..."*: Leo Lyons quote; author interview, 2012.

32 *"One of the guys would come up with a riff ..."*: Leo Lyons quote; author interview, 2012.

33 *"The other 3 UFOs Phil, Andy and Pete have proved a s ..."*: Michael Schenker quote; interviewer unknown, *Pop*, August, 1975.

34 *"Perhaps all this bad luck is a sign of something good ..."*: Michael Schenker quote; interviewer unknown, *Pop* magazine, August, 1975.

35 *"Bizarrely coincidentally, almost as soon as I got ..."*: Danny Peyronel quote; author interview, 2012.

36 *"I telephoned Alexandra when I reached my decision ..."*: Danny Peyronel quote; author interview, 2012.

37 *"UFO were really big in Germany at the time ..."*: Danny Peyronel quote; author interview, 2012.

38 *"There are no bands around in Britain today that I can ..."*: Phil Mogg quote; Geoff Barton interview, *Sounds*, 1977.

39 *"Well, they [Chrysalis] gave me £1500 and it's £25 an hour ..."*: Leo Lyons quote; author interview, 2012.

40 *"I think it's pretty common that when a band does its first record ..."*: Leo Lyons quote; author interview, 2012.

41 *"He'd turn up later saying he turned up late ..."*: Leo Lyons quote; author interview, 2012.

42 *"Yeah, there was tension ..."*: Leo Lyons quote; author interview, 2012.

43 *"No Heavy Petting represents a change in the ..."*: Danny Peyronel quote; author interview, 2012.

44 *"... I don't have any memories of having to ..."*: Danny Peyronel quote; author interview, 2012.

45 *"By the third one they [Chrysalis] started to wake up ..."*: Leo Lyons quote; author interview, 2012.

46 *"I saw them live a couple of times ..."*: Leo Lyons quote; author interview, 2012.

47 *"All in all? Great fun, very exciting tours and shows ..."*: Danny Peyronel quote; author interview, 2012.

48 *"I never actually liked Jethro Tull at all ..."*: Phil Mogg quote; Robert L. Smith interview, *Goldmine*, 1980.

49 *"We're confidence; it might be confidence in Jim Beam ..."*: Phil Mogg quite; Cliff Michalski interview, *Scene*, June, 1976.

CHAPTER THREE
Lights Out – The Michael Schenker Years Part 2 (1977–1978)

50 *"1977 is going to be our most successful year ..."*: Phil Mogg quote; interviewer unknown, *Bravo*, December, 1976.

51 *"My biggest influences were Bill Evans and Victor Feldman, two extraordinary talent jazz pianists ..."*: Paul Raymond quote; Jason Ritchie, *Get Ready To Rock*, 2005.

52 *"Paul seems very, very good ..."*: Andy Parker quote; Mike Daley interview, *Way Ahead*, 1977.

53 *"Doesn't everyone know this one by now? I didn't 'leave' ..."*: Danny Peyronel quote; author interview, 2012.

54 *"We decided to make a big chance on this album ..."*: Andy Parker quote; Mike Daley interview, *Way Ahead*, 1977.

55 *"John Burgess, he was a record producer ..."*: Leo Lyons quote; author interview, 2012.

56 *"I thought they [UFO] wrote some amazing ..."*: Ron Nevison quote; author interview, 2012.

57 *"Schenker wrote these amazing epic riffs ..."*: Ron Nevison quote; author interview, 2012.

58 *"He would do his little demos at home ..."*: Ron Nevison quote; author interview, 2012.

59 *"With the* Lights Out *album they presented ..."*: Ron Nevison quote; author interview, 2012.

60 *"I think this album condenses the better moments ..."*: Phil Mogg quote; Peter Crescenti interview, *Circus*, 1977.

61 *"I still learn English language ..."*: Michael Schenker quote; interviewer unknown, *Bravo*, December, 1976.

62 *"Honestly we are all exhausted ..."*: Michael Schenker quote; interviewer unknown, *Pop*, July, 1977.

63 *"He just went ..."*: Phil Mogg quote; Peter Douglas interview, *Beat Instrumental*, 1978.

64 *"Michael and I got along great and he was very warm towards me ..."*: Danny Peyronel quote; author interview, 2012.

65 *" ... we're not talking about great guitar players ..."*: Ron Nevison quote; author interview, 2012.

66 *"That was the thing – we wanted the album to..."*: Pete Way quote; Peter Douglas interview, *Beat Instrumental*, 1978.

67 *"No real reason ..."*: Phil Mogg quote; Geoff Barton interview, *Sounds*, 1978.

68 *"Phil's wrong about that ..."*: Ron Nevison quote; author interview, 2012.

69 *"The punk thing, well some of that is well ..."*: Phil Mogg quote; Pete Makowski interview, *Sounds*, 1981.

70 *"Yeah, but you see in American arenas ..."*: Pete Way quote; Garry Bushell interview, *Sounds*, 1980.

71 *"He [Mogg] would walk around and fight people ..."*: Michael Schenker quote; Joel Reese interview, *Chicago Daily Herald*, 2001.

72 *"Having a German in an English band ..."*: Ron Nevison quote; author interview, 2012.

73 *"I think Michael thought we'd have him back ..."*: Pete Way quote; Harry Doherty interview, *Melody Maker*, 1979.

74 *"Oh, definitely. Extremely big ..."*: Michael Schenker quote; Joel Reese interview, *Chicago Daily Herald*, 2001.

75 *"He's one of the best lead guitarists around ..."*: Phil Mogg quote; Bob Edmands interview, *NME*, 1978.

76 *"I didn't feel comfortable with ..."*: Michael Schenker quote: *Kerrang!* article by Garry Bushell, 1983.

77 *"It was a shock when Schenker left ..."*: Phil Mogg quote; Kirk Blows interview, *RAW*, 1991.

CHAPTER FOUR
The Wild, The Willing And The Innocent – Moving On With Paul Chapman
(1979–1981)

78 *"We look very sexual on stage ..."*: Phil Mogg quote; Joe Robinson interview, *Waxpaper*, May, 1976.

79 *"The UFO line-up with Michael, Pete, Andy, Paul and myself ..."*: Phil Mogg quote; Del James interview, *RIP*, 1988.

80 *"Yeah, from Sheffield onwards things really ..."*: Paul Chapman quote; Geoff Barton interview, *Sounds*, 1979.

81 *"Well that's not really their fault or my fault ..."*: Ron Nevison quote; author interview, 2012.

82 *"UFO was a great experience for me on a number ..."*: Ron Nevison quote; author interview, 2012.

83 *"I'll tell you about Strangers In The Night as far ..."*: Ron Nevison quote; author interview, 2012.

84 *"We only need to satisfy ourselves ..."*: Phil Mogg quote; Michael Ameen interview, *Trouser Press*, 1979.

85 *"Judas Priest had the nerve to put amplifiers ..."*: Phil Mogg quote; Harry Doherty interview, *Melody Maker*, 1979.

86 *"I first saw UFO in 1978 on the Obsession tour at Birmingham ..."*: Brian Tatler quote; author interview, 2012.

87 *"UFO had some great songs and great riffs but it ..."*: Brian Tatler quote; author interview, 2012.

88 *"It was a shame that we had to split up after ..."*: Michael Schenker quote; Matthew Honey interview, *Hard Roxx*, 1997.

89 *"I was frogmarched away by the police in handcuffs with Angus Young's ..."*: Paul Raymond quote; Jason Ritchie interview, *Get Ready To Rock*, 2005.

90 *"England is still our home ..."*: Paul Chapman quote; David Fricke interview, *Circus*, 1979.

91 *"To say we're more contemporary for this year ..."*: Phil Mogg quote; Bob Edmands interview, *NME*, 1978.

92 *"Initially, we wanted Ted Templeman to produce the album ..."*: Phil Mogg quote; Steve Gett interview, *Melody Maker*, 1980.

93 *"... we felt that the combination of the two ..."*: Phil Mogg quote; Ronnie Gurr interview, *Record Mirror*, 1980.

94 *"I think it's a valid attempt to try and do a few things ..."*: Phil Mogg quote; Garry Bushell interview, *Sounds*, 1980.

95 *"A while after their manager called to ask me ..."*: John Sloman quote; author interview, 2012.

96 *"Around this time, a piece appeared in Sounds with the headline ..."*: John Sloman quote; author interview, 2012.

97 *"... I was writing and recording new Heep ..."*: John Sloman quote; author interview, 2012.

98 *"Paul is no longer with us because his ideas no ..."*: Phil Mogg quote, *NME* article, 1980.

99 *"Bit daunting having so much new material to ..."*: Neil Carter quote; author interview, 2012.

100 *"I tend to keep myself to myself on tours ..."*: Neil Carter quote; Brian Harrigan interview, *Melody Maker*, 1982.

101 *"The bulk of the backing tracks were recorded ..."*: Neil Carter quote; author interview, 2012.

102 *"Sometime later I was at home with my girlfriend watching TV ..."*: John Sloman quote; author interview, 2012.

103 *"Phil was always the dominant force and ..."*: Neil Carter quote; author interview, 2012.

104 *"There's no concept to it at all ..."*: Phil Mogg quote; Geoff Barton interview, *Sounds*, 1981.

105 *"We were in San Sebastian, Spain, and the ..."*: Colin Hart quote; author interview, 2012.

106 *"However, Ritchie encouraged a dizzy Ian to ..."*: Colin Hart quote; author interview, 2012.

CHAPTER FIVE
Mechanix – The Departure Of Pete Way And Break Up Of The Band
(1982–1983)

107 *"As a band, we've never really placed a great …"*: Phil Mogg quote; Geoff Barton interview, *Sounds*, 1977.

108 *"… we were in Switzerland staying in …"*: Neil Carter quote; author interview, 2012.

109 *"We virtually told him to do what he …"*: Phil Mogg quote; Jill Eckersley interview, publication unknown, 1982.

110 *"There was a lot of experimenting with things …"*: Neil Carter quote; author interview, 2012.

111 *"It would always be individuals coming up …"*: Neil Carter quote; author interview, 2012.

112 *"Actually, for a chance, we had more than enough …"*: Andy Parker quote; Brian Harrigan interview, *Melody Maker*, 1982.

113 *"Maybe it is too American for England and …"*: Pete Way quote; Garry Bushell interview, *Sounds*, 1982.

114 *"And then Mechanix, we'd always used Hipgnosis for our covers …"*: Andy Parker quote; Kelley Simms interview, *Hails And Horns*, 2011.

115 *"Crazy Train time as we were with Ozzy in the States …"*: Neil Carter quote; author interview, 2012.

116 *"We have to keep an eye on Neil …"*: Paul Chapman quote; Karen Harvey interview, *Kerrang!*, 1982.

117 *"We're not businessmen at all, how …"*: Neil Carter quote; Jill Eckersley interview, publication unknown, 1982.

118 *"We started rehearsing down in Sussex and …"*: Phil Mogg quote; Dave Dickson interview, *Kerrang!*, 1983.

119 *"It was always fairly even really and didn't …"*: Neil Carter quote; author interview, 2012.

120 *"I didn't know that my contract with Chrysalis …"*: Pete Way quote; Marko Syrjala interview, *Metal-Rules*, 2007.

121 *"Ozzy's like a mate but I was pretty …"*: Pete Way quote; Mark Day interview, *Rock Power*, 1991.

122 *"…Tommy Aldridge is very, very good; Pete isn't very, very good …"*: Phil Mogg quote; Mick Wall interview, *Metal Fury*, 1983.

123 *"Well, we had to sack Gary Lyons after …"*: Phil Mogg quote; Dave Dickson interview, *Kerrang!*, 1983.

124 *"They went through various contacts and a call came …"*: Mick Glossop quote; author interview, 2012.

125 *"Excellent, a gentleman, and very much on my level ..."*: Neil Carter quote; author interview, 2012.

126 *"I'd heard stories about falling out with Gary and they ..."*: Mick Glossop quote; author interview, 2012.

127 *"They'd recorded rhythm tracks and a ..."*: Mick Glossop quote; author interview, 2012.

128 *"Onstage Phil is fairly static ..."*: Mick Glossop quote; author interview, 2012.

129 *"It was a bit odd at first ..."*: Paul Chapman quote; Jill Eckersley interview, publication unknown, 1983.

130 *"I think we missed Pete's spirit and crazy humour ..."*: Neil Carter quote; author interview, 2012.

131 *"Neil was a very large contributor ..."*: Mick Glossop quote; author interview, 2012.

132 *"I've heard all of this. I've had a lot worse issues with ..."*: Mick Glossop quote; author interview, 2012.

133 *"I think Journey were in my consciousness ..."*: Neil Carter quote; author interview, 2012.

134 *"I really did like the sound of their albums ..."*: Neil Carter quote; author interview, 2012.

135 *"Good songs, good arrangements ..."*: Mick Glossop quote; author interview, 2012.

136 *"We'll use him when we can ..."*: Phil Mogg quote; *Record Mirror* article, 1983.

137 *"Looking back now, we can see it ..."*: Neil Carter quote; Jill Eckersley interview, publication unknown, 1983.

138 *"I wasn't asked to join. They needed a bass player for an upcoming tour ..."*: Billy Sheehan quote; interviewee unknown, *Fullinbloommusic*, 2006.

139 *"I'd met Paul Chapman a few times who lived ..."*: Paul Gray quote; author interview, 2012.

140 *"Next day I went up to London to ..."*: Paul Gray quote; author interview, 2012.

141 *"UFO are on the shelf, the band is there ..."*: Phil Mogg quote; *Kerrang!* article by Dave Dickson, 1983.

142 *"Well, and this is quite well documented, but it was the three ..."*: Neil Carter quote; author interview, 2012.

143 *"... the strain of keeping it all going was too much in the end ..."*: Phil Mogg quote; *Sounds* article, 1983.

144 *"It was O.K. surprisingly given that we all knew ..."*: Neil Carter quote; author interview, 2012.

145 *"... it wasn't the happiest band in ..."*: Paul Gray quote; author interview, 2012.

146 *"I had a lot of personal problems ..."*: Andy Parker quote; Kelley Simms interview, *Hails And Horns*, 2011.

147 *"I didn't really have any problems with ..."*: Mick Glossop quote; author interview, 2012.

148 *"I thought they were pretty good, a tight rock band ..."*: Mick Glossop quote; author interview, 2012.

149 *"I've got a paper round ..."*: Phil Mogg quote; Steve Gett interview, *Kerrang!*, 1983.

150 *"I ended up having to go to the dole office ..."*: Phil Mogg quote, Michael Hann, *The Guardian*, 2012.

151 *"Memory tends to dull the pain ..."*: Neil Carter quote; author interview, 2012.

152 *"I think it was always a bit of a rollercoaster ..."*: Neil Carter quote; author interview, 2012.

CHAPTER SIX
Ain't Misbehavin' – The Turbulent Return Of UFO (1984–1989)

153 *"There is nothing, and I mean nothing ..."*: Phil Mogg quote; Michael Ameen interview, *Trouser Press*, 1979.

154 *"In America they all go to guitar school ..."*: Phil Mogg quote; Chris Welch interview, *Metal Hammer*, 1988.

155 *"This band is worlds apart from the old ..."*: Phil Mogg quote; Dave Dickson interview, *Kerrang!*, 1984.

156 *"I felt nervous because we'd had a major ..."*: Phil Mogg quote; Mark Putterford interview, *Kerrang!*, 1985.

157 *"The problem with Chrysalis is that I don't think ..."*: Phil Mogg quote; interviewer unknown, *Rock Scene*, 1985.

158 *"Lovely bloke, I wouldn't have a bad word ..."*: Paul Gray quote; author interview, 2012.

159 *"... played around for a few days and that was it ..."*: Kevin Elson quote; email to author, 2012.

160 *"... apparently he'd [Elson] taken three days ..."*: Nick Tauber quote; author interview, 2012.

161 *"... he [Elson] spent the best part of the next week ..."*: Paul Gray quote; author interview, 2012.

162 *"I wouldn't start recording until we'd done ..."*: Nick Tauber quote; author interview, 2012.

163 *"It took Tommy a little time to get into the English ..."*: Nick Tauber quote; author interview, 2012.

164 *"I had to push him. I said: 'Come on Phil ..."*: Nick Tauber quote; author interview, 2012.

165 *"I like Phil Mogg. He had all the problems that all ..."*: Nick Tauber quote; author interview, 2012.

166 *"The songs of mine that ended up on the …"*: Paul Gray quote; author interview, 2012.

167 *"I think they [Chrysalis] just wanted to get …"*: Nick Tauber quote; author interview, 2012.

168 *"I would have loved to have worked with them [again] …"*: Nick Tauber quote; author interview, 2012.

169 *"Lovely bloke, very jolly, liked a joke.."*: Paul Gray quote; author interview, 2012.

170 *"I have to be a bit diplomatic here …"*: Paul Gray quote; author interview, 2012.

171 *"If we'd got the mix absolutely right it …"*: Nick Tauber quote; author interview, 2012.

172 *"I'm not saying I'm drinking tea all the time …"*: Phil Mogg quote; interviewer unknown, *Rock Scene*, 1985.

173 *"Phil Mogg had run out of cough medicine …"*: Tony Mills quote; author interview, 2012.

174 *"Landing at the Barrowlands, in Glasgow on …"*: Tony Mills quote; author interview, 2012.

175 *"I'll never forget being very thirsty onstage …"*: Tony Mills quote; author interview, 2012.

176 *"Most of the band were sort of, well …"*: Tony Mills quote; author interview, 2012.

177 *"They were great fun …"*: Paul Gray quote; author interview, 2012.

178 *"I think that band needed two more albums …"*: Nick Tauber quote; author interview, 2012.

179 *"… as soon as we were back in Blighty …"*: Paul Gray quote; author interview, 2012.

180 *"I think we could be a lot bigger that we are …"*: Phil Mogg quote; Merryl Lentz interview, *Hit Parader*, 1988.

181 *"…I think the end result is far preferable …"*: Paul Gray quote; author interview, 2012.

182 *"I had the extreme pleasure as a massive UFO fan…"*: Brian Slagel quote; author interview, 2012.

183 *"I think the direction wasn't really particularly special …"*: Pete Way quote; Marko Syrjala interview, *Metal-Rules*, 2007.

184 *"I can't actually remember how I came to be …"*: Myke Gray quote; author interview, 2012.

185 *"I'm my own worst enemy and I admit that it …"*: Phil Mogg quote; Derek Oliver interview, *Kerrang!*, 1988.

186 *"It was really sad …"*: Paul Gray quote; author interview, 2012.

187 *"started mucking around, writing songs …"*: Phil Mogg quote; Derek Oliver interview, *Kerrang!*, 1988.

188 *"I remember it being very unproductive and a ..."*: Myke Gray quote; author interview, 2012.
189 *"Well, when you work on songs and ..."*: Phil Mogg quote; Garry Sharpe-Young interview, *Metal Forces*, 1988.
190 *"We've got just over an album's worth ..."*: Phil Mogg quote; Del James interview, *RIP*, 1988.
191 *"... in a 'power' sense, undoubtedly and unquestionably Phil ..."*: Danny Peyronel quote; author interview, 2012.

CHAPTER SEVEN
High Stakes & Dangerous Men – Mogg And Way Reunite (1990–1994)

192 *"I don't think any of us realised the band would go on long ..."*: Phil Mogg quote; Dmitry M. Epstein interview, *Let It Rock/dmme.net*, 2002.
193 *"but through Chrysalis, Michael said ..."*: Pete Way quote; Neil Jeffries interview, *Kerrang!*, 1991.
194 *"Paul Chapman was the same, he ..."*: Pete Way quote; Garry Sharpe-Young interview, *Metal Forces*, 1992.
195 *"It might sound funny to say it, but ..."*: Pete Way quote; Lyn Guy interview, *Riff Raff*, 1991.
196 *"Y'know we could of come back years ago but ..."*: Pete Way quote; Garry Sharpe-Young interview, *Metal Forces*, 1992.
197 *"Now when I get up in the morning ..."*: Phil Mogg quote; interviewer unknown, *RAW*, 1993.
198 *"It's very important to be able to ..."*: Pete Way quote; Chris Welch interview, *Metal Hammer*, 1991.
199 *"Now our rehearsals are what's giving ..."*: Pete Way quote; Lyn Guy interview, *Riff Raff*, 1991.
200 *"Phil's attitude was that he didn't wanna know ..."*: Clive Edwards quote; author interview, 2012.
201 *"Most of the time we did the album virtually karaoke..."*: Clive Edwards quote; author interview, 2012.
202 *"We recorded the drums in a rather unusual way ..."*: Kit Woolven quote; author interview, 2012.
203 *"What would happen is after Pete had gone to bed I would ..."*: Kit Woolven quote; author interview, 2012.
204 *"...the thing is they got pissed really quick ..."*: Clive Edwards quote; author interview, 2012.
205 *"It took bloody ages doing mainly Pete's bass parts ..."*: Kit Woolven quote; author interview, 2012.

206 *"It was incredibly frustrating working, first of all in dribs ..."*: Clive Edwards quote; author interview, 2012.

207 *"I spoke to Phil sometime after that album ..."*: Kit Woolven quote; author interview, 2012.

208 *"Phil was always alright with me ..."*: Kit Woolven quote; author interview, 2012.

209 *"When we did the* High Stakes *album ninety percent of it ..."*: Laurence Archer quote; author interview, 2012.

210 *"He [Reid] did for my liking spend far too ..."*: Kit Woolven quote; author interview, 2012.

211 *"While I was mixing he was still writing the ..."*: Kit Woolven quote; author interview, 2012.

212 *"I think he [Mogg] knew and that's ..."*: Laurence Archer quote; author interview, 2012.

213 *"It was one of those never-ending things ..."*: Kit Woolven quote; author interview, 2012.

214 *"To be honest, I don't really remember ..."*: Kit Woolven quote; author interview, 2012.

215 *"We wanted to do quite a bit of writing and we wanted to ..."*: Laurence Archer quote; author interview, 2012.

216 *"We were very pleased with the new material ..."*: Pete Way quote; Chris Welch interview, *Metal Hammer*, 1991.

217 *"I actually think our new record is the best ..."*: Pete Way quote; Kirk Blows interview, *RAW*, 1991.

218 *"...I played it the other day and it's very good. I was surprised myself ..."*: Phil Mogg quote; interviewer unknown, *Revelationz*, 2002.

219 *"I don't know if I was or wasn't ..."*: Kit Woolven quote; author interview, 2012.

220 *"I spent a lot of my time in Los Angeles at that time ..."*: Kit Woolven quote; author interview, 2012.

221 *"Japan was great ..."*: Laurence Archer quote; author interview, 2012.

222 *"We were a very, very energetic band ..."*: Clive Edwards quote; author interview, 2012.

223 *"The touring was great. It was great being with Pete ..."*: Laurence Archer quote; author interview, 2012.

224 *"We were in St. Petersburg in Russia ..."*: Laurence Archer quote; author interview, 2012.

225 *"Phil would reach that point when he was ..."*: Clive Edwards quote; author interview, 2012.

226 *"The thing with Michael's been on and off for ..."*: Phil Mogg quote; Dave Ling interview, *RAW*, 1993.

227 *"It got to the point with the record company ..."*: Clive Edwards quote; author interview, 2012.

228 *"We'd done a lot of that donkey work ..."*: Clive Edwards quote; author interview, 2012.

229 *"Well, basically there was a lull anyway because when ..."*: Laurence Archer quote; author interview, 2012.

230 *"I never liked, since I was a kid, a group ..."*: Phil Mogg quote; Dave Dickson interview, *Kerrang!*, 1984.

231 *"The problem with Phil is he keeps changing ..."*: Nick Tauber quote; author interview, 2012.

232 *"It had nowhere left to go. That t ..."*: Phil Mogg quote; Dave Reynolds interview, *Kerrang!*, 1994.

233 *"I think that when they went out to America ..."*: Laurence Archer quote; author interview, 2012.

234 *"Being in a rock band is like running a business ..."*: Pete Way quote; Kirk Blows interview, *RAW*, 1991.

CHAPTER EIGHT
Swimming With Sharks – The Many Returns Of Michael Schenker
(1995–2002)

235 *"I don't think we ever thought of ourselves as rock stars ..."*: Phil Mogg quote, Michael Hann, *The Guardian*, 2012.

236 *"I'd always known that this classic line-up ..."*: Michael Schenker quote; Bill Landers interview, *Hit Parader*, 1997.

237 *"It was fun to get us back together ..."*: Ron Nevison quote; author interview, 2012.

238 *"We talked about it ..."*: Ron Nevison quote; author interview, 2012.

239 *"I was surprised that Andy made it over ..."*: Ron Nevison quote; author interview, 2012.

240 *"There's no question he's one of the ..."*: Ron Nevison quote; author interview, 2012.

241 *"They're all totally different ..."*: Ron Nevison quote; author interview, 2012.

242 *"With pride. The recording went very natural ..."*: Pete Way quote; interviewer unknown, *Aardschok*, 1996.

243 *"Well, a friend of mine put me in touch ..."*: Simon Wright quote; author interview, 2012.

244 *"Interesting to say the least, never a dull moment! ..."*: Simon Wright quote; author interview, 2012.

245 *"I think he's [Schenker] a brilliant guitar player ..."*: Leo Lyons quote; author interview, 2012.

246 *"Absolutely not true! On the contrary ..."*: Pete Way quote; interviewer unknown, *Aardschok*, 1996.

247 *"Michael would keep to himself most of ..."*: Simon Wright quote; author interview, 2012.

248 *"The lowpoint has to be at the Nakano Sun Plaza ..."*: Paul Raymond quote; Jason Ritchie interview, *Get Ready To Rock*, 2005.

249 *"I don't know why we signed it, the idea was that ..."*: Paul Raymond quote; *Classic Rock* news article, 1998.

250 *"Spirit within UFO has never been better ..."*: Pete Way quote; *Classic Rock* news article, 2000.

251 *"My analysis of it is, as a band goes through a growing ..."*: Pete Way quote; Steph Perry interview, *Rocknotes Webzine*, 2000.

252 *"It had been very painful for me to watch Pete Way ..."*: Michael Schenker quote; Dave Ling interview, *Classic Rock*, 2003.

253 *"He's a funny guy ..."*: Phil Mogg quote; Dmitry M. Epstein interview, *Let It Rock/dmme.net*, 2002.

254 *"I think it's more rocky. More kind of how we ..."*: Phil Mogg quote; interviewer unknown, *Revelationz*, 2002.

CHAPTER NINE
The Wild Ones – The Rebirth Of UFO (2003–2008)

255 *"We take the music seriously, obviously ..."*: Andy Parker quote; Morley Seaver interview, *Antimusic*, 2009.

256 *"Sure you get paid, but it's not about the money ..."*: Pete Way quote; Steph Perry interview, *Rocknotes Webzine*, 2000.

257 *"I did say in other interviews that we maybe we would ..."*: Phil Mogg quote; Jason Ritchie interview, *Get Ready To Rock*, 2002.

258 *"I've always loved Phil ..."*: Laurence Archer quote; author interview, 2012.

259 *"Phil [Mogg] was very nervous about anything that I ..."*: Jason Bonham quote; interviewee unknown, *Live4metal*, 2004.

260 *"It's been great ...."*: Vinnie Moore quote; Marko Syrjala interview, *Metal-Rules*, 2004.

261 *"Robert [Plant] came to see UFO during the English tour ..."*: Jason Bonham quote; interviewee unknown, *Glam-Metal*, 2004.

262 *"He plays bass like John Entwistle a little bit. He's real cool ..."*: Phil Mogg quote; Geoff Barton quote; *Classic Rock*, 2009.

263 *"I personally don't think that it was our strongest show ..."*: Vinnie Moore quote; Ruben Mosqueda interview, *Sleaze Roxx*, 2009.

264 *"To be honest with you, Jason got on my nerves ..."*: Pete Way quote; Marko Syrjala interview, *Metal-Rules*, 2007.

265 *"...when we decided to move back we fixed this one house we had ..."*: Andy Parker quote; Lisa Torem interview, *Penny Black Music*, 2011.

266 *"We've been together for so long, it feels comfortable ..."*: Phil Mogg quote; Phil Freeman interview, *Relix*, 2011.

267 *"This band, is an interesting thing – when I ..."*: Andy Parker quote; Tommy Hash interview, *Ytsejam*, 2012.

268 *"Fortunately for this band, when you mix in everybody's ..."*: Phil Mogg quote; Todd K. Smith interview, *Cutting Edge Rocks*, 2004.

269 *"Phil, Pete and Paul Raymond were great to get ..."*: Simon Wright quote; author interview, 2012.

270 *"Well my impression was Phil, but ..."*: Simon Wright quote; author interview, 2012.

271 *"Just the camaraderie, well the great catalogue of ..."*: Simon Wright quote; author interview, 2012.

272 *"Well, as a musician you try to make something that lasts ..."*: Rob De Luca quote; interviewer unknown, *Get Ready To Roll*, 2008.

CHAPTER TEN
Seven Deadly – More Than 40 Years Of UFO (2009–2013)

273 *"It's exciting to get discovered by a younger generation ..."*: Andy Parker quote; Scott Alisoglu interview, *Teeth Of The Divine*, 2012.

274 *"... what seems to work for him is, he likes to ..."*: Andy Parker quote; Morley Seaver interview, *Antimusic*, 2009.

275 *"... it was the same process as we followed in the past ..."*: Vinnie Moore quote; Chad Bowar interview, *Heavymetal.about*, 2009.

276 *"The initial plan when we were rehearsing was to have a local guy ..."*: Vinnie Moore quote; Ruben Mosqueda interview, *Sleaze Roxx*, 2009.

277 *"Yes, I laid that demon to rest a long time ago ..."*: Paul Raymond quote; *Cutting Edge Rocks* article, 2009.

278 *"Everyone is different. Everyone has their style ..."*: Mick Glossop quote; author interview, 2012.

279 *"We are not in our 40th anniversary ..."*: Phil Mogg quote; Geoff Barton interview, *Classic Rock*, 2009.

280 *"And, unfortunately, because he won't curb his lifestyle ..."*: Andy Parker quote; Lisa Torem interview, *Penny Black Music*, 2011.

281 *"Paul and Vinnie pretty much wrote this album between them with Phil ..."*: Andy Parker quote; Scott Alisoglu interview, *Teeth Of The Divine*, 2012.

282 *"If you live life consciously and you belief that you're ..."*: Michael Schenker quote; Jeb Wright interview, *Classic Rock Revisited*, 2001.

283 *"Poor old Peter. He started off with a good attitude ..."*: Andy Parker quote, Steve Patrick interview, *Hard Rock Heaven*, 2012.

284 *"He's hard to control but he's never been a nasty person ..."*: Laurence Archer quote; author interview, 2012.

285 *"The guy has given his life to rock 'n' roll ..."*: Clive Edwards quote; author interview, 2012.

286 *"I suppose they were a bit like an old married couple ..."*: Kit Woolven quote; author interview, 2012.

287 *"I heard an interview with Andy Parker recently ..."*: Laurence Archer quote; author interview, 2012.

288 *"It does get difficult. I'm not absolutely sure at this stage what ..."*: Andy Parker quote; Scott Alisoglu interview, *Teeth Of The Divine*, 2012.

289 *"Whereas now it's: are we getting paid? ...."*: Phil Mogg quote; Michael Hann interview, *The Guardian*, 2012.

290 *"We go back with UFO from the prime time of Schenker ..."*: Bailey Brothers quote; author interview, 2012.

291 *"Naively, you think we've done a good job myself ..."*: Clive Edwards quote; author interview, 2012.

292 *"Since the first line-up they've never settled ..."*: Nick Tauber quote; author interview, 2012.

293 *"The one thing I love about this band is we've ..."*: Andy Parker quote; Kelley Simms interview, *Hails And Horns*, 2011.